ABOUT THE AUTHOR

Anneka Manning has spent more than
22 years in the food print media as a
food writer and editor. She has worked
for a range of leading food publications
in Australia such as *Australian Gourmet
Traveller*, *VOGUE Entertaining + Travel*,
australian good taste, (which she helped
to launch and make one of Australia's
most successful food magazines),
The Australian Women's Weekly and
Good Living (Sydney Morning Herald).
In addition, Anneka has also compiled
and written a number of successful,
award-winning books, including *good
food* and *more good food*. Anneka believes
that the best food is simple food done
well, relying on sound basics, simple
techniques and good ingredients.
Her food reflects the way she cooks,
eats and entertains in her busy life.
It is good food – realistic, yet inspiring.

Mastering
the Art of
Poultry, Meat & Game

**Classic to Contemporary
A Complete Step-by-Step Guide**

Anneka Manning

Contents

Introduction

To many, meat and poultry cookery can seem dauntingly complex – associated with tricky techniques and equipment that only specialty kitchens have in their cupboards. However, once armed with a little 'meaty' information, as contained in this book, this concept will quickly be dispelled.

Mastering the Art of Poultry, Meat & Game contains over 165 approachable, yet inspirational, recipes for both everyday eating and entertaining — all with clear step-by-step instructions. The comprehensive information such as how to identify different cuts of chicken and how to choose the best quality meat, along with techniques, such as Frenching a rack of lamb, trussing a bird for roasting, carving a leg of lamb and making stock, support the recipes and will help build your poultry, meat and game preparation and cooking skills.

From cooking the perfect steak, to creating a traditional osso bucco, slow-cooking lamb shoulder or whipping up an Asian-inspired chicken stir-fry, *Mastering the Art of Poultry, Meat & Game* will be a constantly reliable companion in the kitchen.

Basics

Buying, storing and preparing poultry

Buying poultry

Poultry can be purchased fresh or frozen from supermarkets, speciality poultry stores and butchers. The price and quality will vary depending on the method of production: commercial, corn-fed, free-range or organic.

Commercial poultry (also called barn and cage poultry) are reared in large sheds in an artificially controlled environment and are the most common variety found in supermarkets.

Corn-fed poultry are also raised by the commercial method, but they receive a high level of corn in their diet which produces creamy-yellow flesh.

Free-range poultry are free to roam outside in a more natural environment during daylight hours and are provided with access to shade, shelter and food, however they are housed in sheds at night.

Organic poultry are free-range, chemical-free poultry that spend approximately 85 per cent of their time outdoors foraging in the grass. Standards are stringent and any feed grown with the addition of chemical fertilisers, pesticides, herbicides or genetic modifications is banned.

When poultry is labelled **chemical-free** it means, strictly speaking, it is free from added hormones (banned in Australia in the 1960s), but may contain other chemicals.

Fresh poultry generally gives a tastier result than frozen poultry. When choosing fresh poultry, either a whole bird or smaller cuts, always buy meat that has a healthy appearance with no defects. Look for light pink, moist and plump flesh. Choose packaging that contains no tears or holes and make sure that all meat is cool to touch. Frozen poultry should be solid and tightly wrapped.

Correct handling and storage of poultry is very important. Make it the last purchase on your shopping trip and put it in the refrigerator or freezer as soon as possible. It's a good idea to keep a chiller bag in the car to transport poultry home, not only when the weather is warm but even on cooler days, as cars are often warm enough for bacteria to multiply, potentially leading to food poisoning.

Storing poultry

For raw poultry, discard the original wrapping and pour off any juices. Loosely wrap in plastic wrap or place in a plastic bag on a large plate to catch any moisture. Refrigerate for up to two days. To avoid cross-contamination, do not allow raw poultry to come into contact with other foods.

Cooked poultry can be refrigerated for up to three days, loosely wrapped in foil or plastic wrap. To avoid risk of contamination by bacteria, don't leave cooked poultry at room temperature for longer than an hour.

Freezing poultry

For raw poultry, place in a plastic freezer bag. Expel all the air, seal the bag securely, then label and date. Freeze poultry in small portions, taking into account the number of people you usually cook for, to hasten thawing and reduce waste.

Thaw poultry on a tray in the refrigerator, allowing 3 hours for each 500 g (1 lb 2 oz). Small packages of frozen poultry can be thawed in the microwave on the defrost setting and should then be cooked immediately, but thawing in the microwave is not recommended for whole birds due to uneven results. Never thaw poultry at room temperature, because bacteria that can cause food poisoning thrives in warm temperatures. For the same reason you should never thaw poultry in water or under running water. Never re-freeze thawed poultry. Cook poultry within 12 hours of thawing.

Cooked poultry dishes, such as casseroles, may be frozen in airtight containers or plastic freezer bags for up to two months. Reduce the temperature of cooked dishes as quickly as possible and cool completely in the refrigerator before packaging to freeze.

Preparing poultry

To prepare poultry, trim any excess fat and sinew from the meat, then rinse very briefly under cold water and pat dry with paper towels. Skin may be removed from some cuts of poultry to reduce the fat content, as fat lies in a layer just beneath the skin. However, cooking with the skin left on contributes to the flavour and tenderness of the meat.

When preparing a whole bird for roasting, remove the neck and giblets from the cavity and trim any pockets of fat. Every part of the bird can be used, so keep the neck and giblets for making stock. Indeed, the whole carcass is suitable for making stock, so think twice before discarding any bones. If you are going to be stuffing a whole bird, do so just before cooking, then truss the bird using kitchen string (see page 21). This will help the bird keep a neat shape during cooking and will ensure it cooks evenly.

After preparing raw poultry always thoroughly wash your hands, chopping boards and knives using hot soapy water before they come into contact with other foods to avoid the risk of cross-contamination. You also need to make sure that the chicken is cooked through properly to kill any bacteria.

Different types of poultry

There's more to poultry than chicken alone. It comprises a variety of edible birds in differing shapes, sizes and flavours.

Chicken is one of the world's most popular meats and is sold according to its size and age, either fresh or frozen. For example, no. 14 chickens are 1.4 kg (3 lb 2 oz) and about three months old. As a general rule, the older the chicken, the more flavour it has.

Spatchcock (also known as poussin) are chickens about six weeks old, weighing about 500 g (1 lb 2 oz). The flesh is very tender, but with little flavour, and benefits from marinating.

Turkeys are large birds with about half the fat content of a chicken. Generally, the older the turkey, the tougher the meat. An average size is a no. 55 turkey, which weighs 5.5 kg (12 lb 1½ oz) and is about three months old. Turkey meat is also available as turkey buffe (breast meat on the bone), breast fillets and hindquarters.

Ducks are not as meaty as chickens, have a much higher fat content and a stronger flavour. The most common varieties used in cooking are the Peking duck and Muscovy duck.

Quails are small game birds about 150 g (5½ oz) in size. They are now available from some supermarkets, as well as poultry shops and butchers. You'll need one to two quails per person.

Geese usually need to be ordered from speciality poultry shops or butchers. They vary in size from 3 to 5 kg (6 lb 12 oz to 11 lb 4 oz) and are generally roasted.

Pheasant are regarded as having the best flavour of all the game birds and weigh about 1.5 kg (3 lb 5 oz).

Squab (pigeon), guinea fowl and partridge are small game birds and need to be ordered from speciality poultry shops or butchers.

chicken

quails

spatchcock

turkey

duck

Different cuts of poultry

Most types of poultry, depending on size, can be cut into similar portions to a chicken.

Whole chickens are usually marked with a number that indicates their size. For example, a no. 18 chicken weighs 1.8 kg (4 lb). A chicken under 1.5 kg (3 lb 5 oz) will usually serve up to four people, while larger birds will serve four to six people. Whole chickens can be split in half, from front to back through the backbone and between the breasts, to produce two halves of approximately equal weight. Your butcher can bone a whole chicken ready for stuffing, or cut it into different portions ready for cooking.

Chicken breast fillets are tender white meat portions. They are sold on the bone or as skinless fillets (both come as double or single breasts). Chicken tenderloins are the small fillets of meat on the underside of the breast, which can be detached and cooked separately.

Wings are white meat portions composed of three sections, the drumette, the flat mid-section and the wing tip.

Marylands, also called **leg quarters**, are dark meat portions and can be further separated into drumsticks and thighs.

Drumsticks are the lower portion of the leg and are a firm meat. **Thighs** are the portion of the leg above the knee joint. Thigh cutlets are partially boned, while thigh fillets are completely boned and skinned.

Minced (ground) chicken can be made at home in a food processor from either breast or leg meat and is also available ready-made from butchers and supermarkets.

Chicken livers are available from butchers and selected supermarkets (see page 25 for preparation).

whole chicken

minced chicken

chicken maryland

chicken livers

chicken drumsticks

chicken breast fillet

chicken wings

chicken thigh cutlets

Jointing a chicken

Cutting up a whole chicken for casseroling, roasting, sautéing or frying is not only a great skill to master, but a relatively easy one. The advantage of jointing your own chicken is that you can buy a whole corn-fed or organic chicken, rather than depend on the lesser-quality chicken pieces on offer at the supermarket. Meat cooked on the bone has greater depth of flavour than meat off the bone and chicken is no exception.

To joint a chicken you need a good large, sharp cook's knife. A pair of poultry shears is handy, but not necessary. Keep the neck, trimmed bones and any other offcuts for making stock; these will keep in the freezer for up to 8 weeks so you have a fair bit of time to accumulate the required amount.

This method will give you eight pieces from a whole chicken and can also be used for other birds.

1 Place the chicken on a chopping board, breast side up. Pull the leg away from the body, then cut through the skin and flesh between the thigh and the body until you reach the thigh joint. Using a large sharp knife and pulling the whole leg away from the body, cut through to the upper leg joint where the thigh joins the body.

2 Bend the leg outwards gently to dislocate the ball and socket joint, then cut between the ball and socket to remove the whole leg from the chicken, cutting far enough into the back side of the upper thigh to remove the 'oyster' from the back of the chicken as you go. Repeat this process with the remaining leg. Bend the leg outwards gently to dislocate the ball and socket joint, then cut through the joint; it is not necessary to cut through bone. Use a large, heavy knife or cleaver to chop the knobbly end off the drumstick to neaten its appearance, if desired.

3 Place the chicken on the chopping board, breast side down. Use poultry shears or a large sharp knife to cut down either side of the backbone to remove it completely. Reserve the backbone and neck for stock.

4 Keeping the chicken breast side down, cut through the middle of the breastbone with poultry shears or a heavy knife to give two breast sections. Neaten the edge of the backbone if necessary.

5 Cut through each breast on a slight diagonal to give two pieces of roughly even weight — the half with the wing will be slightly smaller than the piece from the lower breast.

6 You will now have eight pieces of chicken. The wings and half-breast pieces can be divided again to give 10 pieces in total, if desired.

1 Cut through the skin and flesh between the thigh and the body to the thigh joint. Pull the leg away and cut through to the upper leg joint.

2 Bend the leg outwards gently to dislocate the ball and socket joint. Cut between the ball and socket to remove the leg from the thigh.

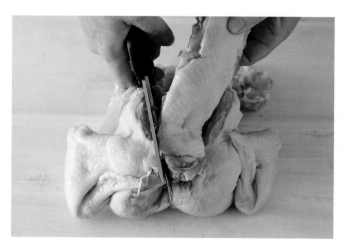

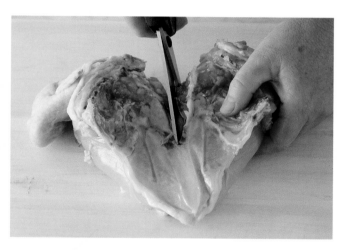

3 Cut down either side of the backbone to remove it completely.

4 Cut through the middle of the breastbone to give two breast sections. Neaten the backbone edge if necessary.

5 Cut through each breast on a slight diagonal to give two pieces of roughly even weight.

6 Once completed you will have eight chicken pieces.

Removing the wishbone

Removing the wishbone before cooking makes it easier to carve a chicken. Allow more time for a larger bird, such as a turkey, as you will find the bone is more embedded.

1 Pull back the skin at the neck cavity and find the V-shaped wishbone with your fingers. Use a small sharp knife to scrape away the flesh on either side of one of the bones until you can grip it with your fingers.

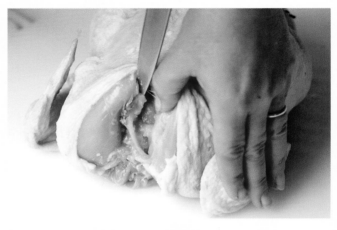

2 Use the tip of the knife to free the top end of the 'V' from the chicken carcass.

3 Scrape away the flesh on either side of the other bone.

4 Gently holding both bones, use the tip of the knife to release the whole wishbone.

Trussing poultry

The main benefit of trussing is to keep the bird's shape during cooking, which ensures it cooks more evenly and will be easier to carve. You can remove the wishbone before trussing if you like.

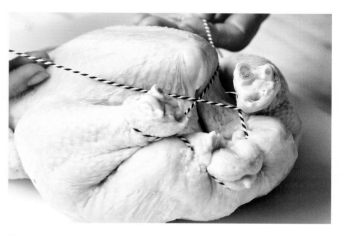

1 Cut a piece of kitchen string about four times as long as the bird. Place the bird on a chopping board, breast side up, and tuck the wings under the body.

2 With the tail of the bird facing away from you, place the middle of the string under the tail. Bring the ends of the string up and around each leg and cross the ends over at the top.

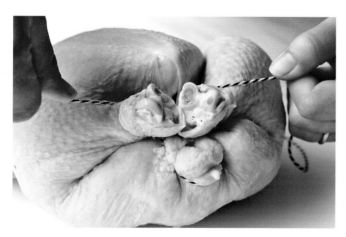

3 Pull each end of the string to draw the legs together, crossing them over each other again.

4 Turn the bird over with the neck cavity facing away from you. Cross the string over the neck skin and tighten to pull the wings to the body. Tie the string securely. Turn the bird onto its back.

Spatchcocking a whole bird

Spatchcocking, also known as butterflying, basically means opening out a whole bird so it will lay flat for cooking, which is particularly handy when barbecuing and also gives a faster roasting time. This useful technique involves cutting out the backbone, then flattening the bird with your hand.

1 Place the bird on a chopping board, breast side down. Use poultry shears or a large sharp knife to cut down either side of the backbone to remove it completely.

2 Turn the bird over so it is breast side up and open it out.

3 Use the heel of your hand to push down on both sides of the bird to flatten it.

TIP When spatchcocking a duck, remove the parson's nose first as it is a highly fatty part of the bird.

Butterflying a chicken breast fillet

This technique will produce a large, thin, flat chicken fillet, perfect for making chicken schnitzel. It's also an excellent way to dress up a fillet — you can stop after step 2 to make a pocket that can be filled, or finish the process and place a filling on top, then roll the chicken up and secure with toothpicks.

1 Place the chicken fillet on a chopping board, skin side down and with the tapered, thin end pointing away from you and the thickest side on the right (or left, if you are left-handed).

2 Place your hand on top of the fillet to steady it, then hold a large sharp knife horizontal to the board and cut through the middle of the chicken to within about 1 cm (½ inch) of the other side. Make sure you don't cut all the way through.

3 Open the chicken fillet out like a book, then use the knife to make more horizontal cuts on the surface of the chicken, near the middle, to further open it out and create an even thickness all over.

4 Cover the breast with a piece of plastic wrap and use a meat mallet or rolling pin to firmly pound the chicken to thin it slightly as required and ensure it is an even thickness.

Trimming chicken wings to make drumettes

A drumette is the middle part of a chicken wing, trimmed to create an elegant mouthful that is perfect for canapés. You can reserve the wing tips for making stock, while the top part of the wings can be marinated and cooked for a casual snack (try the marinade in Honey-glazed chicken wings, page 170).

1 Place a chicken wing on a chopping board and stretch it out. Use your fingers to locate the joint between the wing tip and the middle of the wing, then cut through the joint. Repeat at the other joint. Reserve the middle part of the wing. Repeat to divide all the chicken wings.

2 Use a heavy sharp knife to remove the knuckles from the bones at each end of the middle-wing portions.

3 Hold a middle-wing portion in your hand with the thicker end closest to the base of your palm. Use the thumb of your other hand to push the larger bone from below so that it comes up and out the top. Discard the bone.

4 Stand the middle-wing portion on the chopping board, with the thinner part at the top. Hold the top of the remaining bone tightly between your thumb and first two fingers and push the meat down to the bottom.

5 Use a small sharp knife to clean any meat or sinew from the bone. Repeat with the remaining middle-wing portions.

Mincing chicken

Use well-chilled, free-range, skinless thigh fillets to make minced (ground) chicken. Thighs are the best cut to use as chicken breast is leaner and can be too dry. Before you begin, make sure all of your mincer attachments, or the food processor bowl and blade, are cleaned, sterilised and chilled. Only mince the chicken on the day you'll be using it.

1 Trim the fat from the chicken thighs and roughly chop them, then put the pieces through a mincer.

1 Place the chopped chicken thighs in the bowl of a food processor. Use the pulse button to process briefly until finely chopped.

Preparing chicken livers

Livers need to be as fresh as possible, as they don't keep well, and you should always buy them whole.

1 Trim the livers with a small sharp knife to remove any sinew and gall bladder staining.

2 If the livers are bloody, put them in a glass or ceramic bowl, cover with milk and refrigerate for 3 hours.

3 Rinse the livers and drain on paper towels before use.

Carving a whole chicken

Carving a chicken is a simple process that should ensure everyone gets a selection of white and dark meat. Remember to rest the chicken for at least 10 minutes before carving to set the juices. If you have a cleaver, you can use it to separate the leg and thigh and remove the knobbly end of the leg, however a large heavy cook's knife and a pair of poultry shears will also do the job.

1 Place the cooked chicken, breast side up, on a carving board. Pull the leg and the thigh away from the body to expose the joint that attaches it to the body (between thigh and breast). Use the tip of a sharp knife to probe for the socket and then cut through it, separating the thigh from the carcass.

2 Use a large cleaver to separate the leg and thigh, then chop the knobbly end off the leg to neaten the appearance. Repeat to separate the remaining leg and thigh.

3 Use a small sharp knife to remove the wings from the joints that attach them to the carcass by cutting as closely to the breasts as possible. Or, pull off the wings by gently twisting them away from the carcass.

4 Cut along either side of the breastbone and use your fingers to peel the entire breast off the carcass on both sides. Slice each breast fillet crossways into four to six slices.

5 To serve, place the chicken legs, thighs and wings on a serving plate and place the sliced breast meat to one side.

Carving a large bird

The same principles apply when carving a large bird, such as a turkey — rest it before carving and find the sockets so you can easily cut through them (rather than cutting through bone).

For a large bird, remove and halve the leg portions, then slice off the breast meat, carving thin slices parallel to the centre bone. Remove the wing portions last.

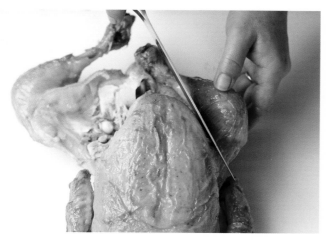

1 Pull the leg and the thigh away from the body to expose the joint that attaches it to the body (between thigh and breast).

2 Use a large cleaver to separate the leg and thigh.

3 Pull off the wings by gently twisting them away from the carcass.

4 Use your fingers to peel the entire breast off the carcass on both sides. Slice each breast fillet crossways into four to six slices.

5 Place the chicken legs, thighs and wings on a serving plate and place the sliced breast meat to one side.

Carving a chicken Chinese-style

The traditional Chinese method of carving up a chicken into serving-sized pieces requires a heavy cleaver and decisive, firm strokes. It is an ideal method for cutting up a whole poached chicken (such as Hainan chicken rice with ginger and spring onion sauce, page 323) or one cooked in an Asian style.

1 Place the chicken on a chopping board, breast side up and legs facing away from you. Use a cleaver or sharp cook's knife to remove each wing at the upper joint nearest the body, cutting through the joint.

2 Cut each wing in half through the second joint and set aside.

3 Turn the chicken around so the ends of the legs are facing you, then cut the thighs and legs off in one piece each by cutting through the joints where the thighs attach to the body.

4 Cut through the second thigh joints to separate the legs from the thighs. You will need to use a cleaver from this point on (if you aren't already). Cut off the end of the leg bone to neaten the leg.

5 Cutting forcefully, divide each chicken leg and each thigh into three pieces, cutting widthways through the bone. Set aside.

6 Stand the chicken carcass upright. Cut neatly through the carcass on either side of the backbone; discard the backbone. Remove and reserve the oysters (the two round pieces of dark meat near the thigh).

7 Turn the chicken breast side up and cut neatly down the breastbone to separate the breast into two. Neaten any protruding backbones.

8 Cut each breast portion widthways into five or six even-sized pieces.

9 To present the chicken, reassemble the various cuts on a platter with the breast pieces on top.

1 Remove each wing at the upper joint nearest the body, cutting through the joint.

2 Cut each wing in half through the second joint.

3 Cut the thighs and legs off in one piece each by cutting through the joints where the thighs attach to the body.

4 Separate the legs from the thighs, then cut off the end of the leg bone.

5 Cut each chicken leg and each thigh into 3 pieces, cutting widthways through the bone.

6 Using a cleaver, cut neatly through the carcass on either side of the backbone.

7 Use the cleaver to neatly cut down the breastbone to separate the breast into two.

8 Turn the chicken breasts skin side up and cut each widthways into five or six even-sized pieces.

9 Reassemble the various cuts on a platter with the breast pieces on top.

Stocks

Home-made stocks are the backbone of good cooking. Once you get into the routine of making and freezing them, you won't go back to ready-made stock. White chicken stock is a great all-rounder, adding a subtle depth of flavour to dishes. Brown chicken stock has a more pronounced flavour due to the caramelisation of the bones and vegetables, and is more suited to richer poultry dishes.

White chicken stock

PREPARATION TIME 15 minutes

COOKING TIME 2 hours 15 minutes

MAKES about 3 litres (105 fl oz/ 12 cups)

2 brown onions
1 leek, white part only
2 celery stalks
½ bunch thyme
4 fresh bay leaves
½ teaspoon black peppercorns
3 kg (6 lb 12 oz) chicken carcass pieces
5 litres (175 fl oz/20 cups) water

1 Coarsely chop the vegetables and put in a stockpot with the thyme, bay leaves and peppercorns. Briefly wash the chicken pieces under cold running water and add to the pot. Add enough water to cover all the ingredients.

2 Bring to the boil over high heat, then reduce the heat and simmer gently for 2 hours, skimming the surface regularly to remove any fat and impurities.

3 Remove from the heat and cool slightly. Ladle through a fine sieve or a sieve lined with a double layer of muslin (cheesecloth) into a clean container and refrigerate until well chilled.

4 Use a slotted spoon to remove the fat that has solidified on the stock's surface.

TIP Stock can be kept in an airtight container in the refrigerator for up to 4 days or frozen for up to 3 months.

Brown chicken stock

PREPARATION TIME 20 minutes

COOKING TIME 2 hours 50 minutes

MAKES about 3 litres (105 fl oz/ 12 cups)

3 kg (6 lb 12 oz) chicken carcass pieces
60 ml (2 fl oz/¼ cup) vegetable oil
2 brown onions
1 leek, white part only
2 celery stalks
2 carrots
½ bunch thyme
4 fresh bay leaves
½ teaspoon black peppercorns
5 litres (175 fl oz/20 cups) water

1 Preheat oven to 200°C (400°F/Gas 6).

2 Briefly wash the chicken pieces under cold running water and place in a large roasting pan, or two smaller roasting pans. Drizzle with 2 tablespoons of oil and turn to coat. Roast for 20 minutes, then turn the bones (and swap the roasting pans if you are using two) and roast for a further 20 minutes, until dark golden. Set aside.

3 Coarsely chop the vegetables. Heat the remaining oil in a stockpot over medium heat. Cook the vegetables for 10 minutes, stirring frequently to ensure even browning. Add the chicken pieces, herbs, peppercorns and enough water to cover all the ingredients.

4 Bring to the boil over high heat. Reduce the heat and simmer gently for 2 hours, skimming the surface regularly to remove any fat and impurities.

5 Remove from the heat and cool slightly. Ladle through a fine sieve or a sieve lined with a double layer of muslin (cheesecloth) into a clean container and refrigerate until well chilled.

6 Use a slotted spoon to remove the fat that has solidified on the stock's surface.

VARIATIONS

Duck stock: Use duck carcass pieces instead of chicken. Add ½ teaspoon juniper berries with the herbs.

White chicken stock

1 Briefly wash the chicken under cold running water and add to the vegetables, thyme, bay leaves and peppercorns in the stockpot.

2 Simmer the stock gently for 2 hours, skimming the surface regularly to remove any fat and impurities.

3 Ladle the stock through a fine sieve into a clean container. Discard the chicken pieces, vegetables and herbs.

4 While the stock is chilling, the fat will solidify and rise to the surface, making it easy to remove and discard.

Brown chicken stock

1 Roast the carcass pieces for 40 minutes, turning the bones halfway through cooking, until dark golden.

Duck confit

In south-west France confiting duck was traditionally a seasonal process to preserve the duck meat through the use of salt. Farmers' wives made it in the lead-up to Christmas, before the birds reared for foie gras were slaughtered. Nowadays, although ducks are reared year-round, we still make salt confits because we want the flavours to penetrate through the meat and fat.

PREPARATION TIME 20 minutes
(+ 9 hours chilling, and cooling)

COOKING TIME 2½ hours

MAKES 6 confit marylands

6 duck marylands (approximately
    1.7 kg/3 lb 12 oz) or 12 legs
105 g (3½ oz/⅓ cup) rock salt
2¼ garlic bulbs (about 30 cloves),
    cloves peeled
1 bunch thyme
2 tablespoons black peppercorns,
    coarsely crushed
3 fresh bay leaves
Zest of 1 orange, removed using a
    vegetable peeler, white pith removed
1.2 kg (2 lb 11 oz/5½ cups) rendered
    duck fat (see tip), approximately

1 Wash the duck and pat dry with paper towels. Place in a glass or ceramic dish. Put the salt, garlic, thyme and peppercorns in a food processor and pulse until coarsely ground.

2 Rub the salt mixture into the duck, then add the bay leaves and orange zest. Cover and refrigerate for 6 hours.

3 Preheat the oven to 120°C (235°F/ Gas ½). Wash the duck under cold running water, rubbing to remove any salt, herbs and spices. Pat dry with paper towels. Place in an ovenproof dish or roasting pan just large enough to fit all the duck in a tight, single layer.

4 Gently heat the duck fat in a saucepan over low heat until melted. Pour over the duck to cover. (How much fat you need will depend on the size of your dish or roasting pan.)

5 Partially cover the dish or pan with foil. Cook the duck for 2½ hours or until the meat is tender and starting to fall away from the bone. The oil should barely simmer — you should only be able to see the occasional small bubble. To test if it is cooked, pierce the duck with a fork to check that the flesh is soft and meltingly tender.

6 Remove from the oven and cool the duck to room temperature in the fat. Use a slotted spoon to carefully remove the cooled duck from the fat and place it on a baking tray, skin side up. Cover and refrigerate for 3 hours or until the flesh is firm.

7 Slowly pour the duck fat through a fine sieve into a jug. Discard any liquid and herbs from the bottom of the dish or pan, and the contents of the sieve.

8 The confited marylands can be stored in a sealed sterilised dish or container, covered in the reserved duck fat, in the refrigerator for up to 1 month.

> **TIP** Rendered duck fat is sold in jars or tubs and is available from larger supermarkets, quality butchers and speciality food stores. You can use olive oil instead of duck fat if duck fat is not available.

1 Process the salt, garlic, thyme and peppercorns until they are coarsely ground.

2 Use your hands to rub the salt mixture into the duck.

3 Wash the duck under cold running water, then pat dry with paper towels.

4 Heat the fat until melted, then pour over the duck to cover.

5 When you pierce the duck flesh with a fork it should be soft and meltingly tender.

6 Use a slotted spoon to carefully transfer the duck to a baking tray, skin side up.

7 Slowly pour the duck fat through a fine sieve into a jug.

8 Store the confited marylands covered with the reserved duck fat.

Flavours for poultry

Poultry is a versatile meat, so it teams well with a wide variety of ingredients and lends itself to the two basic forms of marinating. Rubbing a blend of herbs and spices into the skin of poultry is referred to as a 'dry' marinade, while a 'wet' marinade usually includes liquids such as olive oil, vinegar, lemon juice or wine, as well as herbs and spices, plus other possible additions such as garlic and ginger. Both forms of marinating add flavour to the flesh and help tenderise it.

Chicken benefits from the addition of herbs, especially tarragon, thyme and rosemary. Add garlic, lemon juice and olive oil and you have the perfect wet marinade for chicken.

Fattier birds, such as duck, work well with Asian flavours such as soy sauce, ginger, cumin and coriander, to cut through the richness of the meat, rather than add to it. Alternatively, braising duck with red wine, stock and seasonings is also a good combination.

Small birds such as quail and squab, which have very little fat under the skin, respond to a dry marinade rubbed into the skin, followed by a drizzle of olive oil to keep them moist. Wrapping these birds in prosciutto or bacon also adds flavour and prevents them drying out during the cooking process.

Stuffing is one of the best ways to add flavour to a turkey, as the flavours permeate the bird during the long cooking. Stuffings vary greatly, but usually feature herbs and spices, onion, bacon, mushrooms or nuts added to breadcrumbs or rice. Alternatively, you can place a herb butter under the skin.

The following chart lists flavours that team well with poultry, so you can experiment with marinades and stuffings.

SPICES	HERBS	OTHER
Allspice	Basil	Bacon, ham, prosciutto
Cardamom	Bay leaves	Butter
Cinnamon	Chervil	Fennel
Cloves	Chives	Garlic
Coriander	Marjoram	Ginger
Cumin	Oregano	Leeks, onions
Juniper berries	Parsley	Lemons
Mixed dried herbs	Rosemary	Mushrooms
Nutmeg	Tarragon	Olive oil
Paprika	Thyme	Sherry
Pepper (white, black, cayenne)		Soy sauce
Saffron		Tomatoes
		Vinegar (red and white wine, sherry)
		Wine (red and white)

Buying, storing and preparing meat and game

Buying meat and game

Meat from different animals has varying characteristics, but in general you should look for meat that is richly coloured and not slimy or with any strong odours. Fat should be creamy in colour, not yellow, and the meat should look appealingly moist. Avoid meat with dark patches or an excess of fat or gristle. When buying pork, avoid meat that is very pale or excessively lean. Pork that has a good flavour will be pinkish-red in colour and exhibit a good amount of fat. Avoid grey-looking or sticky pork with overly yellow fat, as this will be past its best. Finally, make sure you get the right cut of meat for the recipe you intend to make — all cuts have different amounts of fat and connective tissue, depending on where in the carcass they come from.

Storing meat and game

All fresh meat has bacteria present on the surface, so it is prone to spoilage if it's not handled or stored properly, or used promptly. Fresh beef, veal and lamb can be stored in the refrigerator for up to four days, although minced (ground) meats should be used within two days. Pork does not keep so well, as its fat turns rancid quickly. Use pork within three days of purchase and minced pork within two days.

Vacuum-packed meat will keep for weeks, refrigerated in the original packaging, so check the use-by date and only open the package just before using. Meat from the supermarket usually comes in oxygen-flushed sealed containers that are designed to prolong freshness and colour, so leave them in the packaging until ready to use and be guided by the use-by date on the packaging.

For meat that is not in special packaging, remove the original wrappings and place the meat on a tray, then loosely wrap in clean plastic wrap. It is important to allow the meat to 'breathe', to preserve freshness and colour. Larger cuts are best stored on a rack over a tray so they don't sit in their own blood. Keep all fresh meat separate from other foods in your refrigerator, as the blood and juices they lose during storage can easily contaminate other foods.

Freezing meat and game

All meat and game can be frozen. The larger the cut, or animal, the longer it will keep in the freezer. Minced (ground) meat can be frozen for six to eight weeks, while larger cuts, such as a large roast, can be frozen for up to eight months. All meat should be well wrapped, in several layers of plastic wrap and then foil, to prevent freezer burn, which causes the outside of the meat to become extremely dry. Game birds, depending on size, can be frozen for two to four months. Whole rabbits can be frozen for up to four months.

Preparing meat and game

Most meat requires some trimming, or 'cleaning', before cooking, depending on the recipe and cut of meat. The thin white tissue surrounding tender cuts, such as fillet, is called silverskin and needs to be removed before cooking. Hard gristle also needs to be removed from some cuts of steak and stewing meat. Recipes will often call for excess fat to be removed and while a special boning knife is best for this, any long, slim and very sharp knife will do the job effectively. A boning knife, designed to be highly manoeuvrable, is also best for removing silverskin and general trimming.

Always prepare meat on a board that is used only for that purpose, and one that can be scrubbed well in very hot water afterwards. Never prepare cooked and raw meat on the same surface, as dangerous bacteria can be transferred from one to the other, potentially causing food poisoning. Use knives that have been sharpened well to avoid accidents and wasteful trimming — knives that are blunt are less accurate than those that are very sharp.

Terms to describe meat and game

Grass fed Different countries have different legal definitions for what constitutes 'grass fed'. In some countries, cattle can be kept in sheds and fed hay all their lives, yet still qualify as grass fed. So, grass fed does not necessarily mean 'pasture' fed (ie, animals that have been reared outdoors). However, it is generally accepted that grass fed means meat (mostly beef, though the term can also be relevant for lamb) from animals that have primarily lived on a diet of foraged grass.

Grain fed Modern, industrial-scale meat production has spawned the need to feed animals a diet with a greater energy density than their natural diet, so they can grow at a faster, more efficient rate. There are many factors at play here, such as a scarcity of pasture due to lack of rain or a harsh climate that has led to animals being kept indoors over winter. Grain feeding, where cattle (and sometimes sheep) are fed grains, soy and other nutrients in addition to grass or hay, provides a cost-effective alternative to grass feeding. Grain-fed meat has good marbling, paler fat than grass-fed meat and tends to be more consistently tender. It also has a milder flavour. The chief problem with grain feeding, however, is that cows and sheep are ruminants. This means their stomachs are designed to digest grass. Feeding grains to ruminants on a long-term basis can wreak havoc on their digestive systems.

Grass finished and grain finished An animal is said to be 'grain finished' when it has lived as a grass-fed animal but spends the last weeks, or even months, of its life eating a diet rich in grains. Conversely, an animal has been 'grass finished' when it has had a diet of grains but is fed grass in the last weeks or months of its life. Finishing is another word for 'fattening', the time before an animal is processed when it gains weight and condition. Grass-fed animals have naturally higher levels of omega 3s and other nutrients, so introducing grass into the diet of a grain-fed animal raises these levels and makes the meat appealing to those who prefer grass-fed meat. Grain finishing puts weight on the animals very quickly and results in well-marbled meat. A boost of grain can be a cheap, quick way to fatten a grass-fed animal before slaughter.

Organic The term 'organic' is subject to legal definitions that vary from country to country. However, in relation to meat, the term organic is generally held to mean meat that has been raised without the use of chemical fertilisers or pesticides in its feed, with no genetically modified foods or food additives and no irradiated feed. Organically raised animals are not pushed to grow and gain weight faster than is natural and are therefore free of growth hormones.

Dry aged Meat is aged before it is eaten, especially game, beef and, to a lesser extent, lamb. The ageing process develops flavour and tenderness, and can be dry or wet (see below). Dry ageing involves hanging large primal cuts of meat in a humidity- and temperature-controlled environment for up to 28 days. During this time the meat dries out slightly as liquid evaporates, and natural enzymes work on the meat and tenderise it. The flavour of the meat deepens. Dry ageing is expensive due to the time and space it requires and only really top-quality meat, with large amounts of well-distributed fat, benefits from it. There is also significant shrinkage through moisture loss and the crust that forms on the outside of the meat needs to be removed before cooking. However, the flavour and texture of dry-aged beef are incomparable.

Game is dry aged by being hung, whole, in a cool dry place for up to two weeks. This develops those strong 'gamey' flavours, while the enzymes that flourish during dry ageing work on the meat and tenderise it. Without hanging, game wouldn't have its characteristic flavour and it would be tough.

Wet aged This is a fairly modern process that involves ageing meat in vacuum-sealed plastic bags for a few days to retain moisture. It doesn't require the space, time or controlled temperatures of dry ageing so it is far more cost-effective. It is normal for the meat to smell quite strong and feel a little slimy when it comes out of the bag.

Hormone free Some countries, including Australia, allow the use of hormone growth promotants. These are often naturally occurring hormones and they enable farmers to raise bigger cattle on less food in the shortest amount of time. They save the grower money and there are various schools of thought as to the effects of these, if any, on the consumer.

Grain Meat is muscle tissue and muscle is made up of fibres that run parallel to each other. These fibres are called the 'grain' of the meat. In some cuts, such as beef tenderloin, the grain is easy to see as it runs the length of the meat. When carving meat, it is important to cut across the grain — if you carve along the grain, the meat will be chewy and stringy.

Marbled meat Marbled meat refers to the appearance that intramuscular fat gives to meat, particularly red meat. It shows as a fine network of white fat throughout the flesh, in a marbled effect. Breeding and diet affect marbling — cattle fed on grain, for example, exhibit well-marbled meat. Marbling is highly desirable, as the fat melts into the flesh as the meat cooks, adding succulence and depth of flavour.

Cuts of beef

Blade and chuck are two muscles from the sides of the shoulder blade. They are hard-working muscles full of connective tissue that require long, slow cooking. Just beside the blade is the oyster blade.

Brisket covers a large area from the underbelly of the animal to the breast. At the breast end it is called the point end brisket. This is leaner than the naval end brisket, which is fatty and coarse textured. Skirt, hangar and flank steaks come from this region of the animal.

Cube roll and rib eye is a prime cut behind the blade/chuck. It can be butchered into a boneless roast (scotch fillet), a standing rib roast, rib cutlets or rib eye/scotch fillet steaks.

Knuckle, also called round or thick flank, is a firm-textured cut from muscles that run lengthways down the rear leg. Round steak, minute steak and knuckle medallion are all taken from this cut.

Mince is finely chopped cheaper cuts and offcuts of beef. Ready-made minced (ground) beef is mechanically ground, but you can make mince by finely chopping beef by hand. This versatile cut is ideal for burgers, meatballs and sauces.

Rump is a large group of four muscles that sits behind the sirloin. These are butchered into cuts known as the cap, rost biff and tri tip. Whole beef rumps can weigh around 6 kg (13 lb 8 oz), but they are often cut into steaks and schnitzels.

Shin is the shank meat from the foreleg. It is also called gravy beef and is a flavoursome stewing cut. Shins can also be cut into shin steaks with the bone left in (sold as osso buco).

Short ribs and spare ribs are cut from the same bones as the rib eye but they occur below it, so they are well marbled. Short ribs are meatier than spare ribs.

Silverside, found just under the rump near the rear of the animal, comprises two leg muscles. The outer muscle has a coarse, fibrous grain and is mostly used for corned beef.

Sirloin, also called strip loin, is a tender prime cut and is the next cut along the spine from the cube roll. It is sold as a large, long tender roast or cut into steaks that are called boneless sirloin, porterhouse or New York cut steaks.

Tenderloin, or eye fillet, is a muscle attached to the sirloin. When the tenderloin and sirloin are attached, the cut is

tenderloin

rump

oyster blade

boneless sirloin
steaks

diced gravy beef

rib eye steaks

known as shortloin and if it's cut through the bone, it makes T-bone steaks. On its own, the tenderloin is a very tender, lean cut that can be cooked as a whole piece (the thick end is known as the chateaubriand), cut into steaks known as fillet or eye fillet, or diced for stir-frying.

Topside is a very lean cut, found on the top inside of the rear leg. It is available as a whole piece, steaks or schnitzel.

mince

shin

silverside

short ribs

topside

T-bone steak

round steak

Cuts of veal

Veal is the meat from young calves (up to one year old) and it is prized for its delicate flavour and tenderness. In Australia, veal is a by-product of the dairy industry and the calves have access to light, pasture, milk and iron.

Backstrap or striploin is the veal equivalent of beef sirloin.

Blade is one of the main forequarter (shoulder) muscles, and is well suited to roasting or casseroling when diced.

Breast, also called the brisket, is the large area of flesh that runs along the end of the rib cage around the belly. The meat has large open fibres and is fatty and flavoursome.

Chuck, another name for the neck, is a braising cut.

Leg is the rear end of the calf and yields the knuckle, rump, topside and silverside. These are sliced thinly to make schnitzel, also called escalopes and scallopini.

Mince is finely chopped cheaper cuts and offcuts of veal. It has a milder flavour than minced (ground) beef and is often combined with minced pork to give a more delicate flavour than minced pork alone.

Osso buco is the shank of the calf, sliced through the bone. This is the genuine osso buco cut, rather than beef shin.

Rack makes a succulent rib roast or can be butchered into cutlets. When the bone is removed, it's called loin and can be cut into medallions.

Rump consists of three muscles: the cap, rost biff and tri tip, as for beef. All three muscles are tender cuts, suited to roasting or grilling.

Tenderloin, or eye fillet, is a small, expensive cut that is found under the backstrap and ranges from 500–800 g (1 lb 2 oz–1 lb 12 oz). It can be cut into steaks or it can be roasted, either whole or just the thicker end.

osso buco

blade (rolled)

blade (diced)

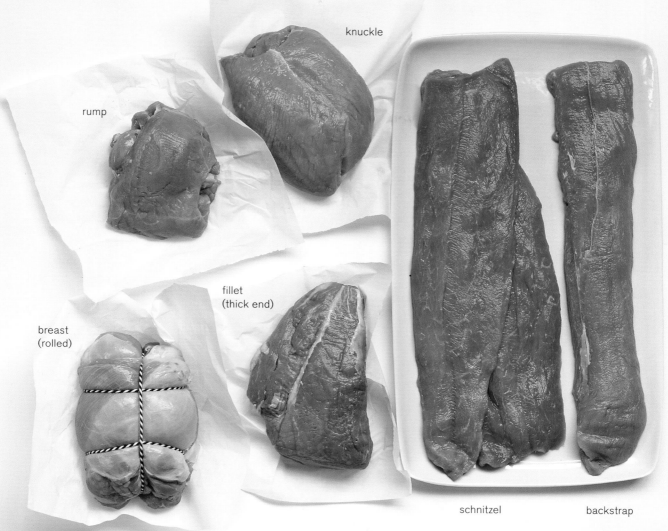

rump

knuckle

fillet
(thick end)

breast
(rolled)

schnitzel

backstrap

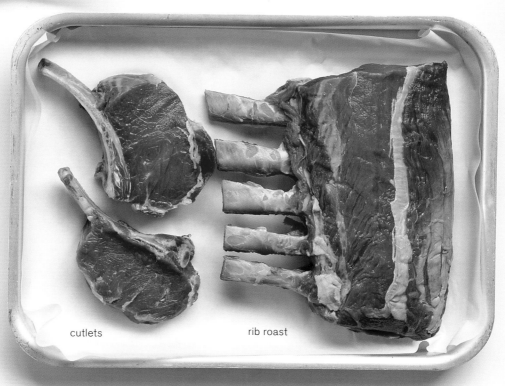

cutlets

rib roast

Cuts of lamb

Breast is the meat on the rib cage that runs from the tip of the rack to the belly. Breast meat is fatty and extremely flavoursome. It is also called 'lamb flaps' and can be used with the bone in or out.

Chump, also called the rump, is the top part of the lamb hindquarter and due to its size (around 250 g/9 oz) makes a perfect roast for one. It is also cut into chops.

Leg is most often cooked whole, although it can be broken up into topside, silverside and knuckle cuts. A whole leg can also be tunnel boned (easy carve) or butterflied and cut into chops, steaks or pieces. A whole leg weighs around 4 kg (9 lb).

Loin is from the middle section of the top of the lamb and contains the sought-after tenderloin (fillet) and backstrap cuts. It can be boned and rolled or cut into loin chops.

Mince is finely chopped cheaper cuts and offcuts of lamb. This versatile cut is ideal for burgers, meatballs and sauces.

Neck can be cooked whole (rib-eye roast) or cut into chops (neck and best end neck). The neck is a hard-working muscle that makes a flavoursome cut of lamb.

Rack runs down the length of the rib cage. It comprises 10 ribs and the section closest to the loin is considered the best part of the cut as the meat is thicker and more tender. For this reason it is often called 'best end'. Racks are cooked whole or as individual cutlets.

Saddle of lamb is arguably the most prized, and certainly the most expensive, of all the lamb cuts. It is a large joint that comprises the two loins, running down to the hip, joined in the middle by the backbone.

Shank can come from the hind or forequarter. Hindquarter shanks are meatier and more succulent than forequarter.

Shoulder is a large cut that can be broken down into a forequarter rack and forequarter chops, or it can be boned and used as a rolled shoulder roast or diced for braising.

loin chops

mince

forequarter chops

backstrap

best end neck chops

chump chops

chump roast

tenderloin (fillet)

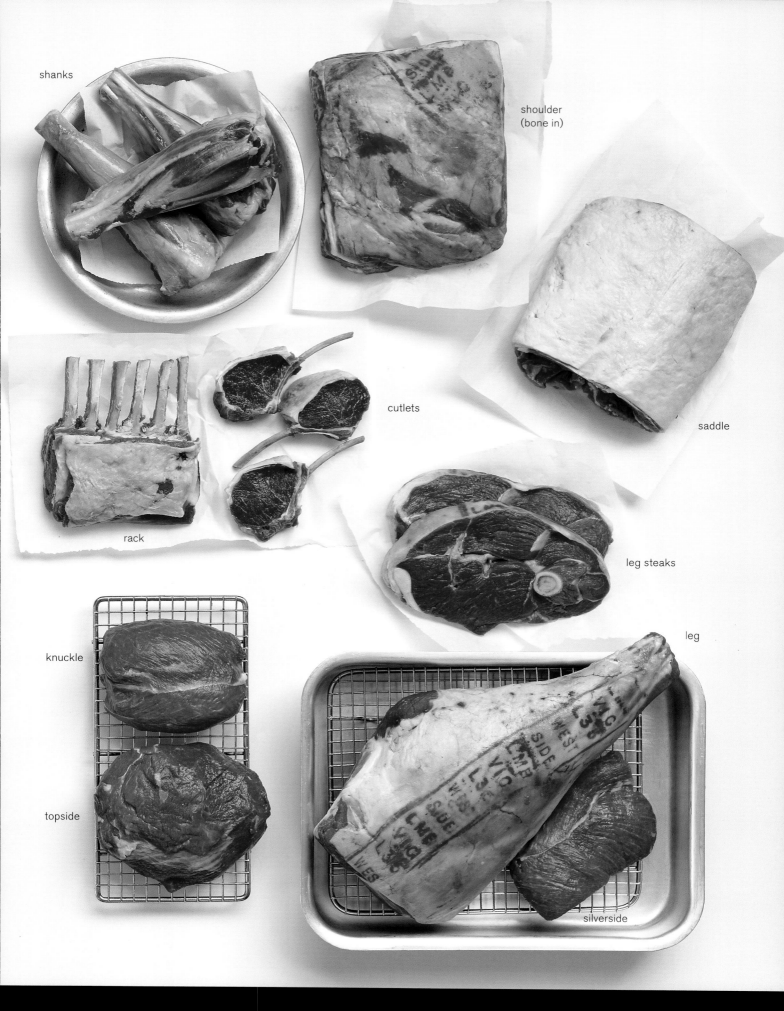

shanks

shoulder
(bone in)

saddle

cutlets

rack

leg steaks

knuckle

leg

topside

silverside

Cuts of pork

Belly is from the stomach region and has a thick layer of fat. It is a tender, juicy and flavoursome cut of pork. When cooked correctly, pork belly has a soft, melting texture. Pork ribs, both American-style and spare ribs, come from this same region of the pig.

Forequarter is a large primal cut from the shoulder region of the pig. The forequarter can be butchered into the shoulder (boned and rolled), suitable for roasting, and smaller cuts such as the scotch fillet, or neck, a boneless rolled roast, forequarter chops and scotch fillet steaks.

Hock is found between the shank and the leg proper. This part of the pig is high in skin, tendon and fat and is loved by many cultures for its sweet, sticky qualities when cooked slowly for a long time. It is a cheaper cut of pork.

Leg is the hind leg of the pig. It can be purchased whole (bone in or boneless) or cut into smaller cuts such as leg steaks and boneless mini roasts.

Loin is considered the finest cut of pork. The whole loin comes on the bone as a rack or boned as a rolled loin. It is also cut into cutlets, chops or steaks that can also be butterflied.

Mince is finely chopped cheaper cuts and offcuts of pork. Like other minced (ground) meats, the quality of commercial minced pork can vary due to differences in fat content.

Ribs are taken from the rib cage. Spare ribs are cut from the belly side, while American-style ribs (back/loin ribs) are taken from under the loin and are the meatier of the two.

Tenderloin (fillet) is a choice cut taken from the base of the loin. This is a lean muscle that does little work and is therefore extremely tender.

loin cutlets

tenderloin

spare ribs

rolled belly

mince

loin steaks

leg steaks

shoulder (boned and rolled)

leg

hock

forequarter roast

belly

scotch fillet

rolled loin

American-style ribs

Cuts of venison, rabbit and goat

Venison

Venison, the meat from deer, has a stronger, more assertive flavour than beef. It is dark red in colour and is lean with little or no marbling of fat. Because it is so lean, it is easily overcooked. Prime cuts, such as fillet and loin, should never be cooked beyond medium-rare or they will be dry. Roasts should be left a little pink in the middle, too. Prime cuts are:

Leg, also called haunch, can be broken down into smaller pieces, notably the rump, topside, silverside and knuckle (shank). The whole leg can be roasted. Topside, silverside and rump can be roasted whole, chargrilled or pan-fried when sliced, and braised or stir-fried when diced.

Loin is a tender cut that is suited to roasting and can be purchased on the bone or off, cut into steaks or cooked whole. Boned loin is the venison equivalent of beef sirloin.

Saddle consists of both loins on the bone and left connected by the backbone. This is a prime roasting cut.

Shoulder of venison is a tough cut that is best suited to moist cooking methods, such as pot-roasting or braising.

Tenderloin, or eye fillet, is taken from the loin and is a succulent, highly desirable cut that is best roasted or cut into steaks. Porterhouse steaks are cut through the bone, taking in the tenderloin and loin muscles.

Rabbit

Farmed rabbit is widely available and is meatier and far more tender than wild rabbit. It has pale, mild-flavoured meat, reminiscent of chicken in both taste and appearance. It is a very lean meat and care should be taken not to overcook it, particularly when roasting. Rabbit is generally sold whole, rather than in pieces, but it is relatively simple to cut into pieces at home. The most tender part of the rabbit is the saddle — the loin muscle that runs either side of the backbone. Rabbit can be roasted, whole or in pieces, or cut into pieces and braised or pan-fried.

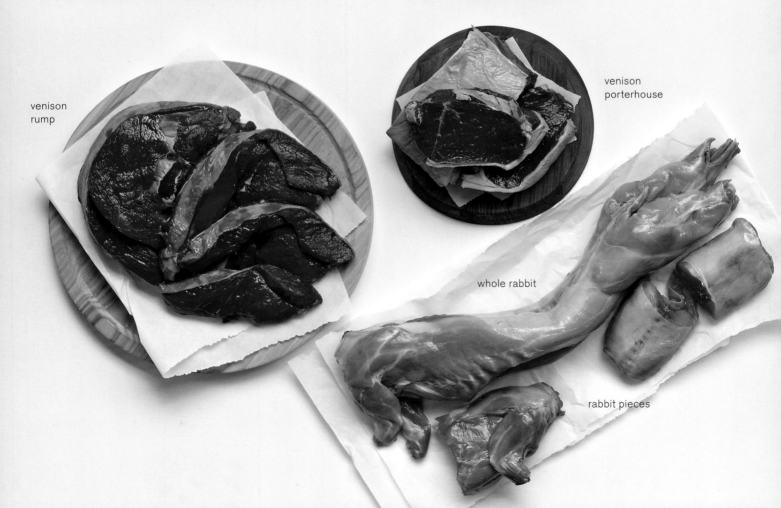

venison rump

venison porterhouse

whole rabbit

rabbit pieces

Goat

Goat is one of the world's most widely consumed meats. The flesh is classified as a red meat and the cuts correspond to those for lamb (it is often cooked quite similarly to lamb). Goat meat, however, is much leaner than lamb. The particularly delicate, tender meat from young goats, or kids, is called cabrito and the meat from mature goats is called chevon. As with lamb, a whole kid can be spit roasted. One of the main cuts is the leg, which is suited to roasting whole or can be cut into smaller boneless mini roasts and escalopes for pan-frying. The loin is another large prime cut that can be left whole, on the bone or boned; both are good for roasting. The loin can also be cut into cutlets for grilling, pan-frying or barbecuing. If it's left attached to the corresponding loin, on the other side of the carcass, it forms the saddle. The shoulder is a large cut that can be roasted or cut into smaller pieces and braised. The breast is often boned and rolled for roasting, while the neck end yields cutlets, for grilling or braising, and the scrag (the end of the neck that can be pot-roasted or braised). Between the neck and the loin is found the best end of neck, which comprises a row of cutlets that can be cooked as a rack or as individual chops for grilling or pan-frying.

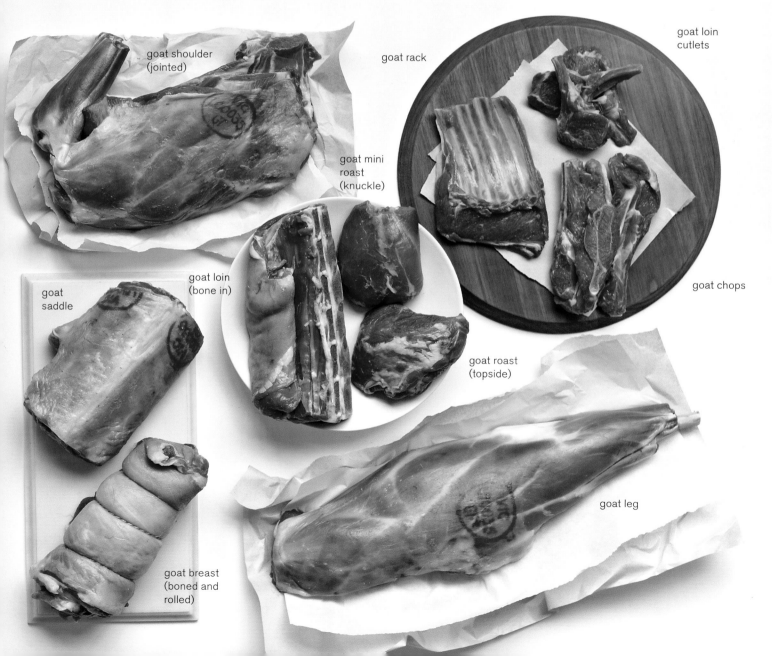

goat shoulder (jointed)

goat rack

goat loin cutlets

goat mini roast (knuckle)

goat loin (bone in)

goat saddle

goat chops

goat roast (topside)

goat breast (boned and rolled)

goat leg

Suitable cooking techniques for cuts of meat

BEEF	
Cut	**Technique**
Tenderloin (eye fillet)	Roasting, poaching, stir-frying, pan-frying, chargrilling
Fillet steak	Pan-frying, chargrilling
Sirloin (whole/roast)	Roasting
Boneless sirloin/New York/porterhouse steak	Chargrilling, barbecuing
T-bone steak	Pan-frying, barbecuing
Topside roast	Roasting, pot-roasting
Topside steak	Stewing, braising
Topside schnitzel/silverside minute steak	Pan-frying
Rump (whole)	Roasting
Rump steak	Chargrilling, barbecuing, pan-frying, stir-frying
Rump schnitzel/rump minute steak	Pan-frying
Brisket/rolled brisket	Stewing, braising
Skirt (rolled)	Stewing, braising
Skirt steak	Pan-frying, chargrilling
Skirt (diced)	Stewing, braising
Shin/gravy (boneless)	Stewing, braising
Shin/osso buco (bone in)	Stewing, braising
Rib eye, whole/standing rib roast	Roasting
Rib cutlet	Pan-frying, chargrilling
Rib eye steak/scotch fillet steak	Pan-frying, chargrilling
Rib eye scotch fillet roast	Roasting
Blade steak	Stewing, braising

BEEF	
Cut	**Technique**
Oyster blade	Chargrilling, pan-frying, stir-frying
Blade minute steak	Pan-frying
Chuck steak	Stewing, braising
Short ribs/spare ribs	Stewing, braising, slow-roasting
Mince	Frying, braising, stewing
Corned beef (topside or silverside)	Poaching
Knuckle/round steak	Pan-frying
Flank steak	Stewing, braising, chargrilling, pan-frying
Chateaubriand	Roasting, chargrilling

VEAL	
Cut	**Technique**
Backstrap/striploin	Poaching, chargrilling, pan-frying, roasting
Blade/shoulder	Roasting, braising
Breast/brisket	Poaching, slow-roasting
Rump	Chargrilling, roasting (whole)
Chuck	Stewing, braising
Leg (whole)	Roasting
Knuckle (diced)	Braising
Schnitzel	Pan-frying
Osso buco	Stewing, braising
Rib roast/loin	Roasting
Cutlet/medallions	Pan-frying, barbecuing
Topside/silverside	Pot-roasting, poaching

LAMB	
Cut	**Technique**
Leg, whole (bone in or tunnel boned)	Roasting, poaching
Butterflied leg	Roasting, barbecuing
Leg (diced)	Pan-frying, stir-frying
Leg steak	Chargrilling, barbecuing, pan-frying
Chump (whole)	Roasting
Chump chop	Chargrilling, pan-frying
Rolled loin	Roasting
Saddle	Roasting
Loin chop	Chargrilling, barbecuing, pan-frying
Eye of loin backstrap	Chargrilling, barbecuing, pan-frying, stir-frying
Mince	Frying, braising, stewing
Tenderloin (fillet)	Chargrilling, barbecuing, pan-frying, stir-frying
Forequarter chop	Chargrilling, barbecuing
Shoulder, whole (boned and rolled)	Roasting
Shoulder (diced)	Stewing, braising
Forequarter rack	Roasting
Rack/best end rack	Roasting
Cutlet	Chargrilling, barbecuing, pan-frying
Shank	Stewing, braising
Neck, fillet roast/ rib eye roast	Roasting, pot-roasting
Neck chop	Stewing, braising
Best neck chop	Stewing, braising
Breast/lamb flaps	Roasting
Silverside/topside	Roasting

PORK	
Cut	**Technique**
Leg, whole and boneless whole	Roasting
Mini leg roast	Roasting
Butterflied steak	Chargrilling, barbecuing, pan-frying
Leg steak	Chargrilling, barbecuing, pan-frying, stir-frying
Hock	Slow-roasting, poaching, braising
Rolled loin	Roasting
Loin rack	Roasting
Loin cutlet	Chargrilling, barbecuing, pan-frying
Loin chop	Chargrilling, barbecuing, pan-frying
Loin steak	Chargrilling, barbecuing, pan-frying, stir-frying
Tenderloin (pork fillet)	Roasting, chargrilling, barbecuing, pan-frying, stir-frying
Belly and rolled belly	Stewing, braising, slow-roasting
Spare ribs	Slow-roasting, barbecuing
Forequarter roast	Roasting
American-style spare ribs	Roasting, stewing, braising
Shoulder (boned and rolled)	Roasting
Shoulder (diced)	Stewing, braising
Mince	Frying, stewing, braising
Scotch fillet	Roasting, pot-roasting
Shoulder chop	Chargrilling, barbecuing
Scotch fillet steak	Chargrilling, barbecuing, pan-frying, stir-frying

Tunnel boning a leg of lamb

Tunnel boning is a technique that involves cutting out the internal bones from a joint of meat, without cutting through the flesh to do so. This makes it easier to carve and leaves a pocket that can be stuffed, if desired. A boning knife, which has a long, thin blade and is designed to be highly manoeuvrable, is the ideal tool for this job. The flesh surrounding the bones is carefully cut away to separate the bones from the meat. With a lamb leg, you work from the top of the leg down to the shank end.

1 If the leg still has the pelvic bone (a large flat bone) attached, this should be removed first. Place the leg on a work surface, with the shank end towards you. Use a sharp boning knife to cut around the exposed edges of the pelvic bone, keeping the knife as close to the bone as possible.

2 As you loosen the bone around the top, gradually and carefully follow the bone deeper into the leg, cutting as close to the bone as possible.

3 When you reach the ball joint of the pelvic bone, cut through the ligaments and then the ball joint to remove the pelvic bone.

4 Following the large leg bone, and cutting as close to the bone as possible, work your knife around the bone to free it from the meat.

5 As you cut deeper into the leg, pull the meat away from the bone for better access. Keep cutting around the leg bone until you reach the shank bone. Continue to cut, pulling the meat away from the exposed bone, until you are at the end of the leg bone and the lamb leg is practically inside out.

6 Remove the shank bone by cutting it free of any meat or ligaments at the end of the leg, then pull the bone out and restore the lamb to its original shape. Reserve the bones to make lamb stock (see page 60).

Butterflying a leg of lamb

Butterflying is a similar technique to tunnel boning, but you cut from the outside, all the way down the leg, to expose the bone and then open the leg out into one large flat piece. A whole butterflied leg of lamb is ideal for barbecuing or chargrilling.

1 Put the lamb on a work surface, shank towards you, and hold the leg by the shank bone. Use a sharp boning knife to cut any large connective tendons away from the end of the shank bone.

2 Make a straight cut up the length of the leg, starting at the shank end and working towards the top.

3 Starting at the top of the leg, cut away the flesh from either side of the bone, working your way down to the shank end of the leg and using your hands to ease the meat back as necessary for better access.

4 Work the knife around the pelvic bone at the top of the leg to loosen and remove it.

5 Work the knife under the leg and shank bones, cutting as close to the bones as possible, to separate them from the meat.

6 Open the lamb out, cutting into the meat if needed to even the thickness of the leg. Reserve the bones to make lamb stock (see page 60).

Trimming a beef tenderloin

You can buy a tenderloin (eye fillet) that is already trimmed of fat and sinew, but you will pay a premium for it. With a sharp boning knife and a little know-how, you'll find trimming the meat yourself is a simple technique that is satisfying to master.

1 Lay the tenderloin on a work surface and locate the chain muscle, which runs the length of the tenderloin. Use your hands to gently separate as much of the chain muscle from the tenderloin as possible.

2 Use a sharp boning knife to carefully cut away any chain muscle that you could not easily pull off.

3 Trim away any fat or connective tissue that remains on the tenderloin.

4 Carefully cut away small sections of the silverskin (the fine silver membrane) that covers parts of the fillet. To begin, hold your knife flat and work it under a roughly 1 cm (½ inch) wide piece of silverskin at one end of the fillet, then cut under it to release the silverskin from the meat.

5 Hold the end of the released silverskin taut with one hand while you work your knife under the silverskin to remove a strip of it.

6 Hold your knife flat against the silverskin and continue cutting, trying to avoid removing any meat, until all the silverskin is released and discarded.

Frenching a lamb rack or cutlets

Frenching, also known as french trimming, involves exposing and then cleaning the bones on a cut of meat. The purpose of frenching is to give a neat and professional presentation to the cooked dish. Without it, the thin seams of meat and fat that cling to the bones can shrivel, burn and look unsightly when cooked. French trimming is classically used for lamb cutlets and lamb rack, although it is now a common treatment for shanks and standing rib roasts as well.

1 Stand the rack on its end so you can easily see the fat 'eye' of meat that runs at the base of the bones.

2 Turn the meat fat-side up, then score a straight horizontal line across the fat from one side of the rack to the other, about 3.5 cm (1⅖ inches) above the eye. Use a boning knife to follow the score mark and cut through the fat, right down to the bones.

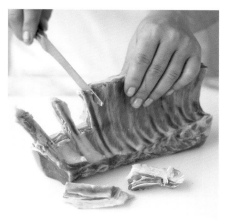

3 Stand the rack on its end again, with the fatty side facing you, and use the tip of the knife to cut through the meat between the bones, cutting all the way through to the other side of the rack.

4 Turn the rack over and, using the cuts as a guide, score along the bones. This mark should coincide with the cut through the fat and will ensure the final frenching is neat.

5 Turn the rack over again and pull the fat off the bones above the cut. Use the knife to cut away any fat that will not easily lift off.

6 Use your knife to scrape the bones perfectly clean, making sure the cuts between the bones above the eye are straight and neat.

Tying meat for cooking

Meat is tied using kitchen string to make it more compact and give it a neat, uniform shape that will help it cook evenly. Larger pieces, such as a whole beef roast, and smaller pieces, such as eye fillet steaks, are both tied for these reasons. Large roasts that have been boned also benefit from tying as they would otherwise cook with an uneven shape.

1 Place the meat on a work surface, fat side up (if there is any fat). If it is a long piece of meat, fold the thin end under by 8–10 cm (3¼–4 inches) to ensure the meat is more or less the same thickness all the way along. Tie kitchen string (see tip) around the meat, about 2.5 cm (1 inch) from one end and with the knot on top.

2 Gently pull about 2.5 cm (1 inch) of string along the meat.

3 Put one finger on the string to hold it in place, then bring the remaining string under and around the meat.

4 Thread the string under the piece your finger is holding, then pull it tight to secure.

5 Repeat the process of pulling the string about 2.5 cm (1 inch) along the meat, bringing it under and around the meat and then looping it under your finger, until you reach the end of the meat.

6 If your string isn't long enough, simply tie another piece to it and continue tying the meat.

7 Turn the meat over, then run the string along the other side, pulling it under and around the original loops until you reach the opposite end of the meat.

8 Tie the string once at the end and cut off the excess.

TIP The string should be approximately four times as long as the meat when tying a tenderloin.
To tie a fillet steak for neater presentation, place the steak, flat side down, on a work surface and loop the string around it, positioning the string midway along the width of the steak. Tie it firmly at the front to form the steak into a tidy round shape. Remove the string before serving.

Perfect pork crackling

Crackling is the crisp crust of a pork roast that forms when the meat is cooked with the rind in place. When properly prepared and cooked, the crackling forms a brittle cap on the meat which lifts off for serving and can then be cut into portions to enjoy with the tender roast.

1 Wipe off any moisture on the rind using paper towels. The rind must be perfectly dry or it will not crisp in the oven. You can even use a hair dryer on a cool setting to make sure every last bit of moisture is gone.

2 Score the rind all over in thin, parallel lines. A Stanley knife is ideal for this as the rind is difficult to cut, even with the sharpest chef's knife. Cut through the skin and fat, taking care not to cut through to the meat. This allows the heat to reach the fat, which will then bubble up through the cuts and over the rind, basting the rind during cooking and helping it crisp. If you score into the meat, juices will escape and the meat may be dry.

3 Rub the rind all over with olive oil, then rub salt into all the incisions.

4 Put the pork on a rack or trivet in a roasting pan, skin side up, to allow air to circulate around the base. Roast the pork in an oven preheated to 220°C (425°F/Gas 7) for 20–25 minutes.

5 Reduce the oven temperature to 180°C (350°F/Gas 4) and roast until the meat is just cooked through. Use a pastry brush to baste the rind 2–3 times with fat from the base of the pan during cooking.

6 To remove the crackling, use a thin sharp knife to help lift it away from the pork. Cut the crackling into thin pieces, using the score marks as guides, to serve.

Carving a leg of lamb

Transfer the cooked, rested leg of lamb to a chopping board or carving tray, with the flattest side down for greatest stability. Most lamb legs come with the shank bone severed, but still attached, to make it easier to fit the joint in a roasting pan. To remove the shank, cut it where the bone has been severed.

1 With the tip of your knife, identify the side of the lamb where the shank bone is closest to the surface. This is the side you will start carving from. Use a carving fork to keep the meat stable while you cut slices 5–8 mm (¼–⅜ inch) thick. Carve 6–8 slices from this side, depending on the size of the leg and the thickness of your slices.

2 Turn the lamb so the carved side is facing down, then begin carving from the rounded, thigh end of the roast. Carve parallel slices into the lamb, slicing downwards until you hit the leg bone for each.

3 Beginning at the slice closest to the shank bone, carve lengthways, as close to the leg bone as possible, to free the carved slices from the leg.

Spit roasting

Spit roasting is an old cooking technique that predates modern ovens and methods of butchery. An entire animal, or bird, is threaded onto a horizontal spit and cooked over a heat source while being turned constantly for even cooking. The turning allows the fat and juices to run over the surface of the meat and prevent it drying out. For successful spit roasting, make sure the heat is low and the meat is threaded evenly onto the skewer so that the weight is well balanced.

This means the spit itself will be easier to turn and the meat will cook evenly as a result.

Some ovens and outdoor barbecues have a built-in rotisserie apparatus, which is a convenient way to spit roast. When choosing meat for spit roasting, ensure it is fairly even in thickness so it cooks at the same rate. The ultimate spit roast is a whole animal, such as a pig, though this requires special equipment and 8–10 hours cooking over a fire.

Beef stock

Making your own stock is not difficult. Once the ingredients are simmering in the pan, it requires nothing more than a quick skim every now and then, however it does take a long time to cook. Because of this, it's best made in large quantities. Good stock should be clear, not cloudy, and lightly jellied from the collagen and other connective tissue remaining on the bones. All stocks freeze well.

PREPARATION TIME 20 minutes

COOKING TIME 9 hours

MAKES about 5 litres
(175 fl oz/20 cups)

2 kg (4 lb 8 oz) raw beef bones,
  cut into small pieces (ask your
  butcher to do this for you)
2 tablespoons olive oil
1 large carrot, coarsely chopped
1 onion, coarsely chopped
1 leek, trimmed, washed and
  coarsely chopped
2 celery stalks, chopped
3 tomatoes, chopped
1 bay leaf
2 thyme sprigs

1 Preheat the oven to 200°C (400°F/ Gas 6). Put the bones in a flameproof roasting pan and cook, turning occasionally, for 35–40 minutes, until well browned all over.

2 Meanwhile, put the oil and vegetables in another flameproof roasting pan, toss to coat and roast for 40–50 minutes, until golden and tender.

3 Remove the bones from the oven and transfer to a large stockpot. Place the roasting pan over medium heat, add

1 litre (35 fl oz/4 cups) water and bring to a simmer, scraping any caramelisation from the base of the pan. Pour the water over the bones.

4 Remove the vegetables from the oven and transfer to the stockpot. Place the roasting pan over medium heat, add 1 litre (35 fl oz/4 cups) water and bring to a simmer, scraping any caramelisation from the base of the pan. Pour the water into the stockpot. Add the herbs and enough water to just cover the bones and vegetables.

5 Bring the stock to a gentle simmer, using a large spoon to skim the surface to remove any impurities.

6 Reduce the heat to low and cook for 8 hours, skimming the surface regularly. Do not allow the stock to boil or it will become cloudy. Strain the stock into a large bowl or container and discard the solids.

7 Cool the stock to room temperature, then skim any fat from the surface. Store in an airtight container in the refrigerator for up to 4 days or freeze in airtight containers or sealed freezer bags for up to 2 months.

VARIATIONS

Veal stock: Use veal bones instead of beef bones and do not cook the bones or vegetables in the oven. Put the veal bones in a stockpot, cover with water and bring to a simmer over medium heat, skimming the surface to remove any impurities. Add the vegetables and herbs and enough extra water to just cover. Return to a simmer, then reduce the heat to low and cook for 8 hours, skimming the surface regularly. Finish and store as for beef stock. Veal stock is used for delicate sauces and soups where the strong flavour and colour of beef stock is not required.

Lamb stock: Use lamb bones instead of beef bones. For a brown lamb stock, roast the bones and vegetables first, as for beef stock. For regular lamb stock, follow the method for veal stock. Cook the stock on the stovetop for 3 hours instead of 8 hours, skimming the surface regularly. Finish and store as for beef stock. Use lamb stock in lamb braises and lamb-based soups and to finish sauces for lamb dishes.

1 Roast the bones in a large flameproof roasting pan until well browned all over.

2 Roast the vegetables in another large flameproof roasting pan until golden and tender.

3 Bring the water to a simmer, scraping any caramelisation from the base of the pan.

4 Add the bay leaf and thyme sprigs to the stockpot.

5 Simmer the stock, using a large spoon to skim the surface to remove any impurities.

6 Strain the stock into a large bowl or container.

Flavours for meat and game

Certain flavours enhance particular meats. The lean, gamey and pronounced flavours of venison cry out for spices, port, chestnuts and juniper berries, however these flavours would overwhelm the delicate nature of veal and rabbit.

Once you understand the principles of cooking techniques, such as constructing a braise, deglazing a pan or making a gravy or jus, it's easy to improvise or experiment with other flavours. If a recipe, for example, calls for braising lamb shoulder with rosemary, capers and white wine, there's no reason you can't adapt it for, say, the same cut of pork and substitute sherry, ginger and star anise. The list below is not comprehensive, but provides guidelines to get you started.

PORK	BEEF	LAMB	VEAL	VENISON	RABBIT
fennel (seeds and the fresh vegetable)	dried mushrooms	mint	tarragon	juniper berries	lemons
oranges and lemons	rosemary	rosemary	capers	allspice	rosemary
wine vinegar	thyme	thyme	garlic	cinnamon	anchovies
pears	oregano	parsley	chives	peppercorns	green peppercorns
apples	basil	anchovies	lemons	port	pancetta
prunes	garlic	garlic	mustard	red wine	white wine
mustard	horseradish	lemons	anchovies	sage	red wine
sage	paprika	saffron	sorrel	rosemary	thyme
rosemary	mustard	parmesan cheese	olives	marjoram	garlic
Asian flavours, such as ginger, star anise, cinnamon, soy sauce and sherry	brandy	capers	Marsala	thyme	mustard
	red wine	white wine		garlic	brandy
white wine	pepper	olives		oranges	
	chilli	pine nuts		star anise	
	soy sauce	quince		raisins	
	oyster sauce	allspice		prunes	
	pickles	paprika		chestnuts	
		cinnamon			
		cardamom			

Rubs and marinades

Rubs and marinades are flavour-enhancing combinations of herbs, spices, sauces and/or other aromatics. The longer they are in contact with the meat or poultry, the stronger the flavour will be. Marinades are based on liquids such as wine, yoghurt, sherry or vinegar, and they add flavour as well as tenderise. They can be applied up to a day ahead. Rubs can be wet, with a thick, paste-like texture, or dry. Dry rubs can be stored in airtight containers in a cool, dark place for up to 6 months, while wet rubs are best made and used fresh. All rubs burn easily, so are best used for barbecuing on low, indirect heat.

Spiced Indian marinade

MARINATES 1 kg (2 lb 4 oz) meat/poultry

260 g (9¼ oz/1 cup) Greek-style yoghurt
2 garlic cloves, crushed
2½ teaspoons finely chopped ginger
2 teaspoons garam masala
2 teaspoons ground cumin
1 teaspoon turmeric
1 teaspoon chilli powder
2 lemons, zest finely grated and juiced

Combine all the ingredients in a large glass or ceramic bowl. Add the meat and stir to coat, then cover with plastic wrap and refrigerate for 4 hours or overnight.

Soy sauce and honey marinade

MARINATES 1 kg (2 lb 4 oz) meat/poultry

80 ml (2½ fl oz/⅓ cup) vegetable oil
60 ml (2 fl oz/¼ cup) soy sauce
60 ml (2 fl oz/¼ cup) Chinese rice wine or sweet sherry
1½ tablespoons honey
2½ teaspoons sesame oil
½ teaspoon Chinese five-spice
1 tablespoon finely chopped ginger
2 garlic cloves, crushed

Combine all the ingredients in a large glass or ceramic bowl. Add the meat and stir to coat, then cover with plastic wrap and refrigerate for 4 hours or overnight.

Greek tomato and oregano marinade

MARINATES 1 kg (2 lb 4 oz) meat/poultry

125 ml (4 fl oz/½ cup) extra virgin olive oil
2 ripe tomatoes, chopped
2 garlic cloves, crushed
Juice of 1 lemon
1 large onion, finely grated
1 fresh bay leaf, bruised
2 tablespoons oregano leaves, chopped
1 teaspoon freshly ground black pepper

Process the oil, tomatoes and garlic in a food processor until well combined. Combine with the remaining ingredients in a large glass or ceramic bowl. Add the meat and stir to coat, then cover with plastic wrap and refrigerate for 4 hours or overnight.

Smoky barbecue marinade

MARINATES 1 kg (2 lb 4 oz) meat

125 ml (4 fl oz/½ cup) extra virgin olive oil
1 onion, finely chopped
2 garlic cloves, crushed
80 ml (2½ fl oz/⅓ cup) red wine vinegar
2½ tablespoons tomato sauce (ketchup)
1½ tablespoons worcestershire sauce

1½ tablespoons dijon mustard
1½ teaspoons smoked paprika
2 fresh bay leaves, bruised

Combine all the ingredients in a large glass or ceramic bowl. Add the meat and stir to coat, then cover with plastic wrap and refrigerate for 4 hours or overnight.

Italian anchovy rub

MARINATES 1 kg (2 lb 4 oz) meat/poultry

6 anchovy fillets, chopped
80 ml (2½ fl oz/⅓ cup) balsamic vinegar
60 ml (2 fl oz/¼ cup) olive oil
2 tablespoons dried basil or oregano
1 tablespoon freshly ground black pepper
4 garlic cloves, finely chopped

Combine all the ingredients in a small bowl. Put the meat in a glass or ceramic bowl, add the rub and use your hands to mix well. Cover with plastic wrap and refrigerate for 4 hours or overnight.

Jerk rub

MARINATES 1.2 kg (2 lb 10½ oz)
beef or pork steaks

1 tablespoon onion powder
2 teaspoons ground dried thyme
2 teaspoons caster (superfine) sugar
1 teaspoon allspice
1 teaspoon cayenne pepper
1 teaspoon freshly ground black pepper
½ teaspoon ground nutmeg

Combine all the ingredients in a small
bowl. Put the meat in a glass or ceramic
bowl, add the rub and use your hands to
mix well. Cover with plastic wrap and
refrigerate for 4 hours or overnight.

Cumin, oregano and chilli rub

MARINATES 4 beef steaks or
4 chicken thighs or pieces

2 teaspoons chilli powder
2 teaspoons dried oregano
1½ teaspoons sea salt
1 teaspoon ground cumin
1 teaspoon freshly ground black pepper
2 garlic cloves, crushed

Combine all the ingredients in a small
bowl. Put the meat or poultry in a
glass or ceramic bowl, add the rub and
mix well. Cover with plastic wrap and
refrigerate for 4 hours or overnight.

Sauces

A prime cut of meat or poultry needs little more than a sauce to lift it to the sublime. These simple sauces, ranging from a creamy classic to a spicy salsa, will fast become favourites. If you are pan-frying, use the same frying pan with the pan juices to cook the Creamy mushroom and Green peppercorn sauces.

The perfect gravy

MAKES about 750 ml (26 fl oz/3 cups)

160 ml (5¼ fl oz/⅔ cup) wine (see tip)
750 ml (26 fl oz/3 cups) good-quality
   ready-made or home-made stock
   (see pages 30 or 60) (see tip)
2 tablespoons plain (all-purpose) flour

1 Remove the roasted meat from the roasting pan and keep warm. Use a spoon to skim off the fat and place it in a small saucepan. Pour the pan juices into a bowl and set aside.

2 Place the roasting pan over medium heat, covering two burners if possible, and add the wine, scraping any caramelisation from the base of the pan. Add the stock and pan juices and bring to the boil. Remove and set aside.

3 Heat the reserved fat over medium heat, then stir in the flour. Cook, stirring, for 2 minutes.

4 Add the stock mixture to the saucepan and whisk until the gravy is smooth and thickened.

TIP You can use red or white wine in the gravy, or extra stock if you prefer.
   Use a stock that is appropriate to your roast (beef stock for beef roast, etc). If you don't have stock, use water.
   Make sure you roast your meat in a flameproof roasting pan and then deglaze the pan well, as this is where most of the gravy's flavour comes from.

Creamy mushroom sauce

MAKES about 375 ml (13 fl oz/1½ cups)

30 g (1 oz) butter
350 g (12 oz) small button mushrooms,
   sliced
2 tablespoons white wine
125 ml (4 fl oz/½ cup) good-quality
   ready-made chicken stock
125 ml (4 fl oz/½ cup) thin
   (pouring/whipping) cream
1 garlic clove, crushed
1 tablespoon snipped chives

1 Stir the butter and mushrooms in a frying pan over medium heat for 5 minutes or until tender and golden.

2 Add the wine, stock, cream and garlic, and bring to the boil. Cook for 5 minutes, stirring constantly, until the sauce thickens slightly. Stir in the chives and serve immediately.

Tomato sauce

MAKES about 750 ml (26 fl oz/3 cups)

2 tablespoons olive oil
1 onion, finely chopped
2 garlic cloves
2 x 400 g (14 oz) tins chopped tomatoes
2 teaspoons balsamic vinegar
Large pinch of sugar

1 Heat the olive oil in a saucepan over medium heat. Add the onion and garlic and cook, stirring occasionally, for 5 minutes or until softened.

2 Add the tomatoes, vinegar and sugar and bring to a simmer. Reduce the heat to low and cook, stirring occasionally, for 10 minutes or until reduced slightly.

Green peppercorn sauce

MAKES about 435 ml (15¼ fl oz/ 1¾ cups)

250 ml (9 fl oz/1 cup) good-quality
   ready-made or home-made beef or
   chicken stock (see pages 30 or 60)
250 ml (9 fl oz/1 cup) thin
   (pouring/whipping) cream
2–3 teaspoons canned green
   peppercorns, drained and rinsed
1 tablespoon brandy

1 Heat the stock in a frying pan over low heat, stirring often, until boiling, then add the cream and peppercorns. Boil for 8–10 minutes, stirring constantly, until thickened slightly. Add the brandy and boil for 1 minute. Serve immediately.

Red wine jus

MAKES about 125 ml (4 fl oz/½ cup)

1 tablespoon olive oil
½ cup raw beef trimmings
3 French shallots, finely diced
½ carrot, finely diced
½ celery stalk, finely diced
375 ml (13 fl oz/1½ cups) red wine
500 ml (17 fl oz/2 cups) good-quality ready-made or home-made veal or beef stock (see page 60)
20 g (¾ oz) butter, chopped

1 Heat the oil in a large frying pan over medium heat, add the meat trimmings and shallots and cook for 2 minutes, stirring constantly, until browned.

2 Add the carrot and celery and cook for 2 minutes, stirring constantly, until browned. Add 125 ml (4 fl oz/½ cup) of the red wine and stir with a wooden spoon, scraping any caramelisation from the base of the pan. Add the remaining wine and simmer, stirring occasionally, for 8–10 minutes or until it has almost evaporated. Add the stock and simmer for 8–10 minutes, until reduced by half.

3 Strain the sauce through a fine sieve into a small saucepan, pressing down on the solids to release the liquid. Discard the solids.

4 Cook the sauce over medium heat for 3–4 minutes or until reduced to about 125 ml (4 fl oz/½ cup). Set aside until required.

5 To serve, bring to the boil in a small saucepan over medium heat, then whisk in the butter until glossy.

Béarnaise sauce

MAKES about 310 ml (10¾ fl oz/ 1¼ cups)

80 ml (2½ fl oz/⅓ cup) white wine vinegar
80 ml (2½ fl oz/⅓ cup) white wine
1 French shallot, thinly sliced
1 garlic clove, thinly sliced
3 black peppercorns
3 egg yolks, at room temperature
225 g (8 oz) unsalted butter, melted
1 tablespoon chopped tarragon

1 Put the vinegar, wine, shallot, garlic and peppercorns in a small saucepan over medium–high heat and simmer for 5 minutes or until reduced to 80 ml (2½ fl oz/⅓ cup). Strain into a jug and set aside to cool slightly.

2 Put the egg yolks in a heatproof bowl that will sit comfortably over a saucepan. Add the reduction and whisk to combine. Place the bowl over a saucepan of barely simmering water (making sure the base of the bowl doesn't touch the water). Whisk for 2 minutes or until thick and foamy. Add the melted butter, a little at a time, whisking constantly until a thick creamy sauce forms. Stir in the tarragon.

3 Cover the sauce with plastic wrap, pressing it onto the surface to prevent a skin forming, and set aside in a warm place until required.

> **TIP** If the béarnaise sauce starts to separate, remove it from the heat and beat in 1 tablespoon of cold water. This can often save it, but not always. The sauce will split if it gets too hot, so make sure you beat in the butter drop by drop, especially at first. Don't let the sauce overheat as the yolks will curdle.

Tomato salsa

SERVES 4–6

4 plum (roma) tomatoes
1 red onion, finely chopped
1 bird's eye chilli, halved, seeded and thinly sliced
¼ cup chopped coriander (cilantro) leaves
1–2 tablespoons lime juice, to taste
½ teaspoon salt

1 Cut the tomatoes in half horizontally and use a teaspoon to scoop out the seeds. Finely chop the tomato flesh.

2 Combine the tomatoes, onion, chilli, coriander, lime juice and salt in a bowl. Cover and refrigerate for 1 hour for the flavours to develop before serving.

> **TIP** You can change the flavour of the salsa to a Mediterranean one by omitting the chilli, replacing the lime juice with lemon juice or red wine vinegar, and replacing the coriander with chopped mint or basil, or a mixture of the two. A few tablespoons of chopped olives or capers would be a great addition, too.
> This salsa is also delicious tossed through hot pasta.

Accompaniments

When you cook a succulent piece of meat or poultry, such as a steak, roast, pot-roast or braise, the simplest of accompaniments are all that are needed. Classic side dishes such as mashed potato, fries and roast vegetables are universally popular and well worth mastering.

Perfect fries

1 Use a large sharp knife to cut off the sides of 1.5 kg (3 lb 5 oz) peeled floury or all-purpose potatoes (such as desiree or pontiac) to make them square or rectangular. Cut the potatoes into slices about 7 mm (⅜ inch) thick, then cut into sticks about 7 mm (⅜ inch) wide. Put in a bowl, cover with cold water and refrigerate for 4 hours or overnight.

2 Drain the potatoes well, then spread out on paper towels and dry thoroughly.

3 Line 2 baking trays with paper towels. Heat 2 litres (70 fl oz/8 cups) safflower or other mild-tasting vegetable oil in a large saucepan or deep-fryer until it reaches 150°C (300°F) or until a cube of bread dropped into the oil turns golden brown in 35 seconds. Cook the potato sticks, in small batches, stirring gently to keep them separate, for about 3 minutes or until cooked through (they will not be coloured). Use a slotted spoon to transfer to the lined trays.

4 Increase the oil temperature to 180°C (350°F) or until a cube of bread dropped into the oil turns golden brown in 15 seconds. Cook the potato chips, in small batches, stirring gently to separate them, for 4–5 minutes or until deep golden brown and crisp. Transfer to trays lined with fresh paper towels, season with sea salt and serve. Serves 6

Roast potatoes

1 Preheat the oven to 200°C (400°F/ Gas 6). Allow 1–1½ floury or all-purpose potatoes (such as desiree or pontiac) per person. Peel the potatoes, cut in half if large, and cook in salted boiling water for 5–6 minutes. Drain and cool slightly.

2 Use the tines of a fork to gently rake the surface of each potato. Place the potatoes in a roasting pan in a single layer, then drizzle generously with olive or vegetable oil to coat.

3 Roast the potatoes for 50 minutes or until tender, deep golden and crisp.

Roast vegetables

Roast vegetables have a rich deep flavour, with crisp golden exteriors and soft, moist interiors. Many vegetables can be roasted, although root vegetables are the most popular. Cut the vegetables into uniform pieces and coat lightly in olive oil to encourage a crisp exterior and keep them moist. Always roast vegetables in a single layer in a roasting pan and do not crowd the pan. The hot air needs to circulate around the vegetables so they can brown and cook evenly. Allow a raw weight of about 200–250 g (7–9 oz) vegetables per person and cook at 180–200°C (350–400°F/Gas 4–6).

Beetroot These are best cooked on their own as they take a long time and can release dark juices. Choose beetroot that are not too large. Trim the stems and scrub them, but do not peel. Dry well, place in a roasting pan and roast for 1 hour 20 minutes or until tender. Cool slightly and then peel, if desired.

Carrots and parsnips Trim and peel, then cut smaller vegetables in half lengthways and large ones into thick rings or chunks. Coat in olive oil and cook for 30–60 minutes, until tender.

Cauliflower Cut or divide into florets, coat well in olive oil and roast for 45 minutes or until tender.

Fennel Trim the green ends and remove any tough outer layers. Cut into thin wedges and coat well in olive oil. Roast for 45–50 minutes, until tender.

Onions Cut in half, leaving the root intact. Coat well in olive oil, then roast for 45–50 minutes, until very tender.

Pumpkin Remove the skin and seeds and cut into wedges or chunks. Coat in olive oil and cook for 35–40 minutes, until tender.

Sweet potato Peel and cut into wedges, chunks or thick slices. Coat in olive oil and cook for 35 minutes or until tender.

Mashed potato

1 Cut 850 g (1 lb 14 oz) peeled all-purpose potatoes (about 5) into 4–5 cm (1½–2 inch) pieces. Place in a saucepan of salted water and bring to the boil over medium heat. Cook for 20 minutes or until very soft, then drain.

2 Return the potatoes to the saucepan and place over medium heat. Use a potato masher to mash the potatoes, then use a wooden spoon to beat in 125 ml (4 fl oz/½ cup) warmed milk, followed by 50 g (1¾ oz) butter. Season with sea salt and freshly ground black pepper, to taste. Serves 6

Useful utensils

With these implements in your kitchen you'll be ready to tackle any type of meat or poultry dish:

Basting brush, to brush marinades over poultry while grilling or barbecuing. You can now buy basting brushes with silicone bristles to prevent them singeing.

Basting spoons have a deep bowl to scoop up pan juices and pour over meat or poultry while roasting.

Casserole dishes in varying sizes are used when making soups and braised or pot-roasted dishes. Heavy-based dishes with lids are preferable.

Food processor, with small and large bowl, for blending soups and sauces or seasoned butters.

Frying pans in varying sizes for pan-frying small cuts or browning meat or poultry before adding it to braised dishes. Heavy-based non-stick pans are ideal.

Kitchen string, for trussing poultry or tying meat or boned stuffed birds into shape for roasting, poaching or braising.

Knives: Boning knife, a small sharp knife with a 10–12 cm (4–4½ inch) stainless-steel blade, with a slight curve, suitable for boning whole birds or large cuts of meat. **Heavy cook's knife** with a ridged blade, for halving small birds. **Carving knife and fork** for carving roasted birds or large cuts of meat.

Meat thermometer used to test whether meat or poultry is cooked. Insert it into the thickest part of the meat, avoiding any contact with the bone. The suggested temperature for poultry to reach before it is safe to consume is 85°C (185°F),

unless the poultry is stuffed, in which case the temperature in the centre of the stuffing should be about 74°C (165°F).

Mortar and pestle, used to pound herbs and spices, forming pastes to rub into meat or poultry or to add to marinades. The mortar can be made of hard wood, ceramic or stone.

Poultry shears, stainless-steel scissors that are designed to cut through chicken bones and flesh.

Roasting pans and baking trays, large enough to contain a whole bird or large cuts of meat. A **roasting rack** that fits in the roasting pan or sits over a baking tray is also useful.

Sauce whisks and balloon whisks are handy for mixing sauces and incorporating butter and cream to finish a dish.

Steaming basket, sized to fit over a wok, for steaming portions of meat or poultry.

Stockpot with lid, at least 8 litres (280 fl oz/32 cups) capacity, suitable for stocks, soups and some stews.

Tongs, used for gripping and lifting meat or poultry. A short pair and a long pair are useful.

Wok, for stir-frying and deep-frying meat or poultry.

Frying and
Sautéing

Chicken with tomatoes, capers and basil

SERVES 4   **PREPARATION TIME** 15 minutes   **COOKING TIME** 25 minutes

1½ tablespoons olive oil
3 garlic cloves, thinly sliced
4 skinless chicken breast fillets
250 g (9 oz) cherry tomatoes
60 ml (2 fl oz/¼ cup) white wine
60 ml (2 fl oz/¼ cup) good-quality
   ready-made chicken stock
2 tablespoons baby capers, rinsed
   and drained
1 cup basil leaves, torn
Cooked fresh pasta, to serve

1 Heat the oil in a large frying pan over medium heat. Cook the garlic for 3 minutes or until softened and lightly golden. Use a slotted spoon to remove the garlic from the pan *(pic 1)*.

2 Increase the heat to medium–high. Add the chicken fillets and cook for 2 minutes. Reduce the heat to medium and cook for another 8 minutes. Turn the chicken, add the tomatoes *(pic 2)* and cook for 5 minutes or until the chicken is cooked through and the tomatoes start to soften. Remove the chicken and tomatoes from the pan and cover loosely with foil to keep warm.

3 Return the garlic to the pan with the wine and stock, scraping any caramelisation from the base of the pan with a wooden spoon, and bring to the boil. Reduce the heat and simmer for 4 minutes or until reduced by half *(pic 3)*. Stir in the capers and basil. Return the chicken and tomatoes to the pan and toss to coat.

4 Serve the chicken and tomatoes with the pasta and drizzle over the sauce.

1

2

3

TIP The cooking time will vary slightly according to the thickness of the chicken breasts. Cooking the chicken on high heat for the first 2 minutes will colour it nicely, then reducing the heat to medium will allow the chicken to cook through without drying out.

Spicy chicken stir-fry

SERVES 2–3　　**PREPARATION TIME** 15 minutes (+ 30 minutes soaking)　　**COOKING TIME** 12–15 minutes

3 dried Chinese mushrooms

300 g (10½ oz) skinless chicken
　　breast fillets

2 tablespoons peanut or vegetable oil

2 garlic cloves, crushed

5 cm (2 inch) piece ginger, cut into
　　matchsticks

1 fresh small red chilli, or to taste,
　　seeded and finely chopped

1 brown onion, cut into thin wedges

150 g (5½ oz) green beans,
　　cut diagonally into 4 cm
　　(1½ inch) lengths

½ red capsicum (pepper), seeded
　　and cut into thin strips

2 tablespoons oyster sauce

2 tablespoons fish sauce

1 teaspoon light brown sugar

2 tablespoons chopped coriander
　　(cilantro) leaves (optional)

Cooked rice stick noodles or
　　jasmine rice, to serve

1 Soak the mushrooms in a bowl of warm water for 30 minutes. Remove the mushrooms from the liquid and squeeze to remove any excess liquid *(pic 1)*. Reserve the liquid. Trim and discard the stems, then thinly slice the mushrooms.

2 Cut the chicken into short, thin strips. Heat 1 tablespoon of the oil in a wok over medium–high heat. Add the garlic, ginger and chilli and stir-fry for 30 seconds, until aromatic but without browning *(pic 2)*. Increase the heat to high, add the chicken strips and stir-fry for 3 minutes or until lightly browned and just cooked through. Transfer to a plate and set aside.

3 Heat the remaining oil in the wok over high heat. Add the onion, beans, capsicum and mushrooms, and stir-fry for 3–4 minutes or until the vegetables are tender crisp *(pic 3)*.

4 Combine the oyster sauce, fish sauce and sugar. Add to the wok with the chicken and stir-fry for another 2 minutes or until heated through.

5 Serve sprinkled with coriander, if desired, and accompanied by rice stick noodles or rice.

Chicken, mint and pea risotto

SERVES 4 **PREPARATION TIME** 15 minutes **COOKING TIME** 40 minutes

1.25 litres (44 fl oz/5 cups) good-quality ready-made or home-made chicken stock (see page 30)

2 tablespoons olive oil

500 g (1 lb 2 oz) skinless chicken thigh fillets, cut into 3 cm (1¼ inch) pieces

1 brown onion, diced

550 g (1 lb 4 oz/2½ cups) arborio rice

125 ml (4 fl oz/½ cup) white wine

140 g (5 oz/1 cup) frozen peas

100 g (3½ oz/1 cup) finely grated parmesan cheese, plus extra, to serve

¼ cup finely shredded mint leaves, plus whole leaves, extra, to serve

1 Put the stock in a medium saucepan and bring to the boil over high heat. Remove from the heat and set aside.

2 Meanwhile, heat the oil in a large saucepan over high heat. Cook the chicken, in 2 batches, stirring occasionally, for 4 minutes or until it is browned *(pic 1)*. Remove the chicken from the pan and set aside.

3 Reduce the heat to medium, add the onion to the pan, and cook, stirring, for 5 minutes or until softened. Add the rice and stir to coat in the oil *(pic 2)*.

4 Stir in the wine and bring to the boil. Cook for 1 minute, stirring, or until the wine is absorbed. Add a ladleful of warm stock and cook, stirring, until it is absorbed. Continue to add the stock, a ladleful at a time, stirring until absorbed. After 10 minutes, return the chicken to the pan *(pic 3)*. Continue to cook, adding a ladleful of stock at a time, for another 10 minutes or until the rice is almost tender. Stir in the peas and cook for 5 minutes or until the rice is tender, but firm to the bite, and the chicken is cooked through. Remove from the heat. Stir in the parmesan and shredded mint and set aside, covered, for 1 minute.

5 Serve sprinkled with the extra mint leaves and extra parmesan.

Thai chicken cakes

Fans of the classic Thai fishcakes will love this chicken adaptation. They are not only incredibly more-ish, they're also a cinch to make.

MAKES 25 **PREPARATION TIME** 20 minutes **COOKING TIME** 30 minutes

500 g (1 lb 2 oz) skinless chicken thigh
  fillets, minced (ground) (see page 25)
1 egg
2 tablespoons red curry paste
1 tablespoon sugar
2 tablespoons fish sauce
3 kaffir lime leaves, finely shredded
  (pic 1)
2 tablespoons chopped coriander
  (cilantro) leaves
2 spring onions (scallions), white part
  only, thinly sliced
3 cm (1¼ inches) lemongrass, white
  part only, thinly sliced
Vegetable oil, for greasing and
  deep-frying

DIPPING SAUCE
125 ml (4 fl oz/½ cup) rice wine vinegar
110 g (3¾ oz/½ cup) sugar
1 teaspoon salt
2 long red chillies, seeded and
  finely chopped

1 To make the dipping sauce, place all the ingredients in a small saucepan over medium heat (pic 2). Stir to dissolve the sugar and bring to the boil. Reduce the heat and simmer for 5 minutes or until slightly reduced. Set aside.

2 Place the minced chicken in a food processor and pulse for 2 minutes or until it forms a smooth paste. Add the egg, curry paste, sugar and fish sauce and pulse to combine. Transfer the mixture to a bowl and stir in the lime leaves, coriander, spring onions and lemongrass until well combined.

3 Grease a baking tray with a little oil, then lightly grease your hands with oil to prevent the chicken mixture sticking to them. Shape heaped tablespoons of the mixture into patties about 6 cm (2½ inches) in diameter (pic 3). Place the patties on the greased baking tray.

4 Half-fill a deep saucepan with oil and heat to 160°C (315°F), or until a cube of bread dropped into the oil turns golden brown in 30–35 seconds. Deep-fry the chicken patties in batches, using a lightly oiled palette knife to lift them from the tray and carefully put them in the oil, for about 4 minutes, turning halfway through cooking, until golden and cooked through. Use a slotted spoon to transfer onto paper towels to drain while you cook the remaining patties. Serve the chicken cakes warm with the dipping sauce.

1

2

3

Pine nut, parmesan and parsley stuffed chicken

SERVES 6   **PREPARATION TIME** 35 minutes (+ 5 minutes resting)   **COOKING TIME** 25 minutes

40 g (1½ oz/¼ cup) pine nuts, toasted
and coarsely chopped
115 g (4 oz/⅔ cup) green olives,
pitted and coarsely chopped
100 g (3½ oz/⅓ cup) fresh
sourdough breadcrumbs
80 g (2¾ oz/¾ cup) finely grated
parmesan cheese
¼ cup chopped flat-leaf (Italian) parsley
1 egg, lightly whisked
6 x 180 g (6¼ oz) chicken breast fillets
with skin, butterflied (see page 23)
9 thin slices prosciutto
(about 200 g/7 oz)
2½ tablespoons olive oil
Mixed baby leaf salad and boiled
potatoes, to serve

1 Combine the pine nuts, olives, breadcrumbs, parmesan and parsley in a bowl. Season with salt and freshly ground black pepper. Add the egg and mix until well combined.

2 Lay a butterflied chicken breast on a chopping board, cut side up. Spoon one-sixth of the filling onto the chicken, shaping it into a neat log running lengthways down the centre of the breast (*pic 1*). Roll the chicken up around the filling to form a neat shape. Tear 3 of the prosciutto slices in half lengthways. Wrap 3 pieces of prosciutto around each chicken roll, overlapping them slightly so they just cover the chicken (*pic 2*).

3 Use kitchen string to tie up each chicken roll at 2 cm (¾ inch) intervals (*pic 3*) to secure.

4 Preheat the oven to 180°C (350°F/ Gas 4).

5 Heat the oil in a large ovenproof frying pan (see tip) over medium heat. Add the chicken and cook, turning often, for 8 minutes or until browned all over. Transfer the pan to the oven and cook for 12–14 minutes or until the chicken is just cooked through. Remove from the oven, cover loosely with foil and set aside for 5 minutes to rest.

6 Remove the string. Cut the chicken into 1 cm (½ inch) thick slices. Serve immediately with salad and potatoes.

1

2

3

TIP If you don't have an ovenproof frying pan that will fit in your oven, use a normal frying pan and then transfer the chicken to a roasting pan to finish the cooking in the oven.

Chicken schnitzel

SERVES 4 **PREPARATION TIME** 25 minutes (+ 30 minutes chilling) **COOKING TIME** 50 minutes

4 small (about 200 g/7 oz each)
   skinless chicken breast fillets,
   tenderloins removed and reserved
   for another use
120 g (4¼ oz/2 cups, lightly packed)
   fresh breadcrumbs
25 g (1 oz/¼ cup) almond meal
2 tablespoons finely chopped flat-leaf
   (Italian) parsley leaves
75 g (2¾ oz/½ cup) plain
   (all-purpose) flour
2 eggs, lightly whisked
80 g (2¾ oz) butter
60 ml (2 fl oz/¼ cup) olive oil
Green oak leaf salad (dressed with
   a light sour cream, vinegar, sugar
   and salt dressing) and lemon
   wedges, to serve

1 Cut each chicken fillet in half crossways. Place the pieces, one at a time, between 2 sheets of plastic wrap and use a flat meat mallet or rolling pin to gently pound until about 1 cm (½ inch) thick *(pic 1)*. Be careful not to tear the chicken.

2 Spread the breadcrumbs over a baking tray. Toast in the oven for 15–20 minutes, stirring often, until dried but not coloured. Cool on the tray. Transfer to a food processor with the almond meal and parsley, and process until combined. Transfer to a large plate or tray. Put the flour on a plate or sheet of non-stick baking paper and season well with salt and freshly ground black pepper.

3 Working with one piece at a time, toss the chicken in flour to lightly coat, then dip in the egg, allowing any excess to drain off. Coat with the breadcrumb mixture, pressing it firmly onto the fillets with your fingers *(pic 2)*. Place on a plate or tray and refrigerate for at least 30 minutes.

4 Preheat oven to 120°C (235°F/Gas ½).

5 Line a baking tray with paper towels. Heat 50 g (1¾ oz) of the butter and 2 tablespoons of the oil in a large heavy-based frying pan over medium–high heat until the butter is foaming. Cook the schnitzel in batches for 3–4 minutes each side, turning once *(pic 3)*, or until golden brown and just cooked through, adding more butter and oil as necessary. Place on the lined tray and keep warm in the oven while cooking the remaining batches. Serve with the salad and lemon wedges.

Duck breast with chargrilled vegetables and red capsicum sauce

This is a wonderful dish for summer. The vegetables can be cooked outdoors on a barbecue, if you like. Finishing off the pan-fried duck breast in the oven ensures even cooking.

SERVES 4 **PREPARATION TIME** 20 minutes (+ 25 minutes cooling/resting) **COOKING TIME** 50 minutes

4 x 250 g (9 oz) duck breast fillets
1 tablespoon aged balsamic vinegar
2 tablespoons extra virgin olive oil
2 zucchini (courgettes), trimmed
1 eggplant (aubergine), trimmed
12 asparagus spears, trimmed
80 ml (2½ fl oz/⅓ cup) light olive oil
120 g (4¼ oz) haloumi, cut into 4 slices
90 g (3¼ oz) baby rocket (arugula)

RED CAPSICUM SAUCE
1 red capsicum (pepper)
⅓ cup chopped basil leaves
40 g (1½ oz/¼ cup) pine nuts, toasted
1 teaspoon tarragon mustard
1 garlic clove, crushed
1 tablespoon lemon juice
60 ml (2 fl oz/¼ cup) extra virgin olive oil

1 Trim the excess fat from the duck breasts and use a sharp knife to score the skin in a diamond pattern, without going through to the flesh *(pic 1)*. Combine the vinegar and extra virgin olive oil in a bowl, add the duck breasts, cover and refrigerate for 1 hour.

2 Meanwhile, to make the red capsicum sauce, preheat the oven to 200°C (400°F/Gas 6). Put the capsicum on a baking tray and roast, turning occasionally, for 30 minutes or until the skin blisters and blackens *(pic 2)*. Transfer to a bowl, cover with plastic wrap and set aside for 15 minutes. Remove the skin and seeds, then put the capsicum flesh and juices in a

food processor. Add the remaining ingredients, season to taste and process until smooth. Cover and refrigerate until ready to use.

3 Cut the zucchini and eggplant into 5 mm (¼ inch) thick slices. Combine with the asparagus and 60 ml (2 fl oz/¼ cup) of the olive oil, and season with salt and pepper. Heat a chargrill pan or barbecue grill over high heat and cook the vegetables, in batches if necessary, until lightly charred and tender *(pic 3)*. Cool to room temperature.

4 Heat a large non-stick frying pan until hot and cook the duck breasts, skin side down, for 2 minutes or until well browned. Turn and seal the other side. Transfer to a baking tray, skin side up, and roast for 7 minutes for medium-rare. Remove from the oven, cover loosely with foil and set aside for 10 minutes to rest. Meanwhile, reheat the chargrill on medium–high heat. Brush the haloumi with the remaining oil and cook for 30 seconds each side or until nicely charred and heated through (see tip).

5 Slice the duck breasts diagonally. Place the rocket leaves on plates with a spoonful of the red capsicum sauce and top with the chargrilled vegetables and haloumi, then the sliced duck. Serve with the remaining red capsicum sauce.

TIP Chargrill the haloumi just before serving, as it becomes rubbery when it cools.

Chicken pad thai

SERVES 2 **PREPARATION TIME** 10 minutes (+ 15 minutes soaking) **COOKING TIME** 10 minutes

85 g (3 oz) medium rice stick noodles
80 ml (2½ fl oz/⅓ cup) fish sauce
2 tablespoons white sugar
2 tablespoons grated palm sugar
    (jaggery) (see tip)
2 tablespoons tamarind purée (see tip)
    or oyster sauce
1 tablespoon tomato sauce (ketchup)
1½ tablespoons vegetable oil
2 eggs, lightly whisked
½ teaspoon shrimp paste (see tip)
½ red onion, cut into thin wedges
300 g (10½ oz) skinless chicken breast
    fillets, thinly sliced
¼ teaspoon chilli powder
4 spring onions (scallions),
    cut into batons
60 g (2¼ oz/½ cup) bean sprouts,
    trimmed, to serve
Coriander (cilantro) sprigs, to serve
2 tablespoons chopped roasted
    peanuts, to serve
1 teaspoon white sugar, extra
¼ teaspoon chilli powder, extra
Lime wedges, to serve

1 Soak the noodles in hot water for 10–15 minutes, until just tender *(pic 1)*. Drain well.

2 Put the fish sauce, sugar, palm sugar, tamarind and tomato sauce in a small saucepan over low heat and stir until the palm sugar dissolves *(pic 2)*. Remove from the heat and set aside.

3 Heat a wok over high heat and add 2 teaspoons of the oil, swirling it around the wok to coat the side. Add the egg and tilt the wok *(pic 3)* to create a thin layer of egg (it will cook almost immediately). Remove from the wok, roll up and coarsely chop. Set aside.

4 Return the wok to high heat and add the remaining oil, swirling it around the wok to coat the side. Add the shrimp paste, onion and chicken and stir-fry for 2 minutes or until the chicken is just cooked. Add the noodles, fish sauce mixture, chilli powder and spring onions and cook for 2–3 minutes or until the noodles have absorbed the sauce. Stir in the egg and then transfer to a serving plate. Serve topped with the bean sprouts, coriander sprigs and chopped peanuts. Place the extra sugar and chilli powder at the edge of the dish for seasoning and serve with lime wedges.

1

2

3

TIP Tamarind purée is extracted from tamarind pods and is sold ready to use. It has a sour, fruity taste. Tamarind purée is an important element in pad thai and, along with the palm sugar and shrimp paste, gives this dish an authentic Thai flavour. All of these ingredients can be found at Asian supermarkets.

Portuguese rice with chicken

Using paprika and saffron, this aromatic chicken and rice dish is reminiscent of paella. It is important to think ahead and marinate the chicken overnight to get the full intensity of the spices. You could use smoked paprika, if desired, for an extra dimension of flavour.

SERVES 4   **PREPARATION TIME** 20 minutes (+ overnight marinating and 15 minutes standing)   **COOKING TIME** 25 minutes

1 tablespoon olive oil
1 large brown onion, finely chopped
1 large carrot, finely chopped
1 celery stalk, finely chopped
2 garlic cloves, crushed
Large pinch of saffron threads
220 g (7¾ oz/1 cup) medium-grain white rice
400 g (14 oz) tin chopped tomatoes
375 ml (13 fl oz/1½ cups) good-quality ready-made or home-made chicken stock (see page 30)
2 tablespoons flat-leaf (Italian) parsley
Lemon wedges, to serve

SPICED CHICKEN
2 teaspoons sweet paprika
1 teaspoon ground fennel
1 tablespoon olive oil
600 g (1 lb 5 oz) skinless chicken thigh fillets, halved lengthways

1 To make the spiced chicken, put the paprika, fennel, oil and chicken in a glass or ceramic bowl. Season with sea salt and freshly ground black pepper *(pic 1)*. Toss to coat the chicken. Cover and refrigerate overnight to marinate.

2 Heat a large non-stick frying pan over medium–high heat and cook the chicken for 2–3 minutes or until golden brown *(pic 2)*, turning often to ensure even colouring. Remove from the pan and set aside.

3 In the same pan, heat the olive oil over medium heat. Add the onion, carrot and celery and cook, stirring occasionally, for 5 minutes or until softened. Add the garlic and cook, stirring constantly, for 1 minute. Add the saffron and rice and stir to coat. Add the tomatoes and stock and stir to scrape any caramelised bits from the base of the pan.

4 Return the chicken to the pan, distributing it evenly throughout the rice mixture *(pic 3)*.

5 Bring to the boil, then reduce the heat to low, cover and simmer for 15 minutes. Remove from the heat and stand, covered, for a further 15 minutes. Sprinkle with parsley and serve with lemon wedges.

1

2

3

Chicken meatballs in fresh tomato sauce

While not for Italian traditionalists, these chicken meatballs make a great family meal, either served with vegetables or tossed through pasta. They can also be served as a canapé — make them half as big and serve with the tomato sauce in a bowl for dipping.

SERVES 4 **PREPARATION TIME** 20 minutes **COOKING TIME** 35 minutes

500 g (1 lb 2 oz) minced (ground)
   skinless chicken thigh fillets
   (see page 25)
2½ tablespoons chopped green olives
2 tablespoons roughly chopped
   oregano leaves
1 tablespoon roughly chopped
   parsley leaves
2 garlic cloves, crushed
25 g (1 oz/¼ cup) finely grated
   parmesan cheese
30 g (1 oz/½ cup) fresh breadcrumbs
1 egg, lightly whisked
1 teaspoon sea salt flakes
¼ teaspoon freshly ground black pepper
2 tablespoons olive oil
1 tablespoon oregano leaves

FRESH TOMATO SAUCE
750 g (1 lb 10 oz) very ripe tomatoes
1 tablespoon olive oil
1 brown onion, finely chopped
2 garlic cloves, finely chopped
80 ml (2½ fl oz/⅓ cup) white wine
60 g (2¼ oz/¼ cup) tomato paste
   (concentrated purée)
2 teaspoons balsamic vinegar
1–2 teaspoons sea salt flakes,
   or to taste
2–3 teaspoons sugar, or to taste

1 Place the chicken, olives, oregano, parsley, garlic, parmesan, breadcrumbs, egg, sea salt and pepper in a large bowl. Mix with your hands until well combined.

2 Wet your hands to prevent the mixture sticking to them. Roll heaped tablespoons of the mixture into balls (*pic 1*), place on a greased baking tray and refrigerate while making the sauce.

3 Meanwhile, to make the fresh tomato sauce, use a small sharp knife to cut the core out of the top of each tomato. Plunge the tomatoes into a saucepan of boiling water for 15 seconds. Use a slotted spoon to remove the tomatoes from the pan (*pic 2*) and transfer to a bowl of iced water. Pinch the skin between your thumb and a paring knife to peel it off in strips. Roughly chop the peeled tomatoes (reserving any juice) and set aside. Heat the oil in a large heavy-based frying pan over medium heat. Cook the onion and garlic for 8 minutes or until softened and just beginning to colour. Add the wine and boil until it has mostly evaporated. Add the tomato paste and cook, stirring, for 2–3 minutes, then add the chopped tomatoes and any reserved juice. Reduce the heat to low and simmer, stirring occasionally, for 10 minutes or until reduced to a good sauce consistency. Add the vinegar, and the sea salt and sugar to taste. You are looking to balance the flavours — this can vary depending on the ripeness of the tomatoes. Set aside.

4 Heat half the olive oil in a large non-stick frying pan over medium heat. Cook half the meatballs, turning occasionally, for 5 minutes or until golden brown and cooked through (*pic 3*). Use a slotted spoon to transfer the meatballs to the pan with the tomato sauce. Add the remaining oil to the frying pan and repeat with the remaining meatballs. Reheat the sauce with the meatballs over medium heat until just simmering. Gently stir through the oregano and serve.

1

2

3

Pan-fried duck confit with baby beetroot salad

This is a perfect Sunday lunch dish — the beetroot salad provides a good balance, with the acid in the dressing cutting through the richness of the duck. You can confit the duck up to 1 month ahead.

SERVES 4   **PREPARATION TIME** 30 minutes (+ 10 minutes cooling)   **COOKING TIME** 1 hour 10 minutes

4 confit duck marylands
(see page 32)
10 baby beetroot (beets),
leaves still attached
3 thyme sprigs
70 ml (2¼ fl oz) olive oil
315 g (11¼ oz/1 cup) rock salt
1 teaspoon fennel seeds
12 French shallots, peeled
20 baby carrots, scrubbed and trimmed
60 ml (2 fl oz/¼ cup) extra virgin olive oil
1½ tablespoons good-quality
red wine vinegar

1 Remove the thigh bone from each maryland by carefully easing it away from the tender duck meat, twisting and breaking it away from the joint *(pic 1)*. Removing this bone improves the presentation and makes eating the leg easier. Remove any cartilage from the tips of the drumsticks and trim any excess fat from around the marylands, neatening their shape. Use a small sharp knife to scrape the bones to remove any excess meat and sinew *(pic 2)*.

2 Preheat the oven to 200°C (400°F/ Gas 6). Cut a double layer of foil, 30 x 40 cm (12 x 16 inches).

3 Trim the beetroot leaves 2 cm (¾ inch) from the top of the beetroot, reserving them for the salad. Gently scrub the beetroot to remove any soil or grit and place on the foil. Add the thyme, 1 tablespoon of olive oil and a little sea salt and seal the edges of the foil. Spread the rock salt over a baking tray and place the beetroot parcel on top

(this will prevent the beetroot burning). Cook for 45 minutes or until tender. Set aside for 10 minutes or until cool enough to handle (beetroot is easier to peel while it's still quite hot). Wearing disposable rubber gloves, use your fingers to gently remove the skin, being careful to leave the stem and point of the beetroot intact *(pic 3)*. Cut each beetroot in half lengthways. Set aside.

4 Meanwhile, crush the fennel seeds using a mortar and pestle until they are coarsely ground. Heat a large, non-stick ovenproof frying pan (see tip) over medium heat. Add 2 tablespoons of olive oil and the shallots and cook, tossing occasionally, for 6 minutes. Add the fennel and carrots and toss gently. Transfer the vegetables and oil to a large roasting pan and roast for 15 minutes or until the carrots are tender.

5 While the vegetables are cooking, wipe out the frying pan, add the remaining oil and heat over medium heat. Cook the duck, skin side down, for 2 minutes, then place in the oven with the vegetables and cook for 12 minutes or until the skin is crisp and golden.

6 Wash, dry and trim about 100 g (3½ oz) of the reserved beetroot leaves and put them in a bowl. Add the warm carrots, shallots and beetroot and season with salt and pepper. Combine the extra virgin olive oil and vinegar, drizzle over the salad and gently toss. Divide the salad among serving plates and top with the duck to serve.

1

2

3

TIP If you don't have an ovenproof frying pan that will fit in your oven, use a normal frying pan and then transfer the chicken to a roasting pan to finish cooking in the oven.

Herbed chicken fingers with lemon mayonnaise

SERVES 8 as a starter or snack **PREPARATION TIME** 15 minutes (+ 30 minutes chilling) **COOKING TIME** 12 minutes

**4 skinless chicken breast fillets
(about 1 kg/2 lb 4 oz)**
**165 g (5¾ oz/1½ cups) ready-made
dry breadcrumbs**
**1 tablespoon chopped flat-leaf
(Italian) parsley**
1 tablespoon chopped oregano
**75 g (2¾ oz/½ cup) plain
(all-purpose) flour**
3 eggs, lightly whisked
125 ml (4 fl oz/½ cup) olive oil

LEMON MAYONNAISE
**235 g (8½ oz/1 cup) whole egg
mayonnaise**
1 small garlic clove, crushed
1–2 tablespoons lemon juice, to taste
½ teaspoon finely grated lemon zest

1 Cut the chicken fillets into long strips about 2 cm (¾ inch) wide. Combine the breadcrumbs, parsley and oregano in a bowl *(pic 1)*. Put the flour in a plastic bag, season well with salt and freshly ground black pepper and add the chicken strips *(pic 2)*. Toss until the chicken is coated and then remove, shaking off any excess flour.

2 Dip the chicken, one strip at a time, in the egg, allowing any excess to drain away *(pic 3)* and then coat with the breadcrumb mixture, pressing it on with your fingers. Place the coated chicken pieces on a foil-lined tray, cover and refrigerate for 30 minutes.

3 Meanwhile, make the lemon mayonnaise. Put all the ingredients in a small bowl and mix well. Cover and refrigerate until needed.

4 Heat the oil in a large heavy-based frying pan over medium heat. Add half the chicken strips and cook for 3 minutes each side or until golden and just cooked through. Transfer to paper towels to drain. Repeat with the remaining chicken pieces. Serve warm with the lemon mayonnaise.

1

2

3

Chicken satay

SERVES 4   **PREPARATION TIME** 20 minutes (+ 1 hour soaking/chilling)   **COOKING TIME** 8–10 minutes

700 g (1 lb 9 oz) skinless chicken
   breast fillets
1 tablespoon peanut oil
½ teaspoon ground turmeric
2 teaspoons ground cumin
90 g (3¼ oz/⅓ cup) crunchy
   peanut butter
140 ml (4¾ fl oz) tin coconut milk
1 garlic clove, crushed
1 long red chilli, seeded, finely chopped
1 teaspoon finely grated ginger
2 teaspoons fish sauce
2 teaspoons kecap manis
1 tablespoon lime juice
Steamed jasmine rice, to serve
Coriander (cilantro) leaves and
   lime halves, to serve

1 Soak 12 bamboo skewers in cold water for 30 minutes to prevent scorching *(pic 1)*.

2 Cut the chicken fillets into long strips about 2 cm (¾ inch) wide and thread onto skewers *(pic 2)*. Place the skewers in a single layer on a baking tray. Brush with the combined oil, turmeric and half the cumin *(pic 3)*. Cover and refrigerate for 30 minutes.

3 Preheat a large frying pan, chargrill pan or barbecue grill on medium–high heat and cook the skewers, turning occasionally, for 8–10 minutes or until the chicken is cooked through.

4 Meanwhile, combine the peanut butter, coconut milk, garlic, chilli, ginger, fish sauce, kecap manis, lime juice and remaining cumin in a small saucepan over medium heat. Cook, stirring, until warm. Serve the skewers with the steamed rice, satay sauce, coriander and lime halves.

Chicken paella

SERVES 4   **PREPARATION TIME** 20 minutes (+ 5 minutes standing)   **COOKING TIME** 45 minutes

650 g (1 lb 7 oz) ripe tomatoes
1 litre (35 fl oz/4 cups) good-quality
   ready-made or home-made chicken
   stock (see page 30)
2 pinches of saffron threads
1.7 kg (3 lb 12 oz) whole chicken, jointed
   into 10 pieces (see page 18)
2 tablespoons olive oil
2 (about 270 g/9½ oz) chorizo, sliced
2 brown onions, diced
1 red capsicum (pepper),
   seeded and diced
3 garlic cloves, thinly sliced
1 teaspoon sweet or smoked paprika
440 g (15½ oz/2 cups) arborio rice
125 ml (4 fl oz/½ cup) dry white wine
¼ cup chopped flat-leaf (Italian) parsley
Lemon wedges, to serve

1 Cut a shallow cross on the base of
each tomato *(pic 1)*. Place in a heatproof
bowl, cover with boiling water and set
aside for 1 minute. Drain, then peel
and discard the skin. Dice the flesh,
reserving any juices. Set aside.

2 Put the stock in a saucepan, add the
saffron and bring to the boil. Reduce
the heat and simmer for 1 minute.
Remove from the heat and set aside.

3 Season the chicken pieces with sea
salt. Heat the oil in a 38 cm (15 inch)
paella pan (see tip) over medium–high
heat and cook the chicken pieces and
chorizo for 5–6 minutes or until they
are golden brown, turning often to
ensure even colour. Remove from the
pan and set aside.

4 Add the onions and capsicum to the
pan, reduce the heat to medium–low
and stir, scraping any caramelised bits
from the base of the pan, for 4 minutes
or until the onion is golden. Add the
garlic and paprika and cook, stirring
constantly, for 1 minute. Add the rice
and stir to coat with the onion mixture.
Add the wine, tomatoes and reserved
juices, and stock and stir to combine.

5 Return the chicken and chorizo to
the pan, distributing them evenly and
pressing into the rice mixture *(pic 2)*.

6 Bring to the boil and simmer
vigorously, uncovered, for 10 minutes
without stirring *(pic 3)*. Reduce the heat
and simmer for 15–20 minutes more,
without stirring, or until the chicken is
cooked, the rice is tender and the liquid
has been absorbed. Keep a close eye on
it so it doesn't burn (see tip).

7 Remove from the heat, cover with a
tea towel (dish towel) and set aside for
5 minutes. Serve sprinkled with parsley
and accompanied by lemon wedges.

1

2

3

TIP If you don't have a paella pan
you could use a very large frying
pan or split the mixture between
two pans. To ensure even cooking
and prevent burning you may need
to turn the pan around occasionally
so there is an even distribution
of heat. However, a good paella
will always have a 'sucarrat' — a
deep-brown crust that forms on
the base. If this crust forms without
burning it is a sign of a good paella.

Chicken liver pâté with marmalade and melba toast

To make a perfect chicken liver pâté, the most important thing is that the livers are still pink and juicy in the centre, not overcooked. You can substitute duck livers if you like.

SERVES 6–8 as an appetiser **PREPARATION TIME** 30 minutes (+ cooling/chilling) **COOKING TIME** 20 minutes

125 g (4½ oz) unsalted butter

2 French shallots, finely chopped

600 g (1 lb 5 oz) chicken livers, cleaned (see page 25) to give 500 g (1 lb 2 oz)

½ teaspoon thyme leaves

½ teaspoon tarragon leaves

1 tablespoon brandy

1 tablespoon orange liqueur (such as Grand Marnier or Cointreau)

125 g (4½ oz) butter, extra, melted and cooled

100 ml (3½ fl oz) thin (pouring/ whipping) cream

8 slices white bread (each about 1 cm/½ inch thick)

Good-quality sweet orange marmalade, to serve

1 Melt 50 g (1¾ oz) of the unsalted butter in a large frying pan over medium heat until foaming. Add the shallots, reduce the heat to low and cook, stirring occasionally, for about 5 minutes, until soft. Add the chicken livers and herbs and stir over medium heat for 2 minutes or until the livers are lightly browned *(pic 1)*. Season to taste. Add the brandy and orange liqueur, tip the pan slightly and flambé (see tip).

2 Set the frying pan aside for 5 minutes or until the mixture cools slightly. Transfer to a food processor and process until smooth. Add the extra melted butter and process until smooth. Add the cream and process until the mixture is very smooth and well combined *(pic 2)*. Push through a fine sieve, then spoon into twelve 60 ml (2 fl oz/¼ cup) dishes, three 250 ml (9 fl oz/1 cup) dishes or a 750 ml (26 fl oz/3 cup) terrine dish. Smooth the top and set aside to cool slightly.

3 Heat the remaining 75 g (2¾ oz) of butter in a small saucepan over medium heat until foaming — don't allow it to burn. Pour through a double layer of muslin (cheesecloth) into a jug to remove the milky solids. Pour over the back of a spoon onto the pâté in the dish/es to cover evenly *(pic 3)*. Cool completely, then cover and refrigerate until ready to serve.

4 Preheat the oven to 160°C (315°F/ Gas 2–3). Toast the bread slices until golden. Use a serrated knife to remove the crusts, then carefully split each slice horizontally and cut each piece into 2 triangles. Place on 2 baking trays, cut side up. Bake for about 5 minutes or until dry and crisp. Cool on the trays.

5 Serve the pâté at room temperature with a little dish of marmalade and the melba toast.

1

2

3

TIP When you flambé a dish, you ignite the alcohol to burn it off and give the dish a slightly singed flavour.

Chicken pasta with basil and lemon

SERVES 4   **PREPARATION TIME** 10 minutes   **COOKING TIME** 15 minutes

600 g (1 lb 5 oz) skinless chicken
  breast fillets
2 tablespoons olive oil
400 g (14 oz) spaghetti
200 g (7 oz) thin asparagus spears,
  trimmed and halved
2 leeks, white part only, sliced
245 g (9 oz/1 cup) sour cream
80 ml (2½ fl oz/⅓ cup) lemon juice
Finely grated zest of 1 lemon
1 cup small basil leaves

1 Brush the chicken with half the olive
oil and season with sea salt and freshly
ground black pepper. Heat a non-stick
frying pan over medium heat. Cook
the chicken for 5 minutes each side or
until golden and just cooked through.
Remove from the pan, set aside to
cool slightly and then use two forks to
coarsely shred the chicken *(pic 1)*.

2 Bring a large saucepan of salted water
to a rapid boil, add the spaghetti and
cook until *al dente*. Add the asparagus
for the final 2 minutes of cooking
(pic 2). It should be bright green and
tender when the pasta is ready. Drain,
reserving a little of the cooking liquid.

3 Meanwhile, heat the remaining oil
in a large saucepan over medium–low
heat. Add the leeks and cook, stirring
occasionally, for 6–8 minutes, until
softened and light golden *(pic 3)*. Add
the sour cream and lemon juice and stir
to combine. Add the shredded chicken
and cook for 1 minute to heat through.
Add the lemon zest and drained pasta
and asparagus, and toss to coat. Add a
little of the reserved cooking liquid if
the sauce is too thick. Taste and adjust
the seasoning, then stir through the
basil and serve.

1

2

3

Chicken san choy bau

SERVES 4   **PREPARATION TIME** 15 minutes   **COOKING TIME** 10 minutes

3 teaspoons sesame oil

600 g (1 lb 5 oz) minced (ground) chicken thigh fillets (see page 25)

2 garlic cloves, crushed

2 teaspoons finely grated ginger

100 g (3½ oz) shiitake mushrooms, finely chopped

227 g (8 oz) tin sliced water chestnuts, drained, chopped

3 spring onions (scallions), thinly sliced

170 g (5¾ oz/1½ cups) bean sprouts, trimmed

2 tablespoons light soy sauce

2 tablespoons oyster sauce

1 tablespoon lime juice

8 iceberg lettuce leaves

15 g (½ oz/¼ cup) crisp fried shallots (see tip)

1 Heat a wok over high heat. Add the oil and swirl it around the wok to coat the side. Add the minced chicken and stir-fry, breaking up any lumps, for 2–3 minutes or until browned *(pic 1)*.

2 Add the garlic, ginger, mushrooms, water chestnuts and spring onions to the wok and stir-fry for 2–3 minutes or until the mushrooms are tender *(pic 2)*. Add the bean sprouts and then the combined soy sauce, oyster sauce and lime juice *(pic 3)*. Toss until combined.

3 Spoon the san choy bau mixture into the lettuce leaves and serve sprinkled with the fried shallots.

TIP You can find fried shallots in the Asian food section at the supermarket. The chicken mince can be replaced with pork mince.

Thai-style chicken fried rice

SERVES 4   **PREPARATION TIME** 15 minutes   **COOKING TIME** 15 minutes

2 tablespoons peanut oil

500 g (1 lb 2 oz) skinless chicken thigh
   fillets, cut into 2 cm (¾ inch) pieces

1 small brown onion, thinly sliced

1 small red capsicum (pepper), seeded
   and thinly sliced

200 g (7 oz) snake beans, trimmed,
   cut into 5 cm (2 inch) lengths

2 garlic cloves, crushed

2 teaspoons finely grated ginger

1 teaspoon chilli paste

2 tablespoons fish sauce

1 tablespoon light soy sauce

2 tablespoons lime juice

750 g (1 lb 10 oz/4 cups) cold cooked
   jasmine rice (see tip)

115 g (4 oz/1 cup) bean sprouts,
   trimmed

¾ cup coriander (cilantro) leaves

15 g (½ oz/¼ cup) crisp fried shallots
   (see tip)

1 Heat a wok over high heat. Add half the oil and swirl it around the wok to coat the side. Stir-fry the chicken, in batches, for 3–4 minutes or until browned *(pic 1)*. Transfer to a plate.

2 Heat the remaining oil in the wok. Add the onion, capsicum and beans and stir-fry for 2–3 minutes or until the vegetables are tender *(pic 2)*. Add the garlic, ginger and chilli paste and stir-fry for 1 minute. Return the chicken to the wok with the fish sauce, soy sauce and lime juice and stir-fry for 1 minute.

3 Add the rice *(pic 3)* and stir-fry for 2–3 minutes or until heated through. Add the bean sprouts and coriander and toss to combine. Serve sprinkled with the fried shallots.

TIP You will need to cook 250 g (9 oz/1¼ cups) jasmine rice for this recipe.
   You can find fried shallots in the Asian food section at the supermarket.

Duck breast with wild rice

Duck breasts are available from butchers and some supermarkets also stock them. If you want, you can substitute chicken breast fillets. The cooking time will remain the same.

SERVES 4   **PREPARATION TIME** 15 minutes   **COOKING TIME** 1 hour

95 g (3¼ oz/½ cup) wild rice, rinsed
2 teaspoons olive oil
50 g (1¾ oz/½ cup) pecans,
    roughly chopped
½ teaspoon ground cinnamon
65 g (2¼ oz/⅓ cup) long-grain
    white rice
2 tablespoons chopped flat-leaf
    (Italian) parsley
4 spring onions (scallions), trimmed,
    thinly sliced
4 x 250 g (9 oz) duck breasts
Shredded zest of 1 orange (see tip)

DRESSING
80 ml (2½ fl oz/⅓ cup) olive oil
1 teaspoon finely grated orange zest
2 tablespoons orange juice
2 teaspoons walnut oil
1 tablespoon finely chopped glacé
    (candied) ginger

1 To make the dressing, thoroughly combine the ingredients and season with salt and pepper. Set aside.

2 Put the wild rice and 300 ml (10½ fl oz) water in a saucepan. Bring to the boil and cook, covered, for 30 minutes or until tender. Drain away any excess water *(pic 1)*.

3 Meanwhile, heat the oil in a large frying pan. Add the pecans and cook, stirring, until golden. Add the cinnamon and a pinch of salt *(pic 2)* and cook for 1 minute, then set aside.

4 Bring a medium saucepan of water to the boil. Add the white rice and cook, stirring occasionally, for 12 minutes or until tender. Drain and mix with the wild rice and pecans in a large, shallow bowl. Add the parsley, spring onions and half the dressing and toss well.

5 Season the duck breasts generously with sea salt. Heat a large non-stick frying pan over medium–low heat and cook the duck breasts for 6 minutes, skin side down. Turn and cook for a further 5 minutes *(pic 3)*. Brown the edges of the duck breasts by holding them one at a time with tongs to ensure they get a little colour on all sides.

6 Tip out any excess fat from the pan, add the remaining dressing and the shredded zest, and cook until bubbling. Remove from the heat, slice the duck diagonally and serve with the rice, drizzling any juices over the top.

1

2

3

TIP This recipe requires long, thin pieces of zest, which can be made with a zesting tool. If you don't have one, use a vegetable peeler to remove long, wide strips of zest, then shred these finely.

Veal medallions with salsa verde

Salsa verde is a terrific accompaniment for veal, as it is salty and packed with flavour. It is also delicious tossed through steamed green vegetables or spooned over roasted meats such as chicken or beef.

SERVES 4 **PREPARATION TIME** 25 minutes (+ 2–3 minutes resting) **COOKING TIME** 20 minutes

600 g (1 lb 5 oz) kipfler (fingerling)
  potatoes, peeled
200 g (7 oz) green beans, trimmed
4 marinated artichokes, halved
8 veal medallions (about 75 g/2¾ oz
  each), at room temperature
1 tablespoon olive oil
Parsley sprigs, to garnish

SALSA VERDE

½ cup firmly packed parsley leaves
½ cup firmly packed basil leaves
⅓ cup firmly packed mint leaves
1 tablespoon salted baby capers,
  rinsed and drained
1 small sweet gherkin, chopped
2–3 anchovy fillets, drained
1 garlic clove, chopped
1 tablespoon dijon mustard
2 tablespoons red wine vinegar
80 ml (2½ fl oz/⅓ cup) olive oil

1 Put the potatoes in a large saucepan, cover with cold water and bring to the boil. Cook for 12–15 minutes or until tender, adding the beans for the last 3 minutes of cooking. Drain well, then cut the potatoes in half lengthways and put in a large bowl with the beans.

2 Meanwhile, to make the salsa verde, put the herbs, capers, gherkin, anchovies, garlic and mustard in a food processor *(pic 1)* and process until finely chopped. With the motor running, add the vinegar and oil and process until well incorporated. Add a little more oil if the consistency is too thick. Season with salt and pepper, to taste. Add the artichokes to the potatoes and beans, then add 2 tablespoons of the salsa verde *(pic 2)* and toss to combine. Transfer the remaining salsa verde to a bowl or small jug and cover with plastic wrap.

3 Heat a large non-stick frying pan over high heat. Brush the medallions with the oil and cook, in batches, for 2 minutes each side *(pic 3)* or until cooked to your liking. Transfer to a plate, cover loosely with foil and set aside for 2–3 minutes to rest.

4 Serve the medallions with the potato, bean and artichoke salad, topped with spoonfuls of the remaining salsa verde and garnished with the parsley sprigs.

TIP Salsa verde is a rustic Italian green sauce made from herbs, capers, vinegar and oil.

Veal saltimbocca

Saltimbocca literally means 'jump in the mouth', which is a good way to describe the more-ish nature of this traditional Italian dish of veal topped with sage and prosciutto. This version is finished with a white wine, butter and caper sauce. Use very tender escalopes of veal, pounded until they are uniformly thin.

SERVES 4 **PREPARATION TIME** 15 minutes **COOKING TIME** 20 minutes

16 sage leaves, plus 2 teaspoons
   chopped sage, extra
8 veal escalopes (about 70 g/
   2½ oz each) (see tip), at room
   temperature
8 slices prosciutto
35 g (1¼ oz/¼ cup) plain
   (all-purpose) flour
2 tablespoons olive oil
80 ml (2½ fl oz/⅓ cup) white wine
2 tablespoons lemon juice
1 tablespoon salted baby capers,
   rinsed and drained
40 g (1½ oz) unsalted butter, chopped
Mashed potato (see page 69) and
   wilted spinach, to serve

1 Place 2 sage leaves down the middle of each escalope, then wrap a piece of prosciutto around each escalope to enclose the sage *(pic 1)*.

2 Place the flour on a large plate and season with salt and pepper. Dust each wrapped escalope in the seasoned flour to lightly coat, shaking off any excess.

3 Heat the oil in a large non-stick frying pan over high heat. Cook the escalopes, in batches, for 1–2 minutes each side *(pic 2)* or until golden brown. Transfer to a large plate, cover loosely with foil and set aside to rest while you make the sauce.

4 Return the pan to medium–high heat, add the wine, lemon juice and capers and simmer for 2–3 minutes or until reduced by half. Whisk in the butter *(pic 3)* until smooth, then stir through the chopped sage.

5 Place 2 saltimbocca on each plate and drizzle with a little of the caper sauce. Serve accompanied by the mashed potato and wilted spinach.

1

2

3

TIP We used butterflied veal loin that was pounded to approximately 5 mm (¼ inch) thick for the veal escalopes. Ask your butcher to do this.

Beef stroganoff

This classic Russian dish is based on beef, which is thinly sliced and cooked in sour cream, paprika, mushrooms and garlic. This version is served with buttered pasta, but steamed rice works well, too.

SERVES 4   **PREPARATION TIME** 20 minutes   **COOKING TIME** 25 minutes

2 tablespoons plain (all-purpose) flour
2 teaspoons smoked paprika
600 g (1 lb 5 oz) beef rump steak,
    at room temperature, trimmed and
    thinly sliced *(pic 1)*
60 ml (2 fl oz/¼ cup) olive oil
2 onions, thinly sliced
250 g (9 oz) button mushrooms,
    wiped clean and sliced
2 garlic cloves, crushed
1 tablespoon tomato paste
    (concentrated purée)
185 ml (6 fl oz/¾ cup) good-quality
    ready-made or home-made beef
    stock (see page 60)
2 tablespoons worcestershire sauce
85 g (3 oz/⅓ cup) sour cream
Cooked fettuccine tossed with butter,
    to serve
2 tablespoons chopped flat-leaf (Italian)
    parsley, to garnish

1 Combine the flour and paprika and season with sea salt and freshly ground black pepper. Toss the beef strips in the seasoned flour to lightly coat, shaking off any excess. Heat half the oil in a large frying pan over high heat. Cook the beef, in batches, stirring occasionally, for 2–3 minutes or until browned *(pic 2)*. Transfer to a bowl and set aside.

2 Return the pan to medium–high heat. Add the remaining oil and onions and cook, stirring occasionally, for 5 minutes or until softened. Add the mushrooms and garlic *(pic 3)* and cook for 3–4 minutes or until the mushrooms are golden.

3 Add the tomato paste and cook, stirring, for 1 minute. Add the stock and worcestershire sauce and stir to combine, then bring to the boil. Reduce the heat and simmer for 2–3 minutes or until slightly thickened. Return the beef to the pan, stir through the sour cream and simmer for 1 minute. Season with salt and pepper, to taste.

4 Divide the fettuccine among serving plates, spoon over the stroganoff and garnish with the parsley.

1

2

3

Crumbed lamb cutlets

This elegant take on a family favourite uses parsley and lemon zest to give the crumb coating added flavour, while preserved lemon and almonds provide crunch and zing to tender-crisp green beans. You could try using other herbs and zests in the crumb coating, such as lemon thyme or orange zest.

SERVES 4   **PREPARATION TIME** 15 minutes   **COOKING TIME** 20 minutes

2 eggs

2 teaspoons dijon mustard

120 g (4¼ oz/2 cups, lightly packed) fresh breadcrumbs, made from day-old bread with crusts removed (see tip)

2 tablespoons chopped flat-leaf (Italian) parsley

Finely grated zest of 1 lemon

8 lamb cutlets, frenched (see page 55), at room temperature

Vegetable oil, for frying

400 g (14 oz) green beans, trimmed

2½ tablespoons extra virgin olive oil

2 teaspoons chopped preserved lemon (rind only) *(pic 1)*

1 tablespoon raw almonds, toasted and coarsely chopped

Mashed potato (see page 69), to serve

1 Whisk the eggs and mustard in a shallow bowl until combined. Mix together the breadcrumbs, parsley and lemon zest in another bowl. Season the cutlets with salt and pepper. Dip the cutlets in the egg mixture, then lightly press into the crumb mixture, one side at a time, to coat generously *(pic 2)*.

2 Heat 1 cm (½ inch) of vegetable oil in a large frying pan over medium–low heat. Cook the cutlets, in batches, for 3–4 minutes each side *(pic 3)* or until cooked to your liking. Transfer to paper towels to drain.

3 Meanwhile, cook the beans in a saucepan of salted boiling water for 3 minutes or until tender. Drain and toss with the olive oil, preserved lemon and almonds.

4 Serve the cutlets with the beans and mashed potato.

1

2

3

> **TIP** You can also use dried plain or wholemeal breadcrumbs, or panko (Japanese) breadcrumbs, available from supermarkets.

Teriyaki beef

In this traditional Japanese dish thin slices of meat are marinated in soy sauce, mirin and sesame oil. It is quick and easy to prepare, with the secret being to slice the meat as thinly as possible. You can substitute another meat, such as pork or chicken, for the beef if you like.

SERVES 4   **PREPARATION TIME** 20 minutes (+ 1 hour marinating)   **COOKING TIME** 15 minutes

1 tablespoon sesame oil
80 ml (2½ fl oz/⅓ cup) mirin
80 ml (2½ fl oz/⅓ cup) soy sauce
600 g (1 lb 5 oz) beef fillet, thinly sliced
    (see tip)
2 teaspoons caster (superfine) sugar
2 tablespoons peanut oil
2 onions, thinly sliced
3 cm (1¼ inch) piece ginger,
    peeled and julienned
1 garlic clove, crushed
Sliced spring onion (scallion), to garnish
Steamed rice and snow peas
    (mangetout), to serve

1 Combine the sesame oil, 1 tablespoon of the mirin and 1 tablespoon of the soy sauce in a shallow glass or ceramic dish. Add the beef and stir to coat, then cover with plastic wrap *(pic 1)* and refrigerate for at least 1 hour. Put the remaining mirin and soy sauce and the sugar in a small bowl, stir until the sugar has dissolved and set aside.

2 Heat half the peanut oil in a large wok or frying pan over high heat. Drain the beef and stir-fry, in batches, for 2 minutes or until browned *(pic 2)*. Transfer to a bowl and set aside.

3 Return the wok to high heat, add the remaining oil and the onions and stir-fry for 2–3 minutes or until the onions are golden. Add the ginger and garlic and stir-fry for 1 minute. Add the mirin mixture *(pic 3)* and cook for 2 minutes. Return the beef to the pan and cook for a further 1 minute.

4 Garnish with the spring onion and serve with steamed rice and snow peas.

1

2

3

TIP Partially freezing the beef will make it easier to slice thinly.

The perfect beef steak

There are five premium cuts of beef steak and while all can be cooked in the same way, the cooking times and end results are a little different. All of these cuts should not be cooked past medium doneness or they will be tough and dry to eat.

Tenderloin or fillet is the most tender, and lean, premium steak. There is little trim with this cut and the ideal size for steaks is 180–200 g (6¼–7 oz). It is best suited to pan-frying, but can also be barbecued.

Rib eye or scotch fillet steak has a lot of fat marbling through the meat, so it is very juicy when cooked. The steaks are available on the bone, with individual steaks weighing around 600 g (1 lb 5 oz), and off the bone, with steaks weighing about 300 g (10½ oz). The steaks on the bone have an even richer flavour.

T-bone steak features a T-shaped bone, hence the name, with meat from the eye fillet on one side and meat from the sirloin on the other. Full-flavoured and juicy, T-bone steaks weigh anywhere from 500 g (1 lb 2 oz) to 1 kg (2 lb 4 oz). Due to the bone, they cook faster than boneless steaks.

Boneless sirloin, or porterhouse/New York cut, steak is a long steak with a cap of fat along the top that is cut from the loin of the cow. It is full-flavoured and a little chewier than most of the other steaks — it needs to be well aged in order to be really tender. A good size for a sirloin steak is about 300 g (10½ oz).

Rump tends to be the cheapest of the premium steaks. Full of flavour and lean, it is prone to being tough so it is important to buy good-quality rump, properly aged, and perhaps marinate it overnight to tenderise it.

Stages of cooking for steaks

The most precise way to determine a steak's doneness is by using a digital instant-read meat thermometer to read its internal temperature. Although steaks are generally the same thickness all the way through, the centre takes the longest to cook so insert the thermometer there. Push it about midway into the steak and leave it there until the reading is done (up to 30 seconds, depending on the brand of thermometer). Do not cut the steak with a knife as all the juices will run out. After cooking, it is essential to rest the steak for 5 minutes to allow the juices to settle. During this time the meat will continue to cook just a little, so bear that in mind when deciding how cooked you would like your steak to be and cook it to a few degrees under the required temperature.

Very rare 120°C (248°F) Also called 'blue', the meat is very pink all the way through and only just warm in the centre.

Rare 125°C (257°F) The meat is still very pink in the centre though it is warm, with a little grey around the edges.

Medium-rare 130–135°C (266–275°F) The meat is pinkish in the middle and very warm, with a thicker band of grey around the edges.

Medium 140–145°C (284–293°F) The meat is quite hot in the centre, still a little pink but with a thick layer of grey around the edges.

Medium-well 150–155°C (302–311°F) The meat is very hot in the centre with only a trace of pink and the interior is predominantly grey.

Well done 160°C (320°F) There is no pink left in the steak at all, it is a uniform grey throughout.

Steak with béarnaise sauce

There is much debate about grass-fed or grain-fed beef and which is the best. In the last decade there has been a big swing towards grain-fed animals. Cattle all start on grass, but grain-fed cattle are then finished in feedlots on high-energy grain which results in even marbling of the meat. In terms of eating (and tenderness) the grain-fed product generally has a consistent melt-in-the-mouth texture, compared to the natural earthy flavour and firmer texture of the grass-fed meat. Try both and decide for yourself and throw some dry-aged meat into the mix for another comparison.

PREPARATION TIME 10 minutes
(+ 5 minutes resting)

COOKING TIME 4–5 minutes

SERVES 4

....

4 x 300 g (10½ oz) boneless sirloin
   steaks, at room temperature
Olive oil, for drizzling
1 quantity béarnaise sauce
   (see page 67)

1 Trim any excess fat from the steaks, leaving just a thin layer of fat to add flavour *(pic 1)*.

2 Preheat a heavy-based frying pan over medium–high heat. Season the steaks generously with sea salt and drizzle with oil to coat *(pic 2)*. Add the steaks to the hot pan and cook, in batches if necessary, for 2–2½ minutes each side *(pic 3)* for medium-rare or until 130–135°C (266–275°F) on a meat thermometer. Transfer the steaks to a plate, cover loosely with foil and set aside for 5 minutes to rest. Serve with the béarnaise sauce.

> **TIP** You can spread a small amount of crushed garlic over the steaks before salting and oiling, if desired.

1 Trim any excess fat from the steaks.

2 Season the steaks generously with sea salt and drizzle with oil to coat.

3 Cook the steaks, in batches if necessary, for 2–2½ minutes each side for medium-rare.

Veal cutlets with apple mustard remoulade

Remoulade is a French mayonnaise-based accompaniment that is often made with thinly sliced celeriac. This version also contains crisp apple, which cuts through the creaminess of the mustard and chive-flavoured mayonnaise. It is also delicious served with roast beef or pork.

SERVES 4   **PREPARATION TIME** 25 minutes (+ 3 minutes resting)   **COOKING TIME** 10 minutes

1 small celeriac, peeled
1 large red apple, cored
60 ml (2 fl oz/¼ cup) lemon juice
85 g (3 oz/⅓ cup) good-quality whole
   egg mayonnaise
2 tablespoons wholegrain mustard
1 French shallot, finely chopped
2 tablespoons snipped chives
1 teaspoon finely grated lemon zest
Freshly ground white pepper
1 tablespoon olive oil
8 small (170 g/6 oz each) or 4 medium
   (220 g/7¾ oz) veal cutlets, frenched
   (see page 55), at room temperature
Lemon cheeks, to serve

1 Finely julienne the celeriac and apple *(pic 1)* and put in a large bowl. Drizzle with 2 tablespoons of the lemon juice and toss to combine (the lemon juice will prevent discolouration).

2 Put the mayonnaise, 1 tablespoon of the mustard, the shallot, chives, zest and remaining lemon juice in a bowl and stir to combine. Add to the celeriac and apple and gently toss together *(pic 2)*. Season with sea salt and freshly ground white pepper. Set aside.

3 Combine the oil and remaining mustard and brush over the cutlets *(pic 3)*. Heat a large non-stick frying pan over high heat. Pan-fry the cutlets for 2 minutes each side, then reduce the heat to medium and cook for a further 2 minutes each side, or until cooked to your liking. Transfer to a plate, cover loosely with foil and set aside for 2–3 minutes to rest.

4 Divide the remoulade and cutlets among serving plates and serve with lemon cheeks.

1

2

3

Lamb stir-fry

Lamb fillet is a lean, tender cut that is easy to prepare and cooks quickly, making it a perfect choice for stir-fries. You could substitute pork fillet if desired. Make sure the wok is hot before you begin cooking to ensure the ingredients cook quickly and retain their true flavours.

SERVES 4   **PREPARATION TIME** 15 minutes   **COOKING TIME** 10 minutes

300 g (10½ oz) lamb fillet,
    fat and sinew trimmed
200 g (7 oz) broccolini, trimmed
1½ tablespoons hoisin sauce
1½ tablespoons light soy sauce
3 teaspoons honey
1½ tablespoons peanut oil
1 garlic clove, sliced
1 long red chilli, thinly sliced
1 red onion, halved and cut into
    thin wedges
2 tablespoons ready-made chicken
    stock or water
⅓ cup mint leaves
Steamed rice, to serve

1 Diagonally slice the lamb into 1.5 cm (⅝ inch) thick pieces *(pic 1)*. Slice off the bottom 5 cm (2 inches) of each broccolini stem and chop into 1 cm (½ inch) pieces. Cut the remaining broccolini stems in half.

2 Combine the hoisin, soy sauce and honey in a small bowl.

3 Heat a wok over high heat, add 1 tablespoon of the oil and cook the garlic and chilli, stirring, for 30 seconds. Add the lamb and stir-fry for 2–3 minutes, until lightly browned *(pic 2)*. Transfer to a bowl.

4 Return the wok to the heat, add the remaining oil and cook the onion, stirring, for 1 minute. Add the 1 cm pieces of broccolini and stir-fry for 1 minute. Add the remaining broccolini and the stock and stir-fry for a further 1 minute *(pic 3)*.

5 Add the hoisin mixture and return the meat to the wok. Stir-fry for 1½ minutes, then toss through the mint. Transfer to a serving dish and serve with steamed rice.

1

2

3

TIP You can substitute broccoli or cauliflower for the broccolini, if you like. Cut off the florets and chop the stems into pieces, as for the broccolini.

Pork cutlets with juniper and sage

This is an earthy dish that is well suited to the cooler months, when Jerusalem artichokes are in season. The bold flavours of crushed juniper and sage work wonderfully with the pork. You can substitute kipfler (fingerling) potatoes for the Jerusalem artichokes when they're out of season.

SERVES 4 **PREPARATION TIME** 20 minutes **COOKING TIME** 25 minutes

2 teaspoons juniper berries
1 teaspoon sea salt flakes
4 pork cutlets, frenched (see page 55), at room temperature (see tip)
750 g (1 lb 10 oz) Jerusalem artichokes, scrubbed
60 ml (2 fl oz/¼ cup) olive oil
20 g (¾ oz) butter, plus 25 g (1 oz) chopped butter, extra
⅓ cup sage leaves
250 ml (9 fl oz/1 cup) sweet white wine
185 ml (6 fl oz/¾ cup) good-quality ready-made or home-made chicken or veal stock (see pages 30 or 60)
Steamed greens, to serve (optional)

CARAMELISED ONION
2 tablespoons olive oil
2 large onions, sliced

1 Use a mortar and pestle to crush the juniper berries. Add the salt and pound until incorporated. Rub over both sides of the cutlets (*pic 1*) and set aside.

2 To make the caramelised onion, put the oil and onions in a medium saucepan over medium heat and cook, stirring often, for 15–20 minutes, until golden brown and caramelised (*pic 2*).

3 Meanwhile, preheat the oven to 210°C (415°F/Gas 6–7). Cut the Jerusalem artichokes into 1 cm (½ inch) thick slices and toss with 2 tablespoons of the oil. Place on a heavy-based baking tray, sprinkle with sea salt and cook for 25 minutes or until golden and tender.

4 While the vegetables are cooking, heat the remaining oil and the butter in a large non-stick frying pan over medium heat until foaming. Add the sage leaves and cook for 1 minute, until the sage starts to gently spit and you can see it becoming crisp. Use a slotted spoon to transfer the sage onto paper towels to drain (*pic 3*). Add the cutlets to the pan and cook for 3 minutes each side or until cooked to your liking. Transfer to a plate, cover loosely with foil and set aside in a warm place to rest.

5 Add the wine to the frying pan, increase the heat to high and cook for 5 minutes, until there is only just enough wine left to coat the base of the pan. Add the stock and cook until reduced by half. Stir in the extra butter, then strain through a fine sieve. Serve the pork cutlets topped with the sage leaves and with the sauce drizzled over. Serve accompanied by the caramelised onion, Jerusalem artichokes and steamed greens, if desired.

1

2

3

TIP You can save time by buying pork cutlets that have already been trimmed or frenched.
Pork loin steaks or trimmed loin chops can be substituted for the cutlets, if desired.

Veal schnitzel with apple coleslaw

This meal will put smiles on the faces of young and old, and anyone in between. It's as classic as they come, but additions like parmesan in the crumb mix and apple in the coleslaw give it a special touch.

SERVES 4 **PREPARATION TIME** 20 minutes **COOKING TIME** 5 minutes

35 g (1¼ oz/¼ cup) plain
   (all-purpose) flour
1 large egg
60 g (2¼ oz/1 cup, lightly packed)
   fresh breadcrumbs (see tip)
25 g (1 oz/¼ cup) finely grated
   parmesan cheese
2 tablespoons finely chopped flat-leaf
   (Italian) parsley
4 veal leg steaks (about 80 g/
   2¾ oz each)
1 tablespoon vegetable oil
20 g (¾ oz) butter
Perfect fries (see page 68) and lemon
   cheeks, to serve

APPLE COLESLAW
375 g (13 oz) green cabbage, cored and
   thinly shredded (see tip)
1 red apple, cored and cut into
   very thin batons *(pic 1)*
½ green capsicum (pepper),
   seeded and thinly sliced
2 spring onions (scallions),
   trimmed and thinly sliced
60 g (2¼ oz/¼ cup) good-quality
   whole egg mayonnaise
1 tablespoon lemon juice

1 To make the apple coleslaw, combine the cabbage, apple, capsicum and spring onions in a large bowl. Whisk the mayonnaise and lemon juice in a small bowl until smooth and season with salt and pepper. Add to the cabbage mixture and toss to coat well. Set aside.

2 Place the flour on a large plate and season well with salt and pepper. Place the egg in a large shallow bowl and whisk lightly with a fork. Combine the breadcrumbs, parmesan and parsley on a separate large plate.

3 Place a steak between 2 sheets of non-stick baking paper. Use a rolling pin to pound the steak until it is about 2–3 mm (¹⁄₁₆–⅛ inch) thick *(pic 2)*. Repeat to flatten the remaining steaks. Cut each steak in half.

4 Working with one steak at a time, dip in the seasoned flour to coat, then tap with your hands to remove any excess. Dip in the egg until coated, then allow any excess to drip off. Finally, place in the breadcrumb mixture and press it on to coat *(pic 3)*. Place on a tray lined with non-stick baking paper. Repeat with the remaining steaks.

5 Heat the oil and butter in a large frying pan over medium–high heat until foaming. Cook the steaks, in 2 batches, for 1 minute each side until golden, crisp and just cooked through. Transfer to paper towels to drain.

6 Serve the schnitzels with the apple coleslaw, perfect fries and lemon cheeks.

1

2

3

TIP You can substitute Japanese (panko) breadcrumbs, available from supermarkets.
   Using a mandolin to shred the cabbage does the job quickly and produces very thin slices.
   You can vary the crust by adding ground nuts or other herbs.

Pan-fried lamb with quince sauce

This is a great recipe for a weeknight dinner party, as it is quick and easy to prepare and the quince sauce is simply stunning. If lamb backstraps are not available, you can substitute lamb fillets.

SERVES 4   **PREPARATION TIME** 15 minutes   **COOKING TIME** 20 minutes

600 g (1 lb 5 oz) lamb backstraps,
   any fat and sinew trimmed *(pic 1)*,
   at room temperature
1 tablespoon olive oil
100 g (3½ oz) quince paste
200 ml (7 fl oz) white wine
Steamed greens, to serve

BLUE CHEESE POLENTA
750 ml (26 fl oz/3 cups) milk
95 g (3¼ oz/½ cup) instant polenta
30 g (1 oz) unsalted butter, chopped
40 g (1½ oz) firm blue cheese
   (such as stilton), chopped (see tip)
¾ teaspoon salt

1 To make the blue cheese polenta, put the milk in a medium saucepan over medium–high heat and bring to the boil. Sprinkle over the polenta in a steady stream while whisking constantly *(pic 2)*. Reduce the heat to low and cook, stirring often with a wooden spoon to prevent the polenta sticking to the base and side of the pan. Keep the heat low to avoid bubbling and spattering. When cooked, the polenta should be creamy and just coming away from the side of the pan. This should take 5–10 minutes, depending on the brand of polenta.

2 Meanwhile, season the lamb with sea salt and cracked black pepper and drizzle with the oil. Heat a non-stick frying pan over high heat. Cook the lamb for 2–3 minutes each side, until well browned and cooked to your liking. Remove from the pan and set aside in a warm place to rest.

3 Add the quince paste and wine to the pan, reduce the heat to medium and simmer for 2–3 minutes. Use the back of a wooden spoon to crush the quince paste as it softens *(pic 3)* and stir it into the wine to form a thick sauce.

4 Stir the butter, cheese and salt through the polenta. Slice the lamb and serve drizzled with the sauce, accompanied by the blue cheese polenta and steamed greens.

1

2

3

TIP You can flavour the polenta with 35 g (1¼ oz/⅓ cup) finely grated parmesan cheese instead of blue cheese if you prefer.

Beef and allspice kofte

Kofte are essentially meatballs. In Turkey there are over 280 different types of kofte, many of which are famous regional variations. The meat was traditionally minced by hand using an enormous knife called a zihr, but this knife is now rarely used, even in Turkey.

SERVES 4   **PREPARATION TIME** 40 minutes   **COOKING TIME** 30 minutes

80 ml (2½ fl oz/⅓ cup) olive oil
8 long thin eggplants (aubergines),
　halved lengthways
8 small vine-ripened tomatoes
600 g (1 lb 5 oz) minced (ground) beef
60 g (2¼ oz/1 cup, lightly packed)
　fresh breadcrumbs
1 onion, grated or very finely chopped
40 g (1½ oz/¼ cup) pine nuts,
　coarsely chopped
1 teaspoon allspice
2½ tablespoons finely chopped parsley
1½ teaspoons salt
1 teaspoon finely ground black pepper
Greek-style yoghurt, lemon wedges,
　Turkish bread and cos (romaine)
　lettuce, to serve

1 Preheat the oven to 180°C (350°F/Gas 4). Brush about 1½ tablespoons of the oil over the eggplants and tomatoes to coat, then place them in a single layer in a roasting pan *(pic 1)*. Bake for 30 minutes or until tender and golden. Remove the tomatoes if they are cooked before the eggplants are ready.

2 Meanwhile, combine the beef, breadcrumbs, onion, pine nuts, allspice, parsley, salt and pepper in a bowl. Use your hands to knead the mixture for 8–10 minutes or until well combined and somewhat elastic *(pic 2)*. (Alternatively, you can use a stand mixer fitted with a paddle attachment to work the mixture, beating it on low speed for 5 minutes or until elastic.)

3 Divide the mixture into 16 equal portions. Use your hands to shape each portion into a torpedo, about 7 cm (2¾ inches) long *(pic 3)*. Heat the remaining oil in a large frying pan and cook the kofte, in batches if necessary, turning often, for 12–15 minutes or until deep golden and cooked through.

4 Serve the kofte with the roasted vegetables, the yoghurt, lemon wedges, Turkish bread and lettuce.

1

2

3

TIP You can also cook the kofte on a barbecue or chargrill pan. Brush with oil and cook over high heat, turning often, for 6–8 minutes, until cooked through.

Veal parmigiana

Although 'parmigiana' means 'from Parma', a town in the north of Italy, parmigiana actually comes from the south of the country. The name is associated with a dish built on layers of cheese (usually mozzarella, though parmesan also works well), tomato sauce and either veal, eggplant or chicken.

SERVES 4   **PREPARATION TIME** 45 minutes   **COOKING TIME** 30–35 minutes

Tomato sauce (see page 66)
4 large veal escalopes (about 600 g/
   1 lb 5 oz in total)
2 eggs
1 tablespoon milk
150 g (5½ oz/2½ cups, lightly packed)
   fresh breadcrumbs (see tip)
1½ teaspoons finely grated lemon zest
50 g (1¾ oz/⅓ cup) plain
   (all-purpose) flour
60 ml (2 fl oz/¼ cup) olive oil
6 slices prosciutto, roughly torn
   lengthways
200 g (7 oz) buffalo mozzarella,
   cut into 5 mm (¼ inch) thick slices
Small handful of basil leaves
Rocket (arugula) salad, to serve

1 Preheat the oven to 180°C (350°F/ Gas 4). Make the tomato sauce. Cut each piece of veal in half widthways, then use a meat mallet to pound each piece until about 3 mm (⅛ inch) thick *(pic 1)*. Take care not to tear the meat.

2 Use a fork to whisk the eggs and milk in a bowl until well combined. Put the breadcrumbs and lemon zest in a separate bowl and toss to combine.

Put the flour in a third bowl, season well with sea salt and freshly ground black pepper and stir to combine. Working with one piece of veal at a time, dust lightly with the seasoned flour, shaking off the excess. Dip in the egg mixture, allow the excess to drain off and then toss in the crumb mixture to coat, pressing the crumbs onto the meat to ensure it is evenly coated *(pic 2)*.

3 Heat the oil in a large frying pan over medium heat and cook the veal, in batches if necessary, for 1–2 minutes each side or until light golden. Spread the tomato sauce over the base of a large roasting pan, then arrange the veal on top in a single layer. Divide the prosciutto among the veal, curling the slices slightly so they fit neatly on top of each escalope, and top each with 1–2 slices of mozzarella *(pic 3)*.

4 Bake for 10–15 minutes or until the cheese has melted and the veal is cooked through. Scatter with basil leaves and serve immediately with rocket salad.

1

2

3

TIP You can use dried breadcrumbs, such as panko (Japanese) breadcrumbs, instead of fresh breadcrumbs, if preferred.

Pork san choy bau

SERVES 8   **PREPARATION TIME** 15 minutes (+ 30 minutes soaking)   **COOKING TIME** 6 minutes

8 iceberg lettuce leaves
60 ml (2 fl oz/¼ cup) peanut oil
1 tablespoon julienned ginger
2 garlic cloves, finely chopped
½ long red chilli, sliced
350 g (12 oz) minced (ground) pork
   (see tip)
¼ red onion, diced
100 g (3½ oz) shiitake mushrooms,
   stems trimmed, diced
1 celery stalk, finely diced
30 g (1 oz) Chinese sausage
   (lap cheong), diced
60 ml (2 fl oz/¼ cup) Chinese rice wine
2 tablespoons oyster sauce
2 tablespoons light soy sauce
2 teaspoons sugar
½ teaspoon sesame oil
1 spring onion (scallion), thinly sliced
40 g (1½ oz) bean sprouts, trimmed
⅓ cup coriander (cilantro) leaves

1 Trim the edges of the lettuce leaves with scissors if they are large (*pic 1*), then soak in a large bowl of cold water for 30 minutes.

2 Heat the oil in a wok over high heat and stir-fry the ginger, garlic, chilli and pork for 1 minute. Add the onion, mushrooms, celery and sausage (*pic 2*) and stir-fry for a further 1 minute.

3 Add the rice wine, oyster sauce, soy sauce, sugar and sesame oil and stir-fry for 2 minutes more or until the pork is just cooked. Add the spring onion, bean sprouts and coriander (*pic 3*) and toss to combine. Remove from the heat. Serve spooned into the lettuce leaves.

1

2

3

TIP Ask your butcher for mince that isn't too lean, as a little bit of fat helps keep the pork tender.

Home-made pork sausages with onion gravy

SERVES 4–6   **PREPARATION TIME** 1½ hours (+ 2½ hours chilling)   **COOKING TIME** 30 minutes

25 g (1 oz) natural sausage casing
(see tip)
500 g (1 lb 2 oz) pork shoulder
375 g (13 oz) pork back fat
250 g (9 oz) skinless chicken thigh
fillets, fat trimmed
100 ml (3½ fl oz) Madeira
2 garlic cloves, chopped
2 teaspoons roughly chopped thyme
1 tablespoon salt
¼ teaspoon Chinese five-spice
1 teaspoon finely ground black pepper
¼ teaspoon ground cumin
⅛ teaspoon cayenne pepper
½ cup roughly chopped parsley
1 tablespoon vegetable oil
Mashed potato (see page 69), to serve
Green peas, to serve

ONION GRAVY
60 ml (2 fl oz/¼ cup) olive oil
600 g (1 lb 5 oz) onions, sliced
1 tablespoon plain (all-purpose) flour
100 ml (3½ fl oz) Madeira
500 ml (17 fl oz/2 cups) ready-made or
home-made beef stock (see page 60)

1 Put the sausage casing in a large bowl in the sink. Fill the bowl with water and hold one end of the casing under the tap. Turn on the tap and allow the water to flow gently through the casing *(pic 1)*.

2 Chop the pork shoulder and back fat and chicken into 2 cm (¾ inch) pieces. Place in a large bowl, add the remaining ingredients (except the oil) and use gloved hands to mix until combined.

3 Set up a mincer/sausage maker with a 6 mm (¼ inch) hole attachment and coarsely mince (grind) the pork mixture. (Use a low speed if electric.)

4 Use your hands to mix the mince again, then attach the sausage filler (with a 2 cm/¾ inch nozzle) to the machine. Push the sausage casing over the nozzle, leaving about 15 cm (6 inches) at the end. Do not tie the end. Feed the pork mixture into the machine, start the machine on low speed and gradually begin to fill the casing *(pic 2)*. Increase the speed to medium–low and continue feeding the pork mixture into the machine.

5 Gently remove the remaining sausage casing from the nozzle. Lay the sausage on the bench and gently squeeze to ensure an even thickness. Gently twist the casing at 10 cm (4 inch) intervals to form 10 even sausages *(pic 3)*. Place in the refrigerator for at least 2½ hours.

6 To make the onion gravy, heat the oil in a saucepan over medium heat and cook the onions, stirring often, for 15–20 minutes, until golden brown. Add the flour and cook, stirring, for 1 minute. Add the Madeira and stir with a wooden spoon, scraping any caramelisation from the base of the pan, until almost evaporated. Add the stock and simmer rapidly for 5–6 minutes, until reduced and thickened.

7 Meanwhile, prick the opposite sides of each sausage 4 times. Heat 2 non-stick frying pans over medium–low heat. Add half the oil to each pan and cook the sausages, turning occasionally, for 12 minutes, until well browned all over. Transfer to a baking tray and bake for 5 minutes or until just cooked through. Serve with the onion gravy, mashed potato and green peas.

2

1

3

> **TIP** Natural sausage casings are made from animal intestines (usually pig or sheep) and are available from most butchers.

Roasting and Baking

Roast chicken with lemon and thyme stuffing

SERVES 4 **PREPARATION TIME** 30 minutes **COOKING TIME** 1 hour 15 minutes

1.5 kg (3 lb 5 oz) whole chicken
60 ml (2 fl oz/¼ cup) extra virgin
   olive oil
1 large brown onion, finely chopped
2 garlic cloves, crushed
160 g (5¾ oz/2 cups, firmly packed)
   coarse breadcrumbs, made from
   fresh crusty bread
2 tablespoons chopped flat-leaf
   (Italian) parsley
Finely grated zest of 1 lemon
3 teaspoons thyme leaves
Steamed vegetables, such as
   asparagus, snow peas (mangetout)
   and sugar snap peas, to serve

GRAVY
1½ tablespoons plain (all-purpose)
   flour
500 ml (17 fl oz/2 cups) good-quality
   ready-made or home-made chicken
   stock (see page 30)

1 Preheat the oven to 200°C (400°F/ Gas 6). Wash the chicken under cold running water, remove the neck and giblets and trim any pockets of fat, then pat dry with paper towels and set aside.

2 Heat 2 tablespoons of the oil in a large frying pan over medium heat. Add the onion and cook, stirring often, for 5–6 minutes or until softened. Add the garlic and cook for 1 minute or until aromatic. Transfer to a bowl. Add the breadcrumbs, parsley, lemon zest, thyme, salt and pepper and mix until well combined. Spoon into the chicken cavity, stuffing it firmly *(pic 1)*.

3 Pull the skin on either side of the cavity together, then secure by threading a small, thin metal skewer through the skin several times *(pic 2)*. Alternatively,

use a trussing needle and kitchen string to sew the skin closed. Rub the chicken all over with the remaining olive oil, then season well with sea salt and freshly ground black pepper. Truss the legs with kitchen string (see page 21).

4 Put the chicken in a small flameproof roasting pan and roast for 15 minutes. Reduce the heat to 180°C (350°F/Gas 4) and roast for another 45 minutes or until the juices run clear when the chicken is pierced through the thickest part (between the thigh and body) *(pic 3)*. Transfer to a warmed plate, cover loosely with foil and set aside.

5 To make the gravy, remove the excess fat from the roasting pan. Place the pan on the stovetop over medium heat. Add the flour and cook, stirring with a wooden spoon, for 3–4 minutes or until smooth and slightly browned. Gradually add the stock, whisking constantly and returning the mixture to a simmer between additions to prevent lumps forming. Simmer, whisking often, for 2–3 minutes or until thickened and smooth. Season with salt and pepper, then strain into a warmed jug.

6 Transfer the chicken to a chopping board and use a large sharp knife to carve (see page 26). Serve immediately with the stuffing, gravy and vegetables.

STUFFING VARIATION
Walnut and currant stuffing: Omit the lemon and thyme. Add 75 g (2¾ oz/ ½ cup) currants and 60 g (2¼ oz/½ cup) chopped toasted walnuts to the onion with the breadcrumbs.

1

2

3

TIP You can replace half the stock in the gravy with 250 ml (9 fl oz/1 cup) dry white wine.

Middle Eastern roasted chicken

This is a really easy dish to prepare, using aromatic spices common in Middle Eastern cooking. Dry-roasting the spices is an essential step as it helps to bring out their full flavour.

SERVES 4   **PREPARATION TIME** 20 minutes   **COOKING TIME** 45 minutes

2 teaspoons cumin seeds
1 teaspoon coriander seeds
1 teaspoon caraway seeds
2 teaspoons fennel seeds
1 teaspoon cayenne pepper
½ teaspoon ground ginger
½ teaspoon ground cassia
2 teaspoons sea salt
½ preserved lemon
4 garlic cloves
60 ml (2 fl oz/¼ cup) olive oil
Pinch of saffron threads
1.6 kg (3 lb 8 oz) whole chicken,
    cut into 8 pieces (see page 18)
½ cup coriander (cilantro) leaves
½ cup mint leaves
Extra virgin olive oil, to serve

1 Preheat the oven to 200°C (400°F/ Gas 6). Place the cumin, coriander, caraway and fennel seeds in a small frying pan over low heat and cook until aromatic. Transfer the spices to a mortar and pestle, add the cayenne, ginger, cassia and salt, and pound to a fine powder. Set aside.

2 Remove the pips, flesh and pith from the lemon. Discard the pips and pith. Slice the rind into thin strips and reserve for a garnish *(pic 1)*. Add the lemon flesh and garlic to the spice powder in the mortar and pestle, and pound to a smooth paste, adding the olive oil gradually and then the saffron.

3 Place the chicken pieces in a large glass or ceramic bowl, add the spice paste and rub it into the chicken using your hands *(pic 2)*.

4 Line a roasting pan with non-stick baking paper. Put the chicken, skin side up, on the lined tray *(pic 3)*. Roast for 20 minutes, basting occasionally with pan juices to develop a good colour and crust. Bake for a further 20 minutes or until cooked through and golden.

5 Transfer the chicken to a platter. Toss the coriander, mint and reserved strips of preserved lemon together. Sprinkle over the chicken and drizzle with a little extra virgin olive oil.

1

2

3

Asian-style chicken drumettes

These drumettes are loaded with flavour and make wonderful finger food. Preparing the drumettes does take a little time, but they look very elegant and are easy to eat as a result.

MAKES 20   **PREPARATION TIME** 10 minutes (+ preparing the drumettes)   **COOKING TIME** 25 minutes

5 coriander (cilantro) stems,
    with roots intact
80 ml (2½ fl oz/⅓ cup) soy sauce
2½ tablespoons honey
2 tablespoons Chinese rice wine
5 teaspoons light brown sugar
2½ teaspoons fish sauce
1 teaspoon sesame oil
¾ teaspoon Chinese five-spice
2 garlic cloves, chopped
1 tablespoon finely chopped ginger
1 small red chilli, finely chopped
20 chicken drumettes (see page 24)

1 Preheat the oven to 200°C (400°F/ Gas 6).

2 Wash the coriander and pick the leaves to use as a garnish. Clean any dirt from the coriander root with the tip of a sharp knife *(pic 1)*, then finely chop the roots and stems.

3 Put the chopped coriander in a shallow 20 x 30 cm (8 x 12 inch) ovenproof dish (3 litre/105 fl oz/ 12 cup capacity) with the soy sauce, honey, rice wine, sugar, fish sauce, sesame oil, five-spice, garlic, ginger and chilli. Stir to combine. Add the drumettes one at a time, coating in the marinade but being careful not to get too much marinade on the bones as they can burn. Lean the bones around the sides of the dish so they're out of the marinade *(pic 2)*.

4 Roast for 10 minutes, then baste the drumettes with the marinade in the dish *(pic 3)*. Cook for a further 10 minutes and baste again. Cook for 5 minutes more or until golden and cooked through. Remove from the oven and set aside for 5 minutes to cool slightly. Coat the drumettes, one at a time, in the marinade and place them on a serving platter. Garnish with the reserved coriander leaves and serve.

1

2

3

TIP You could wrap the bones in small pieces of foil to prevent them browning too much. Remove the foil before serving.

Roasted spatchcocks with flavoured butter

SERVES 4 **PREPARATION TIME** 30 minutes **COOKING TIME** 30 minutes

4 x 500 g (1 lb 2 oz) spatchcocks,
  spatchcocked (see page 22)
1 quantity flavoured butter of your
  choice (see right)
2 tablespoons olive oil
Coriander (cilantro) sprigs, to garnish
Green salad and roast potatoes,
  to serve

1 Preheat the oven to 200°C (400°F/
Gas 6).

2 Working with one spatchcock at a
time, lay the bird on a chopping board,
skin side up and with the neck end
facing you. Push your fingers under the
skin, taking care not to tear it, to create
a cavity between the skin and the flesh,
pushing as far down into the legs as
you can *(pic 1)*.

3 Divide the butter into 4 portions. Use
your fingers to push a portion of butter
under the skin of each bird and spread
it as evenly as you can, pushing it down
into the legs and over the breasts *(pic 2)*.
Take 8 long metal skewers and push one
through the wing, breast and out the
other wing of each bird to retain a neat
shape. Push another skewer through the
lower legs of each bird *(pic 3)*.

4 Brush the skin of the spatchcocks
with oil and season with sea salt and
freshly ground black pepper. Place on
2 baking trays, skin side up, and roast
for 15 minutes. Swap the trays to ensure
even cooking and cook for a further
15 minutes or until the spatchcocks are
golden and cooked through.

5 Garnish the spatchcocks with the
coriander sprigs and serve with a green
salad and roast potatoes.

LIME, CARDAMOM AND HONEY BUTTER

125 g (4½ oz) unsalted butter, softened
1 tablespoon honey
½ teaspoon cardamom seeds, finely
  crushed in a mortar and pestle
2 teaspoons finely grated lime zest
2½ tablespoons lime juice

1 Process all the ingredients in a small
food processor until smooth. Season
with sea salt and ground black pepper.

SAFFRON AND SPICE BUTTER

Large pinch of saffron threads
125 g (4½ oz) butter, softened
1 teaspoon sweet paprika
1 teaspoon ground cumin
½ teaspoon ground cinnamon
½ teaspoon chilli flakes
1 teaspoon finely grated lemon zest
1½ tablespoons lemon juice

1 Combine the saffron with 1 teaspoon
hot water and infuse for 5 minutes.

2 Put the saffron mixture and the
remaining ingredients in a small food
processor. Season with salt and pepper,
and process until combined and smooth.

PANCETTA AND ROSEMARY BUTTER

80 g (2¾ oz) butter, softened
100 g (3½ oz) pancetta,
  very finely chopped
2 garlic cloves, crushed
Large pinch of ground cloves
2 teaspoons chopped rosemary

1 Place all the ingredients in a small
bowl and mash well with a fork to
combine. Season with sea salt and
freshly ground black pepper.

1

2

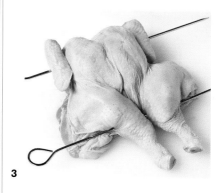

3

> **TIP** The flavoured butters can all
> be made up to 4 days in advance.
> Wrap in plastic wrap or place
> in a snap-lock plastic bag and
> store in the refrigerator. They will
> also keep, stored this way, in the
> freezer for up to 1 month (thaw in
> the refrigerator overnight). Bring
> the butters to room temperature
> before using.

Roast turkey with traditional stuffing and cranberry sauce

Roast turkey is popular festive or party fare as it's such a suitable dish for feeding a crowd. Ask your butcher for a free-range turkey and choose a smaller rather than a larger bird, which can dry out over long cooking. The breadcrumb stuffing can also be used to stuff a chicken (use half the quantity).

SERVES 10–12　　**PREPARATION TIME** 40 minutes (+ 30 minutes cooling and 15 minutes resting)　　**COOKING TIME** 3 hours 20 minutes

5 kg (11 lb 4 oz) whole turkey
8 large thyme sprigs
40 g (1½ oz) butter, melted
750 ml (26 fl oz/3 cups) white chicken
　stock (see page 30)

TRADITIONAL BREADCRUMB STUFFING
50 g (1¾ oz) butter, chopped
2 onions, chopped
2 celery stalks, trimmed, chopped
300 g (10½ oz) bacon, chopped
⅓ cup chopped sage
½ cup chopped flat-leaf (Italian) parsley
1 tablespoon chopped thyme
480 g (1 lb 1 oz/8 cups) breadcrumbs
　made from day-old bread
Finely grated zest of 2 lemons

CRANBERRY SAUCE
100 g (3½ oz) dried sweetened
　cranberries
1 orange, zest finely grated, juiced
100 g (3½ oz) redcurrant jelly
125 ml (4 fl oz/½ cup) port

1 To make the traditional breadcrumb stuffing, heat the butter in a large frying pan over low heat. Add the onions, celery and bacon and cook, stirring occasionally, for 10 minutes or until the onion is soft. Transfer to a large bowl, add the remaining ingredients (*pic 1*) and mix to combine. Season well with salt and pepper. Set aside to cool completely.

2 Preheat the oven to 200°C (400°F/Gas 6). Wash the turkey under cold running water, remove the neck and giblets and trim any pockets of fat, then pat dry with paper towels. Remove the wishbone (see page 20). Spoon a quarter of the stuffing into the neck cavity, cover with the skin and tuck the skin under the wings. Spoon the remaining stuffing into the body cavity, then truss the turkey (see page 21).

3 Place the thyme sprigs in a large roasting pan and put the turkey on top. Brush all over with melted butter and cover the legs loosely with greased foil. Pour the stock around the turkey (*pic 2*) and roast for 1 hour. Reduce the heat to 180°C (350°F/Gas 4). Baste the turkey, remove the foil and roast for a further 2 hours, basting every 30 minutes and covering loosely with greased foil if it is browning too much, or until the juices run clear when pierced through the thickest part. Remove from the pan, cover loosely with foil and set aside in a warm place for 15 minutes to rest.

4 Meanwhile, to make the cranberry sauce, place the cranberries in a bowl, cover with hot water and set aside for 30 minutes. Drain the cranberries, put in a saucepan with the remaining ingredients (*pic 3*) and simmer over low heat for 10 minutes. Set aside to cool.

5 While the turkey is resting, use a metal spoon to remove the excess fat from the pan juices. Season, if necessary.

6 Carve the turkey (see page 26) and serve with the stuffing, pan juices and cranberry sauce.

1

2

3

Chicken baked with pears, pancetta, rosemary and fennel

This simple bake combines some of the best flavours of the Mediterranean and can be dressed up or down as you choose. You can use ready-prepared chicken pieces, however the overall flavour of the dish will benefit if you joint a whole chicken yourself.

SERVES 4   **PREPARATION TIME** 20 minutes (+ 4 hours marinating)   **COOKING TIME** 1 hour 5 minutes

2 teaspoons fennel seeds
3 garlic cloves, crushed
2 rosemary sprigs, leaves removed
   and coarsely chopped
90 g (3¼ oz/¼ cup) honey
60 ml (2 fl oz/¼ cup) white wine
60 ml (2 fl oz/¼ cup) extra virgin
   olive oil
1 teaspoon freshly ground black
   peppercorns
1.5 kg (3 lb 5 oz) whole chicken, cut into
   8 pieces (see page 18)
3 beurre bosc pears (about 550 g/
   1 lb 4 oz), cut into quarters
   lengthways and cored
2 medium fennel bulbs (about 600 g/
   1 lb 5 oz), trimmed and
   quartered lengthways
150 g (5½ oz) thinly sliced pancetta
90 g (3¼ oz/¼ cup) green olives
Boiled or mashed potatoes, to serve

1 Lightly crush the fennel seeds using a mortar and pestle. Put in a large bowl with the garlic, rosemary, honey, wine, oil and pepper and whisk until well combined. Add the chicken and turn to coat *(pic 1)*. Cover with plastic wrap and refrigerate for 4 hours or overnight, turning occasionally if possible.

2 Preheat the oven to 180°C (350°F/ Gas 4). Remove the chicken from the marinade (reserve the marinade) and set aside. Spread the pears and fennel over the base of a large roasting pan and drizzle with 125 ml (4 fl oz/½ cup) of the reserved marinade, tossing to coat *(pic 2)*. Roast for 15 minutes, then remove the pan from the oven.

3 Add the chicken pieces to the pan, skin side up. Lay the pancetta slices over the chicken, taking care as the pan will be hot. You may need to tear the slices to patch any gaps so that the chicken pieces are covered *(pic 3)*. Drizzle the remaining marinade over the chicken, then season well with sea salt.

4 Roast for 45 minutes. Scatter the olives over the top and roast for a further 5 minutes or until the pears and fennel are tender, the chicken is cooked through and the olives are warm.

5 Divide the chicken, pears, olives and fennel among warmed plates and spoon the pan juices over. Serve with boiled or mashed potatoes.

1

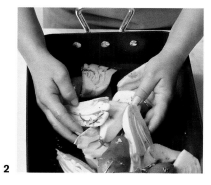

2

3

Roast paprika chicken with currant and almond couscous

Put a new spin on your weekend roast with this recipe. Putting the flavoured butter under the skin of the chicken ensures that the breast meat stays juicy. This method is quite addictive once you taste the results, and it's easy to play around with different ingredients for the butter.

SERVES 4 **PREPARATION TIME** 20 minutes **COOKING TIME** 1½ hours

3 lemons
60 g (2¼ oz) unsalted butter, softened
1 garlic clove, crushed
1 teaspoon paprika
1 teaspoon smoked paprika
1.6 kg (3 lb 8 oz) whole chicken
250 ml (9 fl oz/1 cup) good-quality ready-made or home-made chicken stock (see page 30)
40 g (1½ oz/¼ cup) currants
280 g (10 oz/1½ cups) couscous
30 g (1 oz) butter, chopped
1 small red onion, finely chopped
80 g (2¾ oz/½ cup) raw almonds, toasted and roughly chopped
45 g (1½ oz/¼ cup) dried apricots, finely chopped
½ cup flat-leaf (Italian) parsley leaves, finely chopped

1 Preheat the oven to 180°C (350°F/ Gas 4). Lightly oil a roasting pan. Finely grate the zest from 1 lemon. Halve the lemon, squeeze 1 tablespoon of juice and set aside. Cut the lemon into quarters and set aside. Combine 1 teaspoon of the zest with the butter, garlic, paprika and smoked paprika in a small bowl. Mix well with a fork and season with freshly ground black pepper. Reserve the remaining zest.

2 Wash the chicken under cold running water, remove the necks and giblets and pat dry with paper towels. Slide a finger under the skin of each breast *(pic 1)* to make a pocket (taking care not to break the skin) and loosen the skin on the thickest part of the thigh flesh. Spoon the butter mixture into the cavities between the skin and the flesh *(pic 2)*. Season the chicken with sea salt. Place the lemon quarters in the chicken cavity and tie the legs together *(pic 3)*. Place the chicken in the oiled pan and roast for 1½ hours or until the skin is crisp and the chicken is cooked through.

3 Meanwhile, combine the stock and 125 ml (4 fl oz/½ cup) water in a small saucepan and bring just to the boil.

4 Put the currants, couscous and butter in a large bowl. Pour over the hot liquid, stir to combine and cover with plastic wrap. Set aside for 5 minutes or until the liquid is absorbed. Fluff with a fork.

5 Combine the onion and reserved lemon juice in a small bowl and set aside for 10 minutes. Add to the couscous mixture with the remaining lemon zest and the onion mixture, almonds, apricots and parsley. Season with sea salt and freshly ground black pepper.

6 Halve the remaining 2 lemons and cook, cut side down, in a medium non-stick frying pan or chargrill pan over high heat until browned and caramelised. Cut the chicken into pieces and serve with the couscous and caramelised lemon.

1

2

3

Greek-style chicken pie with tahini sauce

This pie goes a long way and can be served as an entrée or a main course with salad. It is based on a traditional Greek-style pie, but with a new look and tangy sauce to give it a lift.

SERVES 4 as a main or 8 as an entrée   **PREPARATION TIME** 30 minutes (+ 30 minutes marinating)   **COOKING TIME** 1 hour

500 g (1 lb 2 oz/3 cups) chopped
   cooked chicken meat
2 teaspoons dried oregano
125 ml (4 fl oz/½ cup) extra virgin
   olive oil, approximately
2 brown onions, chopped
135 g (4¾ oz/⅔ cup) basmati rice
40 g (1½ oz/¼ cup) currants, soaked in
   hot water for 10 minutes, drained
40 g (1½ oz/¼ cup) pine nuts, toasted
1 bunch silverbeet (Swiss chard), stems
   trimmed, leaves washed and chopped
150 g (5½ oz) fresh firm ricotta, drained
8 sheets filo pastry

TAHINI SAUCE

65 g (2¼ oz/¼ cup) tahini
2 tablespoons water
70 g (2½ oz/¼ cup) plain yoghurt
2 tablespoons lemon juice
½ teaspoon sumac
½ teaspoon ground cumin
2 garlic cloves, chopped
2 tablespoons olive oil

1 To make the tahini sauce, process all the ingredients in a small food processor until smooth. Season with salt and pepper, to taste. Cover and refrigerate.

2 Toss the chicken with the oregano and season with salt and pepper, to taste. Cover and refrigerate for 30 minutes.

3 Meanwhile, heat 2 tablespoons of the oil in a saucepan over low heat and cook the onions, covered, stirring occasionally, for 10 minutes or until soft. Cook the rice in a saucepan of simmering salted water for 10 minutes, then drain and rinse under cold water. Combine the onion, rice, currants and pine nuts and season to taste.

4 Cook the silverbeet (still wet from being washed) in a wok over medium heat, stirring occasionally until wilted. Drain, rinse under cold water and then use your hands to squeeze out excess moisture *(pic 1)*. Combine the silverbeet and ricotta in a bowl and season to taste.

5 Use a pastry brush to brush a 5 cm (2 inch) deep, round 20 cm (8 inch) diameter straight-sided tin with a little of the remaining oil. Keeping the filo pastry under a clean tea towel (dish towel) to prevent it drying out, layer 6 filo sheets around the dish, brushing oil between each and overlapping the sheets to fit the dish and allowing about 10 cm (4 inches) of pastry to overhang the edge *(pic 2)*.

6 Preheat the oven to 180°C (350°F/ Gas 4). Spoon half the rice mixture over the pastry. Top with the silverbeet and ricotta mixture, the chicken mixture *(pic 3)* and the remaining rice mixture. Fold the overhanging pastry over the top of the pie and brush with oil. Fold the remaining 2 sheets of pastry together, brush with oil and scrunch over the pie to create some height, then brush with the remaining oil.

7 Place the pie on a baking tray and bake for 40 minutes, until the pastry is golden and the pie is heated through. Remove from the oven and set aside for 10 minutes before serving. Use a serrated knife to cut wedges of pie and serve with the tahini sauce.

TIP You can use 125 g (4½ oz) of melted butter to brush between the layers of pastry instead of oil for a richer pie.

Chermoula-roasted quails

The Middle Eastern chermoula and the fluffy couscous merge perfectly with the delicate flavour of the quails to produce this more-ish, vibrant dish. Trussing the quails keeps the thighs and drumsticks tight and next to the thin end of the breast, which will prevent overcooking and keep the meat moist.

SERVES 6 as an entrée   **PREPARATION TIME** 35 minutes   **COOKING TIME** 20 minutes

95 g (3¼ oz/½ cup) couscous
80 ml (2½ fl oz/⅓ cup) good-quality
   ready-made or home-made chicken
   stock (see page 30)
1 tablespoon olive oil
1 tablespoon chopped flat-leaf
   (Italian) parsley
1 fresh date, seeded and chopped
2 teaspoons finely chopped dried
   apricots
1 tablespoon chopped toasted almonds
½ teaspoon salt
⅛ teaspoon orange flower water or
   1 teaspoon finely grated orange zest
6 x 200 g (7 oz) quails
Mint leaves, to garnish

CHERMOULA

⅓ cup chopped flat-leaf (Italian) parsley
⅓ cup chopped coriander (cilantro)
   leaves
2 garlic cloves, finely chopped
80 ml (2½ fl oz/⅓ cup) olive oil
3 teaspoons ground cumin
1½ teaspoons sweet paprika
¼ teaspoon ground cinnamon
1 long red chilli, seeded and
   finely chopped
1 teaspoon caster (superfine) sugar
1 lemon, zest finely grated, juiced

1 Preheat the oven to 200°C (400°F/ Gas 6). Place the couscous in a small heatproof bowl. Heat the stock in a small saucepan until boiling, then pour over the couscous, add the oil and stir to combine. Cover with plastic wrap and set aside for 3 minutes or until the stock has been absorbed. Use a fork to stir the couscous to separate the grains *(pic 1)* and then stir through the parsley, date, dried apricots, almonds, salt and orange flower water. Set aside to cool to room temperature.

2 To make the chermoula, combine all the ingredients in a small bowl and then season with sea salt.

3 Wash each quail under cold running water, remove the giblets and pat dry with paper towels. Loosen the skin from around the neck, then remove the neck using poultry shears or a sharp knife, leaving the skin intact. Fold the wing tips under the quails. Season the cavity of each quail with salt and pepper. Carefully ease about 3 tablespoons of stuffing into each bird *(pic 2)*, pushing it into the cavity with a teaspoon or the end of a wooden spoon. Truss the quails (see page 21).

4 Place the quails on a baking tray lined with non-stick baking paper and spoon over the chermoula *(pic 3)*, then rub it into the quails. Roast for 20 minutes or until the juices run clear when the quail is pierced through the thickest part. Remove from the oven and set aside for 5 minutes to rest. Cut each quail in half and serve garnished with the mint leaves.

1

2

3

Roasted spatchcock with cauliflower and white bean mash and roasted grapes

This dish ticks all the boxes for perfect dinner party fare — fast, simple, delicious and impressive. The key to its success is the contrasting textures: the mash, which is not quite a purée, and roasted grapes, which are soft and juicy but still with a slight resistance.

SERVES 4   **PREPARATION TIME** 40 minutes (+ 10 minutes resting)   **COOKING TIME** 40 minutes

4 x 500 g (1 lb 2 oz) spatchcocks
4 sprigs each thyme, rosemary and
    tarragon, all crushed
80 ml (2½ fl oz/⅓ cup) lemon juice
60 ml (2 fl oz/¼ cup) extra virgin
    olive oil
20 g (¾ oz) butter, chopped
500 g (1 lb 2 oz) seedless red grapes
600 g (1 lb 5 oz) green beans,
    trimmed and blanched
50 g (1¾ oz/½ cup) flaked almonds,
    toasted

CAULIFLOWER AND WHITE BEAN MASH
400 g (14 oz) cauliflower florets
400 g (14 oz) tin cannellini beans,
    drained and rinsed
1 garlic clove, chopped
1 tablespoon lemon juice
60 ml (2 fl oz/¼ cup) extra virgin
    olive oil

1 Preheat the oven to 200°C (400°F/ Gas 6).

2 Wash the spatchcocks under cold running water, remove the necks and giblets and pat dry with paper towels. Place a sprig of thyme, rosemary and tarragon in the cavity of each bird. Truss each spatchcock (see page 21).

3 Place the spatchcocks in a large flameproof roasting pan, drizzle with lemon juice and 2 tablespoons of the oil, dot with butter and season well *(pic 1)*. Add enough water to the pan to come 2 cm (¾ inch) up the side.

4 Roast the spatchcocks, basting with the pan juices halfway through cooking, for 40 minutes, until browned and cooked through and the juices run clear when the spatchcocks are pierced at the thickest part. Remove from the oven, transfer to an oven tray, cover loosely with foil and set aside for 10 minutes to rest. Place the roasting pan on the stovetop over medium heat, season the juices and cook over medium heat until reduced to about 150 ml (5 fl oz).

5 Meanwhile, toss the grapes with the remaining tablespoon of oil, place on an oven tray and cook with the spatchcocks for the last 20 minutes *(pic 2)*.

6 To make the cauliflower and white bean mash, cook the cauliflower in a medium saucepan of simmering salted water for about 10 minutes, until very tender. Drain and rinse under cold running water. Put the cauliflower, cannellini beans, garlic, lemon juice and oil in a food processor and season with salt and pepper *(pic 3)*. Using the pulse button, pulse until well combined and smooth. Return the mixture to the pan and heat gently over low heat, stirring occasionally, until warmed through.

7 Toss the beans and almonds together. Serve the cauliflower and white bean mash topped with a spatchcock and drizzled with the pan juices. Spoon the grapes and their juices over and serve accompanied by the beans and almonds.

1

2

3

TIP You can substitute roasted duck or chicken breast fillets with skin for the spatchcocks.

Roasted chicken with lemon and oregano

SERVES 4   **PREPARATION TIME** 15 minutes   **COOKING TIME** 45–50 minutes

600 g (1 lb 5 oz) kipfler (fingerling) or
   new potatoes
4 parsnips, halved
6 garlic cloves, unpeeled
1 lemon, washed and cut into wedges
⅓ cup oregano sprigs
80 ml (2½ fl oz/⅓ cup) extra virgin
   olive oil
4 x 250 g (9 oz) chicken breast fillets
   with skin
Steamed green beans, to serve

1 Preheat the oven to 200°C (400°F/
Gas 6).

2 Wash and dry the potatoes and
cut into slices about 1.5 cm (⅝ inch)
thick. Place in a roasting pan with the
parsnips, garlic, lemon and oregano.
Add 2 tablespoons of the oil, season
with sea salt and freshly ground black
pepper and toss to coat *(pic 1)*. Roast
for 25 minutes or until light golden and
half cooked.

3 Meanwhile, after the vegetables have
been cooking for about 15 minutes,
heat a large non-stick frying pan over
medium heat. Brush the chicken breasts
with 1 tablespoon of the remaining
oil and season with sea salt and freshly
ground black pepper. Cook, skin side
down, for 3–4 minutes or until the skin
is a light golden. Turn and cook for a
further 3 minutes *(pic 2)*.

4 Remove the roasting pan from the
oven. Place the chicken, skin side up, on
top of the potatoes and parsnips *(pic 3)*.
Return to the oven and cook for a
further 10–15 minutes or until the
chicken is just cooked through and the
vegetables are tender.

5 Season the green beans, drizzle with
the remaining olive oil and finish with
a squeeze of lemon from the roasted
lemon wedges. Arrange the chicken on a
platter for guests to help themselves and
serve with the green beans.

1

2

3

Honey and star anise glazed duck

SERVES 4   **PREPARATION TIME** 15 minutes   **COOKING TIME** 1 hour 40 minutes

80 ml (2½ fl oz/⅓ cup) Chinese
   rice wine
80 ml (2½ fl oz/⅓ cup) soy sauce
90 g (3¼ oz/¼ cup) honey
2 tablespoons light brown sugar
1 tablespoon finely shredded ginger
1 long red chilli, thinly sliced
2 garlic cloves, thinly sliced
4 star anise
4 duck marylands (about 1.2 kg/
   2 lb 10 oz), excess fat removed
Steamed jasmine rice and baby
   choy sum, to serve

1 Preheat the oven to 160°C (315°F/
Gas 2–3).

2 Combine the rice wine, soy sauce,
honey, sugar, ginger, chilli, garlic and
2 of the star anise in a small saucepan
over medium–high heat and stir until
the sugar dissolves. Bring to the boil,
then reduce the heat and simmer for
10 minutes. Transfer 80 ml (2½ fl oz/
⅓ cup) of the glaze to a bowl and
reserve for serving.

3 Place the marylands, skin side up,
on a wire rack over a large roasting pan.
Brush all over with half the remaining
glaze *(pic 1)*. Pour 125 ml (4 fl oz/½ cup)
hot water into the pan, add the
remaining star anise and cover tightly
with foil. Roast for 1 hour 20 minutes.

4 Increase the oven temperature to
220°C (425°F/Gas 7). Remove the
foil from the duck, brush with the
remaining glaze *(pic 2)* and roast for a
further 5–10 minutes or until the duck
is very tender and the skin is crisp.

5 Meanwhile, put the reserved glaze
in a small saucepan over medium–high
heat. Bring to the boil, then reduce
the heat and simmer for 1–2 minutes
(pic 3) or until thickened slightly. Serve
the duck drizzled with the glaze and
accompanied by the steamed rice and
baby choy sum.

1

2

3

Roasted spiced chicken drumsticks with spinach, orange and mint salad

SERVES 4   **PREPARATION TIME** 15 minutes (+ 2 hours marinating)   **COOKING TIME** 35 minutes

2½ teaspoons paprika
2½ teaspoons ground cumin
1½ teaspoons ground cinnamon
½ teaspoon salt
80 ml (2½ fl oz/⅓ cup) olive oil
60 ml (2 fl oz/¼ cup) lemon juice
1.5 kg (3 lb 5 oz) chicken drumsticks

SPINACH, ORANGE AND MINT SALAD
1 orange
60 ml (2 fl oz/¼ cup) extra virgin
    olive oil
1½ tablespoons white wine vinegar
200 g (7 oz) baby spinach leaves or
    rocket (arugula) leaves
½ cup mint leaves
25 g (1 oz) sliced raw almonds

1 Put the paprika, cumin, cinnamon, salt, oil and lemon juice in a glass or ceramic container and whisk to combine. Pat the chicken drumsticks dry with paper towels. Add to the spice mixture and toss to coat *(pic 1)*. Cover and refrigerate for 2 hours to marinate.

2 Preheat the oven to 200°C (400°F/ Gas 6). Place the chicken, in a single layer, and any remaining marinade in a large roasting pan or ovenproof dish *(pic 2)* (you might need to use two roasting pans, depending on the size). Roast for 35 minutes or until the chicken is golden and cooked through.

3 Meanwhile, prepare the spinach, orange and mint salad. Use a small sharp knife to remove the skin and pith from the orange. Segment the orange *(pic 3)* and then slice each segment into 3 pieces. Combine the oil, vinegar and a pinch of salt.

4 When the chicken is cooked, put the spinach, orange, mint and almonds in a bowl. Drizzle over the dressing, gently toss and serve with the chicken.

1

2

3

Honey-glazed chicken wings

SERVES 4 as a snack **PREPARATION TIME** 15 minutes (+ 2 hours marinating) **COOKING TIME** 35–40 minutes

12 chicken wings (about 1.2 kg/
   2 lb 10 oz)
2 tablespoons soy sauce
2 tablespoons hoisin sauce
60 ml (2 fl oz/¼ cup) tomato sauce
   (ketchup)
90 g (3¼ oz/¼ cup) honey
1 tablespoon cider vinegar
2 garlic cloves, crushed
2 tablespoons sesame seeds
½ teaspoon Chinese five-spice
1 tablespoon sesame oil

1 Tuck the wing tips into the underside of the chicken wings *(pic 1)*. Combine all the remaining ingredients in a large bowl and mix well. Add the wings to the marinade and mix well to coat *(pic 2)*. Refrigerate, covered with plastic wrap, for 2 hours or overnight to marinate, turning the chicken occasionally.

2 Preheat the oven to 180°C (350°F/ Gas 4). Line a roasting pan with non-stick baking paper and place a wire rack inside the pan.

3 Drain the chicken wings, reserving the marinade, and place on the wire rack *(pic 3)*. Cook, turning and brushing occasionally with the reserved marinade, for 35–40 minutes or until well glazed and cooked through. Serve hot or at room temperature.

Roast chicken with fennel and chilli salt

SERVES 4   **PREPARATION TIME** 20 minutes (+ 10 minutes resting)   **COOKING TIME** 1½ hours

1 tablespoon fennel seeds

3 teaspoons sea salt flakes

1½ teaspoons dried chilli flakes

½ teaspoon freshly ground
   black pepper

2 teaspoons finely grated lemon zest

1 garlic clove, chopped

60 ml (2 fl oz/¼ cup) olive oil

1.6 kg (3 lb 8 oz) whole chicken

1 large lemon, washed, coarsely
   chopped

3 baby fennel bulbs (400 g/14 oz),
   quartered, fronds removed
   and reserved

12 baby new potatoes

4 garlic cloves, unpeeled, squashed

1   Preheat the oven to 180°C (350°F/ Gas 4).

2   Heat a small saucepan over medium heat. Add the fennel seeds and cook, stirring, for 1 minute or until aromatic. Put the fennel seeds in a mortar and pestle and pound until lightly crushed. Add the salt, chilli, pepper, lemon zest and garlic and pound well *(pic 1)*. Gradually add 2 tablespoons of the oil to make a thin paste.

3   Wash the chicken under cold running water, remove the neck and giblets and trim any pockets of fat, then pat dry with paper towels. Place the chopped lemon in a large roasting pan and put the chicken on top. Use your fingers to loosen the skin from the chicken breast. Rub half the fennel seed mixture under the skin *(pic 2)*. Rub the remaining mixture all over the chicken. Roast the chicken for 30 minutes.

4   Toss the baby fennel, potatoes and squashed garlic in the remaining oil. Add to the roasting pan *(pic 3)* and roast for a further 1 hour or until the chicken is cooked through, the juices run clear when the chicken is pierced through the thickest part, and the vegetables are tender. Remove the chicken from the oven, cover loosely with foil and rest for 10 minutes before carving (see page 26). Serve with the vegetables and sprinkled with reserved fennel fronds.

1

2

3

Roasting tips

1 Roasting involves cooking meat and poultry in the oven with no liquid other than fat. It is a relatively simple cooking method that is best suited to larger cuts of meat or poultry. Once it is in the oven a roast requires no more than an occasional baste (spooning the pan juices over the meat), although if the roast has a top cap of fat this is not necessary.

2 Roasting is best suited to tender cuts of meat such as lamb leg, beef rib roast, whole sirloin or eye fillet, or pork loin. These cuts come from parts of the animal where the muscles are not hard working, so they have less connective tissue than tougher cuts.

3 Meat and poultry are usually browned all over first to seal in juices and establish a flavoursome, crusty exterior. This can be done in a little fat on the stovetop or, for large cuts, in a very hot oven for 20 minutes or so. Always make sure your oven is properly preheated before putting a roast inside.

4 Use a roasting pan that is appropriate to the size of the meat or poultry you are cooking. Roasting in a pan that is too large will mean all the juices will evaporate and perhaps burn on the base of the pan, leaving nothing for the gravy. The sides of a roasting pan should be about 8 cm (3¼ inches) high. If the sides are too low the juices will splatter all over the oven, and if they are too high the roast will not brown properly.

5 For poultry, pat both the inside cavity and outside skin well with paper towels before cooking — any excess moisture on the bird can prevent the skin from becoming crisp.

6 Never stuff poultry ahead of time or with warm stuffing, as bacteria can develop.

7 Trussing a whole bird (see page 21) or tying a larger cut of meat (see page 56) will help it cook more evenly and retain its shape for serving.

8 Place the roast on a trivet or rack in the roasting pan if possible. This lets air circulate all around it and stops the bottom from stewing in the juices and fat.

9 Duck is often cooked at a lower temperature than other birds, and for longer, to allow the fat under the skin to render.

10 A meat thermometer is the best way to determine when a roast is cooked. Do not pierce the meat with a knife, as precious juices will run out. Simply insert the thermometer into the thickest part of the roast before cooking, then leave it there and check it as the roast cooks. Avoid inserting the thermometer near any bones. Check the internal temperature of a roasting bird/s about three-quarters of the way through the suggested roasting time and then frequently after that, until the correct temperature is reached. The meat thermometer should read 83°C (180°F) for cooked poultry.

11 Bones conduct heat well and quickly transfer heat to the centre of a joint, so meat or poultry that are on the bone cook faster than meat without a bone.

12 Roasts are cooked at around 180–200°C (350–400°F/ Gas 4–6). Slow-roasting requires a lower temperature (anywhere between 120–160°C/235–315°F/Gas ½–2-3) and a longer cooking time than regular roasting, as the name suggests. This cooking method is ideal for coarse-grained meats, such as topside, and older game birds, which would dry out at normal roasting temperatures. Tender cuts of meat, such as legs, shoulders and loins, are usually roasted normally but they can be slow-roasted. The result will be quite different, as the cooked meat will not be pink and juicy, but incredibly soft and falling apart in unctuous shreds.

13 Roasts should always be rested after cooking. Remove from the oven, cover loosely with foil and set aside at room temperature, covered loosely with foil. Meats can be set aside for up to 30 minutes. For poultry, allow 5 minutes for a small bird (such as quail and spatchcock), 10 minutes for a medium bird (such as chicken) and 15 minutes for a large bird (such as turkey). Resting allows the extremely hot juices to redistribute evenly throughout the roast, making the meat consistently juicy throughout. Resting also gives the fibres a chance to relax, making the meat more tender and easier to carve.

14 Pan juices can be used to make a sauce to serve with the roast. Skim off all the excess fat before using and make the sauce or gravy directly in the roasting pan on the stovetop. Other ingredients may be added to the juices, such as stock or wine (for flavour) and flour (to thicken).

15 Small birds (such as quail) can be pan-roasted. Brown them in a frying pan on the stovetop and then transfer to the oven to finish cooking.

MEAT/CUT	APPROX. SIZE	TEMPERATURE	TIME
Beef			
Rib eye/scotch fillet, rump, sirloin, fillet, tenderloin	For every 500 g (1 lb 2 oz)	200°C (400°F/Gas 6)	Rare 15–20 minutes, medium 20–25 minutes, well-done 25–30 minutes
Silverside, blade, round, topside	For every 500 g (1 lb 2 oz)	160°C (315°F/ Gas 2–3)	Rare 20–25 minutes, medium 25–30 minutes, well-done 30–35 minutes
Lamb			
Backstrap, lamb round or topside mini roast, lamb rump	Regardless of weight	200°C (400°F/Gas 6)	Rare 15–20 minutes, medium 20–25 minutes, well-done 25–30 minutes
Rack of lamb, small rib roast	Regardless of weight	200°C (400°F/Gas 6)	Rare 20–25 minutes, medium 30–35 minutes, well-done 40–45 minutes
Veal			
Fillet, rack, leg, loin/eye of loin, rump and shoulder, boned and rolled loin, rump, breast	For every 500 g (1 lb 2 oz)	200°C (400°F/Gas 6)	Rare 15–20 minutes, medium 20–25 minutes, well-done 25–30 minutes

Poultry			
Quail	200 g (7 oz)	200°C (400°F/Gas 6)	20–25 minutes
Spatchcock	500 g (1 lb 2 oz)	200°C (400°F/Gas 6)	40 minutes
Chicken	1.5 kg (3 lb 5 oz)	200°C (400°F/Gas 6) 180°C (350°F/Gas 4)	15 minutes at 200°C + 1 hour at 180°C
Duck	2.3 kg (5 lb 1¾ oz)	180°C (350°F/Gas 4) 150°C (300°F/Gas 2)	1 hour at 180°C + 1 hour at 150°C
Turkey	5 kg (11 lb 4 oz	200°C (400°F/Gas 6) 180°C (350°F/Gas 4)	1 hour at 200°C + 2 hours at 180°C

Standing rib roast with roasted onions, garlic and rosemary

A standing rib roast is an impressive cut of meat that is perfect for a special occasion. If you are going to use a meat thermometer to determine when the meat is ready, insert it into the centre and look for a reading of 35°C (95°F) for rare; 45°C (113°F) for medium-rare and 65°C (149°F) for well done.

SERVES 6 **PREPARATION TIME** 20 minutes **COOKING TIME** 1 hour 40 minutes–2 hours

140 ml (4½ fl oz) olive oil
2.2 kg (4 lb 15 oz) beef rib roast, fat trimmed, at room temperature (see tip)
3 garlic cloves, crushed
2 tablespoons chopped rosemary leaves
6 red onions
375 ml (13 fl oz/1½ cups) good-quality ready-made or home-made beef stock (see page 60)
2½ tablespoons balsamic vinegar
Roasted potatoes and sweet potatoes and steamed green beans, to serve

1 Preheat the oven to 150°C (300°F/ Gas 2). Heat 2 tablespoons of the oil in a large frying pan over medium–high heat and cook the beef, turning once, for 6–7 minutes or until browned all over *(pic 1)*. Transfer to a plate.

2 Put the remaining 100 ml (3½ fl oz) oil, the garlic and rosemary in a small food processor *(pic 2)* and process until the mixture is smooth.

3 Peel the onions, leaving the root end intact, and cut in half lengthways. Place the beef and onions in a large flameproof roasting pan and brush all over with the oil mixture *(pic 3)*. Roast the beef and onions, brushing with the

oil mixture every 20–30 minutes, for 1¼ hours for medium-rare, 1½ hours for medium or until cooked to your liking. Transfer the beef to a plate, cover loosely with foil and set aside in a warm place for at least 20 minutes to rest.

4 While the beef is resting, increase the oven temperature to 180°C (350°F/ Gas 4) and cook the onions for a further 10 minutes or until deep golden. Transfer to a plate and keep warm. Drain the excess fat from the pan juices, then place the pan over medium heat. Add the stock and vinegar and bring to the boil. Cook, stirring occasionally, for 5 minutes or until reduced slightly.

5 Carve the roast between the bones and serve with the onions and the balsamic pan juices poured over, and accompanied by the roasted potatoes and sweet potatoes and green beans.

1

2

3

TIP Ask your butcher to trim and tie the rib roast for you.

Shepherd's pie

Classic comfort fare, shepherd's pie was originally made using leftover roast mutton, extended with a few vegetables and moistened with broth, but these days it is often made using minced (ground) lamb. It is always baked with a layer of mashed potato on top.

SERVES 4–6 **PREPARATION TIME** 20 minutes **COOKING TIME** 1 hour 10 minutes

Mashed potato (see page 69)
2 tablespoons olive oil
2 brown onions, finely chopped
2 carrots, finely chopped
1 tablespoon tomato paste
   (concentrated purée)
60 ml (2 fl oz/¼ cup) good-quality
   ready-made chicken stock,
   approximately
600 g (1 lb 5 oz) cold leftover roast
   lamb, cut into 5 mm (¼ inch) pieces,
   and any leftover gravy or pan juices
2½ teaspoons worcestershire sauce
2½ teaspoons hot English mustard
½ cup coarsely chopped flat-leaf
   (Italian) parsley
Tomato sauce (see page 66) and
   steamed green vegetables or
   green salad, to serve

1 Preheat the oven to 180°C (350°F/ Gas 4). Make the mashed potato.

2 Meanwhile, heat the oil in a large saucepan over medium heat. Add the onions and carrots and cook, stirring, for 8 minutes or until very soft *(pic 1)*. Add the tomato paste and stir for 1 minute, then add the stock and any gravy or juices from the lamb. Stir to combine and bring to a simmer. Stir through the lamb, then add a little extra stock if the mixture is dry (see tip). Stir in the worcestershire sauce, mustard and parsley and season with sea salt and freshly ground black pepper *(pic 2)*.

3 Spoon the meat mixture into a 2 litre (70 fl oz/8 cup) baking dish. Spoon the mashed potato evenly over the top and use a fork to rough up the surface *(pic 3)*. Bake for 40 minutes or until the juices are bubbling and the potato is golden. Serve immediately with tomato sauce and steamed vegetables or salad.

1

2

3

TIP The amount of stock you will need depends on how much gravy or pan juices you have. The mixture should be just moist.
   You could add grated cheddar or gruyère cheese to the mashed potato for a richer flavour.

Individual beef wellingtons

This old-timer is definitely worth revisiting. Good-quality tenderloin steaks will give the best results, so don't skimp. It can be worthwhile buying a whole beef tenderloin and using it for a few recipes, such as this one and the Perfect roast beef (see page 201).

SERVES 4 **PREPARATION TIME** 30 minutes (+ cooling) **COOKING TIME** 35–40 minutes

4 x 120 g (4¼ oz) beef tenderloin steaks
   (see tip), at room temperature
1 tablespoon olive oil, plus extra,
   for drizzling
20 g (¾ oz) butter
100 g (3½ oz) field mushrooms,
   coarsely chopped
100 g (3½ oz) Swiss brown mushrooms,
   coarsely chopped
1 French shallot, finely chopped
1 garlic clove, finely chopped
1 teaspoon thyme leaves
1 tablespoon Madeira
50 g (1¾ oz) home-made or
   good-quality ready-made chicken liver
   pâté (without any jelly) (see page 103)
12 thin slices prosciutto
4 sheets (24 cm/9½ inches)
   ready-made puff pastry
2 egg yolks, lightly whisked with
   1 tablespoon water
Mixed salad leaves, to serve

1 Heat a heavy-based frying pan over high heat. Season the steaks generously with sea salt and freshly ground black pepper. Drizzle with the extra oil and cook for 1–2 minutes each side. Using tongs, pick up each steak and roll the sides over the hot pan until seared *(pic 1)*. Remove from the pan and set aside to cool to room temperature.

2 Heat the oil and butter in the frying pan over medium–high heat. Add the mushrooms and cook, stirring often, for 3–4 minutes or until golden. Add the shallot, garlic and thyme and cook, stirring, for 2 minutes. Add the Madeira and stir for 1 minute, until it evaporates. Remove from the heat and season to taste. Set aside for 10 minutes to cool, then process briefly in a small food processor until finely chopped. Cool completely, then use a spatula to mix through the pâté until incorporated.

3 Preheat the oven to 220°C (425°F/ Gas 7). Lay 4 pieces of plastic wrap on a work surface. Place 3 slices of prosciutto on each, slightly overlapping. Spread the prosciutto with the mushroom mixture, then place a steak in the centre of each. Wrap the prosciutto tightly around each steak, using the plastic wrap to help lift it over *(pic 2)*. Trim each pastry sheet to a 19 cm (7½ inch) square. Brush the edges with the egg wash, then place a prosciutto parcel on each pastry square. Fold the pastry over as tightly as possible, without stretching it, and press to seal.

4 Place the beef wellingtons, seam side down, on a baking tray lined with non-stick baking paper. Brush the pastry with the egg wash. Use the tip of a small sharp knife to score the pastry, starting at the centre of the top and going all the way down (on a slight angle) to where the pastry meets the baking paper *(pic 3)*. Score the top of each beef wellington about 16 times.

5 Bake for 20 minutes or until the pastry is puffed and golden. Serve with mixed salad leaves.

1

2

3

TIP Ask your butcher to cut the tenderloin steaks to about 3.5 cm (1²/₅ inch) thick.

Roasted veal rack wrapped in prosciutto, stuffed with lemon and anchovies

The mild, sweet flavour of veal always works beautifully with salty ingredients such as prosciutto and anchovies. You could use thinly sliced strips of pancetta instead of prosciutto if you prefer.

SERVES 4　**PREPARATION TIME** 20 minutes (+ 5 minutes resting)　**COOKING TIME** 35 minutes

60 ml (2 fl oz/¼ cup) olive oil
1 brown onion, finely chopped
60 g (2¼ oz/1 cup, lightly packed)
　fresh breadcrumbs
2 teaspoons finely grated lemon zest
4 anchovy fillets, finely chopped
2 tablespoons chopped flat-leaf
　(Italian) parsley
4 medium racks of veal with 2 ribs each,
　frenched (see page 55) (see tip)
4 slices prosciutto, halved lengthways
Mashed potato (see page 69) and
　steamed greens, to serve

1 Heat 2 tablespoons of the oil in a large non-stick frying pan over medium heat. Add the onion and cook, stirring occasionally, for 5 minutes or until softened. Add the breadcrumbs, lemon zest and anchovies and cook, stirring, for a further 2–3 minutes or until the breadcrumbs are golden *(pic 1)*. Transfer to a bowl, stir in the parsley and set aside to cool.

2 Preheat the oven to 200°C (400°F/ Gas 6). Use a sharp knife to make a slit in the centre of the meaty section of each veal rack, approximately 2 cm (¾ inch) wide *(pic 2)*. Stuff each rack firmly with the breadcrumb mixture. Wrap 2 slices of prosciutto around the meaty section of each rack *(pic 3)*.

3 Place the veal racks in a large roasting pan and drizzle with the remaining oil. Roast the veal for 25 minutes or until a meat thermometer inserted into the centre of the thickest part reads 70°C (158°F) for medium veal or until cooked to your liking.

4 Transfer the veal racks to a carving board, cover loosely with foil and set aside for 5 minutes to rest. Cut each rack into individual cutlets and serve with mashed potato and steamed greens.

1

2

3

TIP If you are short of time, you can ask your butcher to trim and french the veal racks for you.

Roasted venison with diane sauce and braised red cabbage

Venison is a very lean meat that is best served rare. When roasting, the general rule of thumb is to cook the meat for 25 minutes per kilogram (2 lb 4 oz) for rare, depending on thickness, followed by 10 minutes resting. The thicker the piece of venison, the longer it will take to cook.

SERVES 4   **PREPARATION TIME** 20 minutes (+ 10 minutes resting)   **COOKING TIME** 30 minutes

1 teaspoon freshly ground black pepper
1 kg (2 lb 4 oz) boneless topside venison (4–5 cm/1½–2 inches thick), silverskin removed, at room temperature
1 tablespoon olive oil
20 g (¾ oz) butter
2 French shallots, finely chopped *(pic 1)*
1 tablespoon cognac
1 teaspoon dijon mustard
2 tablespoons worcestershire sauce
125 ml (4 fl oz/½ cup) thin (pouring/ whipping) cream
Boiled new potatoes, to serve

BRAISED RED CABBAGE
2 tablespoons olive oil
1 red onion, thinly sliced
1 green apple, peeled, cored and cut into 1 cm (½ inch) pieces
500 g (1 lb 2 oz) red cabbage, thinly shredded
2 tablespoons red wine vinegar

1 Preheat the oven to 200°C (400°F/ Gas 6). Sprinkle the pepper all over the venison and press it onto the meat. Heat the oil and butter in a large non-stick frying pan over high heat and cook the venison until browned all over *(pic 2)*. Transfer to a roasting pan and roast for 25 minutes for rare. Remove from the oven, cover loosely with foil and set aside in a warm place for 10 minutes to rest.

2 Meanwhile, to make the braised red cabbage, heat the oil in a large heavy-based saucepan over low heat and cook the onion and apple, covered, until the onion is soft. Increase the heat to high, add the cabbage and stir until combined. Stir in the vinegar and 2 tablespoons water, then reduce the heat to low, cover and cook, stirring occasionally, for 15 minutes, until the cabbage is tender. Season to taste.

3 While the cabbage is cooking, make the diane sauce. Heat the frying pan you browned the venison in over low heat, add the shallots and cook, stirring often, until soft. Add the cognac *(pic 3)* and cook, scraping any caramelisation from the base of the pan. Stir in the mustard, worcestershire sauce and cream, increase the heat to medium and bring to the boil. Reduce the heat to low and simmer for 2 minutes. Season with salt and pepper, to taste.

4 Cut the venison into 1 cm (½ inch) thick slices and serve drizzled with the diane sauce and accompanied by the braised red cabbage and boiled potatoes.

1

2

3

TIP Diane sauce is traditionally served with pan-fried beef steak, but it is also lovely with venison.

Slow-roasted lamb with white bean purée

SERVES 8   **PREPARATION TIME** 40 minutes (+ overnight soaking and 20 minutes resting)
COOKING TIME 2 hours 25 minutes

2.2–2.5 kg (4 lb 15 oz–5 lb 8 oz) leg of
   lamb, excess fat trimmed,
   at room temperature
3 slices pancetta
3 garlic cloves, crushed
1 tablespoon finely chopped
   rosemary
3 anchovy fillets, finely chopped
Pinch of ground cloves
2 tablespoons olive oil
250 ml (9 fl oz/1 cup) white wine
375 ml (13 fl oz/1½ cups) good-quality
   ready-made or home-made chicken or
   veal stock (see pages 30 or 60)
Steamed green vegetables, to serve

WHITE BEAN PUREE

400 g (14 oz/2 cups) dried white beans
   (such as cannellini), soaked overnight
4 garlic cloves, unpeeled
1 fresh bay leaf
4 thyme sprigs
1 brown onion, halved
8 whole cloves

1 Preheat the oven to 160°C (315°F/
Gas 2–3). Use a small sharp knife to
make deep slits all over the lamb.

2 Remove the lean parts of the pancetta
and reserve for another use. Finely chop
the fatty pancetta and use the back
of a spoon to mash with the garlic,
rosemary, anchovies and cloves until
combined. Use your fingers to push a
little mixture into each slit in the lamb
(pic 1), creating more slits if needed.

3 Heat the oil in a large flameproof
roasting pan over medium heat. Add the
lamb and sprinkle with pepper. Cook,
turning occasionally, for 7–8 minutes
or until well browned all over *(pic 2)*.
Remove the lamb. Add the wine to the
pan, scraping any caramelisation from

the base, and bring to the boil. Stir in
the stock. Remove from the heat and sit
a trivet or rack in the pan. Put the lamb
on top and sprinkle well with salt.

4 Cook the lamb for 2 hours 15 minutes
or until the juices run a little pink when
a skewer is inserted into the thickest
part of the leg or a meat thermometer
reads 60°C (140°F) for medium-rare.
Add more liquid to the pan if necessary.

5 Transfer the lamb to a warmed platter
and cover loosely with foil. Set aside in a
warm place for 20 minutes to rest. Pour
the liquid from the pan into a bowl and
set aside for 10 minutes, then skim off
the fat. Pour the juices into a saucepan
and bring to a simmer over medium
heat, then reduce the heat to low.

6 Meanwhile, to make the white bean
purée, drain the beans and place in a
large saucepan with the garlic and herbs.
Stud each onion half with cloves and
add to the pan. Cover with water and
bring to a simmer over medium heat,
skimming any scum that rises to the
surface *(pic 3)*. Reduce the heat to low
and cook for 1 hour or until the beans
are tender. Add more water if necessary
to keep the beans covered. Drain the
beans, reserving the liquid. Discard the
herbs and onion. Squeeze the garlic flesh
from the skins. Process the garlic flesh,
half the beans and 125 ml (4 fl oz/
½ cup) of reserved liquid in a food
processor until creamy and smooth,
adding a little more liquid if the mixture
is too thick. Stir in the whole beans and
season with salt and pepper.

7 Carve the lamb (see page 59) and
serve with the white bean purée, warm
pan juices and steamed vegetables.

1

2

3

Baked leg ham

Baking your own ham leg is a simple process — removing the skin is not difficult, then all you need to do is score and stud the fat with cloves, heat the glaze, brush it on and begin baking. The rewards, beginning with the amazing aroma as it cooks and culminating in the superb flavour, are well worth it.

SERVES 12   **PREPARATION TIME** 40 minutes   **COOKING TIME** 1 hour 10 minutes

6–8 kg (13 lb 8 oz–18 lb) cooked
  ham leg
Whole cloves, for studding

ORANGE AND HONEY GLAZE
125 ml (4 fl oz/½ cup) strained freshly
  squeezed orange juice
115 g (4 oz/⅓ cup) honey
75 g (2¾ oz/⅓ cup, firmly packed)
  dark brown sugar
60 g (2¼ oz/¼ cup) dijon mustard

1 Use a small sharp knife to cut around the ham shank in a zig-zag pattern, about 10 cm (4 inches) from the end. Starting at the other end of the ham, run your fingers between the skin and flesh. Continue sliding your fingers further up the ham until you reach the shank end. You are aiming to keep the fat attached to the ham flesh and remove the skin. Once loosened, carefully remove the skin in one piece *(pic 1)*.

2 Preheat the oven to 180°C (350°F/ Gas 4).

3 To make the orange and honey glaze, put all the ingredients in a small deep saucepan over medium heat. Bring to the boil, then reduce the heat and simmer for 5–10 minutes or until thickened slightly.

4 Score the fat in a diamond pattern, cutting about 1 cm (½ inch) deep and being careful not to touch the flesh. Press a clove into each diamond *(pic 2)*.

Line a heavy baking tray with a double layer of foil (see tip) and place a rack on top. Put the ham on the rack, brush with the glaze *(pic 3)* and bake for 20 minutes. Glaze again and bake for a further 20 minutes, then glaze and bake for a final 20 minutes or until golden. Carve the ham and serve warm or at room temperature.

GLAZE VARIATIONS

Lemon, honey and ginger glaze: Omit the mustard. Replace the orange juice with 185 ml (6 fl oz/¾ cup) strained freshly squeezed lemon juice. Increase the honey to 235 g (8½ oz/⅔ cup). Replace the brown sugar with white sugar. Add the finely grated zest of 3 lemons, 3 teaspoons ground ginger and 3 star anise. Bring to the boil, then reduce the heat and simmer for 10 minutes.

Bourbon and wholegrain mustard glaze: Replace the orange juice with maple syrup. Increase the brown sugar to 220 g (7¾ oz/1 cup, firmly packed). Replace the dijon mustard with wholegrain mustard. Omit the honey. Add 80 ml (2½ fl oz/⅓ cup) bourbon. Bring to the boil, then reduce the heat and simmer for 4 minutes. If the glaze browns too quickly during cooking, cover with foil for the last 20 minutes.

TIP The tray that comes with your oven is perfect for this task as the ham is very heavy. Lining it with foil to catch any glaze that drips and caramelises will make washing up easier.

Pastitsio

Pasta bakes such as this are very convenient, as the meat sauce can be made up to two days ahead, then the pasta and white sauce prepared just before you bake the dish. This is a good alternative to lasagne, and is a simple yet hearty dish.

SERVES 6–8   **PREPARATION TIME** 30 minutes (+ 10 minutes standing)   **COOKING TIME** 2 hours

250 g (9 oz) dried penne

2 eggs, lightly whisked

50 g (1¾ oz/½ cup) coarsely grated cheddar cheese

60 g (1¼ oz/½ cup) coarsely grated parmesan cheese

½ teaspoon freshly grated nutmeg

MEAT SAUCE

1 tablespoon olive oil

1 brown onion, finely chopped

2–3 garlic cloves, chopped

500 g (1 lb 2 oz) minced (ground) beef

400 g (14 oz) tin chopped tomatoes

50 g (1¾ oz/¼ cup) tomato paste (concentrated purée)

1 teaspoon dried oregano

125 ml (4 fl oz/½ cup) white wine

125 ml (4 fl oz/½ cup) good-quality ready-made or home-made beef stock (see page 60) or water

¼ cup flat-leaf (Italian) parsley, chopped

WHITE SAUCE

50 g (1¾ oz) butter

35 g (1¼ oz/¼ cup) plain (all-purpose) flour

750 ml (26 fl oz/3 cups) milk

1 egg, lightly whisked

¼ teaspoon freshly grated nutmeg

25 g (1¼ oz/¼ cup) finely grated parmesan cheese

30 g (1 oz/¼ cup) dry breadcrumbs

1 Preheat the oven to 180°C (350°F/Gas 4). Grease an ovenproof dish (about 23 x 30 x 5 cm/9 x 12 x 2 inches).

2 Cook the pasta in a large saucepan of boiling salted water, following the packet instructions, until *al dente*.

Cool under cold running water and drain. Stir through the egg, cheeses and nutmeg and season with salt and freshly ground black pepper, to taste.

3 To make the meat sauce, heat the oil in a large frying pan. Add the onion and garlic and cook over medium heat for 2–3 minutes or until soft. Add the meat and cook, stirring, for 3–4 minutes or until the meat changes colour.

4 Add the tomatoes, tomato paste, oregano, wine and stock or water. Simmer for 45 minutes. Use a potato masher or fork to break up any lumps in the meat *(pic 1)*. Set aside.

5 To make the white sauce, melt the butter in a saucepan over low heat, then add the flour and stir for 1 minute. Remove from the heat and gradually add the milk, whisking until smooth. Return to the heat and stir until smooth and thick. Simmer for 3 minutes, then set aside. Allow to cool a little before whisking in the egg and nutmeg. Pour 125 ml (4 fl oz/½ cup) of the sauce into the meat mixture *(pic 2)* and stir through with the parsley.

6 Spoon half the pasta mixture evenly over the base of the prepared dish. Spoon over the meat sauce *(pic 3)*, then the remaining pasta mixture. Pour on the white sauce and sprinkle with the combined parmesan cheese and breadcrumbs. Bake for 50 minutes (cover with foil if the top is browning too quickly). Remove from the oven and set aside for 10 minutes before serving.

Meatloaf

Some believe meatloaf is a variation on Italian meatballs, created by Italian immigrants when they moved to America. Others say it's a Depression dish, as it extends meat by adding breadcrumbs. Whatever the case, it remains one of the simplest, and most loved, of all meat dishes.

SERVES 6   **PREPARATION TIME** 20 minutes (+ cooling)   **COOKING TIME** 1 hour 20 minutes

95 g (3¼ oz) fresh breadcrumbs
350 g (12 oz) minced (ground) pork
350 g (12 oz) minced (ground) veal
400 g (14 oz) pork or beef sausages,
 removed from their casings
1 small brown onion, very finely chopped
2 garlic cloves, crushed
1 egg
2 teaspoons thyme leaves
2½ tablespoons dijon mustard
80 ml (2½ fl oz/⅓ cup) tomato sauce
 (ketchup) or barbecue sauce
2 teaspoons salt
1½ teaspoons freshly ground
 black pepper
Mashed potato (see page 69) and
 tomato sauce (see page 66),
 to serve
Coleslaw, to serve

1 Preheat the oven to 180°C (350°F/ Gas 4). Brush the base and sides of an 8 x 19 cm (3¼ x 7½ inch), 1.5 litre (52 fl oz/6 cup) loaf (bar) tin with oil.

2 Put the breadcrumbs, pork, veal, sausage meat, onion, garlic, egg, thyme, mustard, tomato sauce, salt and pepper in a large bowl *(pic 1)*. Use your hands to mix well until smooth.

3 Pack the mixture into the greased tin and smooth the surface *(pic 2)*. Bake for 1 hour 20 minutes or until the juices run clear when pierced with a skewer. Carefully pour any excess liquid from the tin *(pic 3)*, then set aside to cool. Carefully turn out and serve warm or at room temperature with the mashed potato, tomato sauce and coleslaw.

1

2

3

TIP For the best results, use good-quality meats and make sure they're not too lean or the loaf will be dry and not as tasty as it could be.

Roast pork loin stuffed with couscous, millet and apricot

SERVES 4–6   **PREPARATION TIME** 20 minutes   **COOKING TIME** 1 hour 40 minutes

1.8 kg (4 lb) pork loin (including the 'tail'; see tip)
1 tablespoon vegetable oil
1 tablespoon sea salt
125 ml (4 fl oz/½ cup) apple cider
185 ml (6 fl oz/¾ cup) good-quality ready-made or home-made chicken stock (see page 30)
1 tablespoon dijon mustard
steamed greens, to serve

STUFFING

50 g (1¾ oz/¼ cup) instant couscous
30 g (1 oz) butter
1 brown onion, finely chopped
2 bacon rashers, finely chopped (about 120 g/4 oz)
2 garlic cloves, crushed
80 g (2¾ oz/½ cup) dried apricots, chopped
30 g (1 oz) baby spinach
2 tablespoons millet flakes

1 Score the pork skin with a sharp knife at 1.5 cm (⅝ inch) intervals (*pic 1*, and see tip).

2 Preheat the oven to 220°C (425°F/Gas 7). To make the stuffing, place the couscous and 60 ml (2 fl oz/¼ cup) boiling water in a small heatproof bowl, cover and stand for 5 minutes or until the liquid is absorbed. Fluff with a fork.

3 Meanwhile, melt the butter in a large frying pan over medium–high heat. Add the onion, bacon and garlic and cook, stirring, for 5 minutes or until the onion has softened and the bacon is golden brown. Add the apricots and spinach. Cook, stirring, for 2 minutes or until the spinach has wilted. Transfer to a bowl and stir in the couscous and millet flakes.

4 Place the pork, skin side down, on a work surface. Spoon the stuffing next to the loin (*pic 2*) and roll to enclose. Secure with kitchen string.

5 Rub the pork all over with the oil. Sprinkle the sea salt over the pork skin, rubbing it in so it penetrates the scored rind (*pic 3*). Put the pork in a large flameproof roasting pan.

6 Roast for 30 minutes, then reduce the heat to 180°C (350°F/Gas 4) and roast for a further 45–50 minutes or until the pork is just cooked. Cover loosely with foil and stand in a warm place for 10 minutes.

7 Carefully skim the excess fat from the pan, then place over medium heat on the stovetop. Add the cider, stock and mustard, bring to a gentle boil and cook, stirring to remove any caramelised bits stuck on the base, for 10 minutes or until the liquid has reduced by half. Slice the pork and serve with some steamed greens and the sauce.

1

2

3

TIP It's best to buy the pork from your butcher (rather than a supermarket) so that the tail has not been trimmed. This enables you to enclose the stuffing easily.
For good crackling, score the skin with a sharp knife — if you like, use a steel ruler to help create even lines.

Rack of lamb with herb crust

Lamb racks make the perfect quick roast, taking only 20 minutes in the oven. A simple herb crust transforms them into something more special, ideal for an easy dinner party. Any combination of herbs (oregano, rosemary and so on) can be used.

SERVES 4 **PREPARATION TIME** 15 minutes (+ 5 minutes resting) **COOKING TIME** 20–25 minutes

35 g (1¼ oz) fresh white breadcrumbs (see tip)

1 tablespoon snipped chives

1 tablespoon chopped flat-leaf (Italian) parsley

1 tablespoon dijon mustard

½ teaspoon finely grated lemon zest

2 teaspoons salted baby capers, rinsed, drained and chopped

60 ml (2 fl oz/¼ cup) olive oil

4 lamb racks with 3 ribs each (about 200 g/7 oz each), frenched (see page 29)

600 g (1 lb 5 oz) all-purpose potatoes, peeled and cut into chunks

Steamed greens, to serve

1 Preheat the oven to 200°C (400°F/ Gas 6). Put the breadcrumbs, herbs, mustard, lemon zest, capers and 1 tablespoon of the oil in a medium bowl. Season with salt and pepper *(pic 1)* and stir until well combined.

2 Heat 1 tablespoon of the oil in a large non-stick frying pan over high heat. Cook the lamb racks, in batches if necessary, for 1–2 minutes each side *(pic 2)*, then transfer to a large roasting pan. Press one-quarter of the breadcrumb mixture over the meaty part of each rack *(pic 3)*. Roast the lamb for 15 minutes or until a meat thermometer inserted into the centre of the thickest part of a rack reads 60°C (140°F) for medium-rare, or until cooked to your liking.

3 Meanwhile, put the potatoes in a large microwave-safe bowl and add a little water. Cover and cook on high (100%) for 5 minutes. Drain, pat dry with paper towels and transfer to a baking tray. Drizzle with the remaining oil and bake for 15–20 minutes, until golden and cooked through.

4 Transfer the lamb racks to a carving board, cover loosely with foil and set aside for 5 minutes to rest. Cut the racks into individual cutlets and serve with the potatoes and steamed greens.

1

2

3

TIP Two slices of bread, with the crusts removed, should yield about 35 g (1¼ oz) breadcrumbs.

Pork, apple and fennel sausage rolls

Sausage rolls are perennially popular, especially for casual finger food at a party. Making your own, using good-quality ingredients, is so simple and gives such fabulous results that you'll never look back.

MAKES 12   **PREPARATION TIME** 1 hour (+ 1 hour 20 minutes chilling/cooling)   **COOKING TIME** 35–40 minutes

1 tablespoon fennel seeds
1 tablespoon olive oil
1 small fennel bulb, trimmed and
   finely chopped
2 garlic cloves, finely chopped
60 g (2¼ oz/½ cup) chopped pancetta
Pinch of allspice
300 g (10½ oz) good-quality pork
   sausages, removed from their casings
300 g (10½ oz) minced (ground) pork
60 g (2¼ oz/1 cup, lightly packed)
   fresh breadcrumbs
1 small green apple (about 100 g/
   3½ oz), peeled and coarsely grated
¼ cup coarsely chopped flat-leaf
   (Italian) parsley
1 egg yolk
550 g (1 lb 4 oz) block home-made or
   ready-made puff pastry
1 tablespoon sesame seeds
1 egg, lightly whisked with
   2 teaspoons water

1 Heat a small non-stick frying pan over medium heat. Add 3 teaspoons of the fennel seeds and cook, shaking the pan, for 30 seconds or until aromatic. Use a mortar and pestle or spice grinder to grind the seeds to a powder.

2 Heat the olive oil in a medium frying pan over medium–low heat. Add the chopped fennel and cook, stirring, for 5 minutes. Add the garlic and pancetta and cook for a further 5 minutes or until the fennel is golden and tender. Add the ground fennel and the allspice and cook for 30 seconds or until aromatic. Set aside to cool.

3 Combine the sausage meat, minced pork, cooled fennel mixture, breadcrumbs, apple, parsley and egg yolk in a large bowl. Season well with salt and freshly ground black pepper.

4 Preheat the oven to 200°C (400°F/ Gas 6). Line 2 large baking trays with non-stick baking paper.

5 Cut the pastry in half widthways, then roll each piece out on a lightly floured work surface to a 25 cm (10 inch) square. Cut each pastry sheet in half. Divide the mince mixture into 4 equal portions. Shape each portion into a log and place on the centre of each piece of pastry *(pic 1)*. Brush the edges of the pastry well with the egg wash. Fold the pastry over to enclose the filling, overlapping the edges and pressing to seal *(pic 2)*. Transfer to a tray and refrigerate for 20 minutes to rest and chill.

6 Line 2 more baking trays with non-stick baking paper. Place the sausage rolls on a chopping board, seam side down. Cut each roll into 3 equal pieces *(pic 3)*. Transfer to the lined trays, allowing room for spreading.

7 Combine the remaining fennel seeds and sesame seeds in a small bowl. Brush the sausage rolls with the egg wash and sprinkle with the seed mixture. Bake for 15 minutes, then reduce the temperature to 180°C (350°F/Gas 4), swap the trays around and cook for 10–15 minutes more or until puffed and golden.

1

2

3

TIP The uncooked sausage rolls can be frozen, in sealed freezer bags, for up to 2 months. There is no need to defrost them before cooking, but allow an extra 5 minutes to cook them through.

Perfect roast beef

It is hard to beat a tender and juicy roasted fillet of beef. The potato purée is quite indulgent as it's made with cream, but you could substitute milk to make a lighter version.

SERVES 4–6   **PREPARATION TIME** 20 minutes (+ 10 minutes resting)   **COOKING TIME** 45 minutes

1.2 kg (2 lb 11 oz) beef tenderloin, at room temperature
25 g (1 oz/¼ cup) flaked almonds
1 tablespoon vegetable oil
50 g (1¾ oz) butter, chopped
2 teaspoons white wine vinegar
500 g (1 lb 2 oz) green beans, trimmed
Red wine jus (see page 67), to serve

POTATO PURÉE

1.2 kg (2 lb 11 oz) all-purpose potatoes, peeled and chopped
330 ml (11¼ fl oz/1⅓ cups) thin (pouring/whipping) cream
75 g (2¾ oz) butter, chopped

1 Trim any sinew and excess fat from the beef fillet and reserve (see page 54). You need about ½ cup of meat trimmings for the red wine jus — if you don't have enough, trim a little meat from the thin end of the fillet and dice.

2 Preheat the oven to 180°C (350°F/Gas 4). Spread the almonds over a baking tray and cook for 2–3 minutes or until golden. Meanwhile, tie the beef with kitchen string at regular intervals (*pic 1*) (see page 56). Season with sea salt and freshly ground black pepper and drizzle with the oil (*pic 2*).

3 Increase the oven temperature to 200°C (400°F/Gas 6). Heat a large heavy-based frying pan over medium heat. Cook the beef, turning occasionally, for 4–5 minutes or until browned all over. Use tongs to transfer the beef to a rack in a roasting pan and roast for 30 minutes for medium-rare or until cooked to your liking.

4 Meanwhile, to make the potato purée, put the potatoes in a saucepan of salted cold water and bring to the boil over high heat. Reduce the heat to medium and cook for 20 minutes or until tender. Drain well, then push the potatoes through a potato ricer, sieve or mouli. Return to the saucepan. Heat the cream and butter in a small saucepan over medium heat. Add to the potato, then return to low heat and stir with a wooden spoon or spatula until smooth. Season to taste and cover to keep warm.

5 Remove the beef from the oven, cover loosely with foil and set aside in a warm place for 10 minutes to rest.

6 Heat the butter in a small frying pan over medium heat for 2–4 minutes or until foaming and nut-brown in colour. Add the vinegar (*pic 3*) and remove from the heat. Cook the beans in a saucepan of boiling salted water for 3–4 minutes or until tender. Drain and toss with the almonds and butter mixture.

7 Carve the beef into thin slices or thick portions and serve with the beans, potato purée and red wine jus.

Italian meatballs with spaghetti

The addition of milk-soaked bread helps to keep these meatballs moist. To get the most flavour in your meatballs, don't roll the balls too tightly. This allows the sauce to soak into the meatballs during cooking. Spaghetti is the traditional accompaniment, but other long pastas work well, too.

SERVES 4   **PREPARATION TIME** 20 minutes   **COOKING TIME** 1 hour 20 minutes

80 g (2¾ oz) day-old white bread, finely
   chopped (about 3 slices)
125 ml (4 fl oz/½ cup) milk
60 ml (2 fl oz/¼ cup) olive oil
1 brown onion, finely chopped
100 g (3½ oz) pancetta, finely chopped
2 garlic cloves, crushed
125 ml (4 fl oz/½ cup) red wine
500 g (1 lb 2 oz) minced (ground) beef
300 g (10½ oz) mixed minced (ground)
   pork and veal
50 g (1¾ oz/½ cup) finely grated
   pecorino cheese
700 g (1 lb 9 oz) tomato passata
   (puréed tomatoes)
250 ml (9 fl oz/1 cup) good-quality
   ready-made or home-made chicken
   stock (see page 30)
400 g (14 oz) dried spaghetti
Shredded parmesan cheese, to serve

1 Preheat the oven to 180°C (350°F/ Gas 4). Combine the bread and milk in a small bowl and set aside for 10 minutes or until softened *(pic 1)*.

2 Meanwhile, heat 1 tablespoon of the oil in a frying pan over medium heat. Add the onion, pancetta and garlic and cook, stirring, for 5–10 minutes or until softened. Add the wine and bring to the boil. Reduce the heat to low and simmer for 3 minutes or until almost completely evaporated. Transfer to a bowl and allow to cool to room temperature.

3 Combine the bread mixture, onion mixture, meats and cheese in a large bowl. Season with salt and freshly ground black pepper, then mix well.

4 Using wet hands, roll heaped tablespoons of the meat mixture into 25 balls *(pic 2)*. Place in a large baking dish (the meatballs need to fit fairly snugly in the dish).

5 Heat the remaining oil in a large frying pan over medium heat. Add the tomato passata and stock. Bring to the boil. Reduce the heat to low and simmer, uncovered, for 20 minutes or until reduced slightly.

6 Spoon the tomato mixture over the meatballs *(pic 3)*. Cover the dish with foil and bake for 45 minutes.

7 Meanwhile, cook the pasta in a large saucepan of boiling salted water, following the packet instructions, until *al dente*. Drain and return to the pan. Add some of the sauce and toss to combine. Serve the spaghetti topped with the meatballs, remaining sauce and parmesan cheese.

Country-style terrine

Terrines, named after the traditional earthenware dishes they are cooked in, have a coarse, rustic texture. They are simple to make and easily varied by using different meats and flavourings. For a richer, truly authentic terrine, replace one-quarter of the minced veal with finely chopped pork back fat.

SERVES 10   **PREPARATION TIME** 40 minutes (+ overnight chilling)   **COOKING TIME** 1 hour 45 minutes

300 g (10½ oz) rindless bacon rashers
400 g (14 oz) minced (ground) pork
   (see tip)
400 g (14 oz) minced (ground) veal
150 g (5½ oz) chicken livers, cleaned
   and finely chopped (see page 25)
400 g (14 oz) skinless chicken thigh
   fillets, cut into 5 mm (¼ inch) pieces
2½ tablespoons brandy
1 egg, lightly whisked
Large pinch of allspice
Pinch of freshly grated nutmeg
1 tablespoon chopped thyme
45 g (1¾ oz/⅓ cup) pistachios
2 teaspoons salt
1½ teaspoons freshly ground
   black pepper
Crusty French bread, cornichons and
   pickled onions, to serve

1 Preheat the oven to 180°C (350°F/ Gas 4). Lightly brush the base and sides of an 11 x 25 (4¼ x 10 inch), 1.5 litre (52 fl oz/6 cup) terrine mould or loaf (bar) tin with butter to grease.

2 Working with one rasher of bacon at a time, arrange widthways across the base and long sides of the mould, pressing it snugly into the edges and allowing it to overhang the sides. Continue arranging the bacon, pushing the pieces close together so the surface of the mould is covered and allowing long pieces to overhang the sides, until the base and long sides are covered (*pic 1*). You may need to cut some of the rashers to fill any gaps. Use the remaining bacon to cover the short sides of the mould, cutting them to fit.

3 Put the remaining ingredients in a large bowl and use your hands to mix until well combined. Pack the mixture into the bacon-lined mould and use a spatula to smooth the surface (*pic 2*). Bring the overhanging bacon over the mixture to cover, using any remaining pieces of bacon to patch any gaps.

4 Cover the mould tightly with foil (*pic 3*) and place in a roasting pan. Add enough boiling water to the pan to come about halfway up the side. Bake the terrine for 1 hour 45 minutes or until the juices run clear when it is pierced with a skewer and it has shrunk slightly from the sides of the mould.

5 Remove the mould from the pan, uncover and pour off any liquid, then set aside to cool to room temperature. Once cooled, place the mould on a tray, then put a wooden board on top. Put weights (about 2.5 kg/5 lb 8 oz of tinned food works well) on the board and then refrigerate overnight. Remove the weights and board, turn the terrine out and serve with crusty bread, cornichons and pickled onions.

1

2

3

TIP Use minced pork that isn't too lean, as fat will contribute flavour and moistness.
   You can use only minced pork and replace the livers with chopped skinless chicken breast or thigh fillet, if desired.

Lasagne

There are several versions of a traditional Italian meat sauce for lasagne and they vary depending on the region of origin. Here, as is the custom in the north, full-cream milk is added to the sauce for richness. Simmering the sauce over low heat for a long time also adds extra intensity to the flavour.

SERVES 8 **PREPARATION TIME** 40 minutes (+ 10 minutes standing) **COOKING TIME** 2 hours 35 minutes

60 ml (2 fl oz/¼ cup) olive oil
1 brown onion, chopped
1 celery stalk, finely chopped
1 carrot, finely chopped
600 g (1 lb 5 oz) mixed minced
   (ground) pork and veal
2 teaspoons mixed dried herbs
4 garlic cloves, chopped
250 ml (9 fl oz/1 cup) milk
375 ml (13 fl oz/1½ cups) red wine
400 g (14 oz) tin chopped tomatoes
2 tablespoons tomato paste
   (concentrated purée)
250 ml (9 fl oz/1 cup) good-quality
   ready-made chicken stock
50 g (1¾ oz) butter, chopped
300 g (10½ oz) fresh lasagne sheets
125 g (4½ oz) finely grated
   parmesan cheese
¼ cup basil leaves, to serve
Green salad, to serve

BECHAMEL SAUCE
125 g (4½ oz) butter, chopped
125 g (4½ oz) plain (all-purpose) flour
1 litre (35 fl oz/4 cups) warm milk
1 bay leaf

1 Heat the oil in a large frying pan over low heat and cook the onion, celery and carrot for 5 minutes or until soft (*pic 1*).

2 Add the minced meat to the pan and cook over medium heat, stirring to break up any lumps, for 5 minutes, until browned. Stir in the herbs and garlic.

3 Add the milk (*pic 2*), stir to combine and cook over low heat, stirring occasionally, for about 10 minutes, until the milk is absorbed.

4 Stir in the wine, tomatoes, tomato paste and stock and simmer over low heat for 1½ hours or until thick, adding a little hot water if the mixture sticks to the base of the pan. Season with salt and freshly ground black pepper, to taste.

5 Meanwhile, to make the béchamel sauce, melt the butter in a medium saucepan over medium heat. Add the flour and cook, stirring, for 1 minute, until pale and bubbling. Gradually whisk in the milk and slowly bring to a simmer. Add the bay leaf and cook over low heat for 5 minutes, whisking occasionally, until thick. Season to taste, cover with plastic wrap and set aside to cool slightly. Remove the bay leaf.

6 Preheat the oven to 180°C (350°F/ Gas 4).

7 Rub half the butter over the base of a 3 litre (105 fl oz/12 cup) heatproof casserole dish, measuring about 19 x 35 x 7.5 cm (7½ x 14 x 3 inches), and line the base with lasagne sheets. Top with one-third of the meat sauce and one-third of the béchamel sauce. Top with another layer of pasta (*pic 3*). Continue layering (you will have three layers of pasta), finishing with a layer of béchamel sauce. Sprinkle with the parmesan cheese and dot with the remaining butter.

8 Place the dish on a baking tray and bake for 45 minutes, or until browned and bubbling. Remove from the oven and stand for 10 minutes, then scatter with basil and serve with a green salad.

Braising and
Pot-roasting

Classic pot-roasted chicken

SERVES 4   **PREPARATION TIME** 25 minutes   **COOKING TIME** 1 hour 20 minutes

1.6 kg (3 lb 8 oz) whole chicken

3 thyme sprigs, plus extra
   sprigs, to garnish

2 tablespoons olive oil

20 g (¾ oz) butter

1 bunch baby carrots, trimmed
   and peeled

12 baby onions, peeled

3 turnips, about 500 g (1 lb 2 oz), peeled
   and cut into large wedges

1 bay leaf

125 ml (4 fl oz/½ cup) white wine

375 ml (13 fl oz/1½ cups) good-quality
   ready-made or home-made
   chicken stock (see page 30)

1 tablespoon thick (double/heavy)
   cream

MASHED POTATO

800 g (1 lb 12 oz) all-purpose potatoes,
   peeled and cut into large chunks

200 g (7 oz) thick (double/heavy)
   cream

50 g (1¾ oz) butter, chopped

1 Preheat the oven to 200°C (400°F/
Gas 6). Wash the chicken briefly under
cold running water, remove the neck
and giblets and trim any pockets of fat.
Pat the chicken dry with paper towels.
Season the chicken, inside and out, with
salt and pepper. Place a sprig of thyme
inside the cavity of the chicken *(pic 1)*.

2 Heat half the oil in a large heavy
flameproof casserole dish over high heat.
Add the butter. Cook the chicken for
8 minutes or until browned all over.
Remove the chicken from the dish,
discard the oil and wipe over with paper
towels. Heat the remaining oil in the
casserole dish. Add the carrots, onions,
turnips, bay leaf and the remaining

thyme sprigs. Cook, stirring, for
5 minutes or until the vegetables are
lightly browned. Return the chicken
to the dish, breast side up *(pic 2)*. Pour
over the wine and stock, then bring the
liquid to the boil.

3 Cover the casserole dish, put in the
oven and cook for 40 minutes. Remove
the lid and cook for 15 minutes more or
until the chicken is cooked through and
the juices run clear when it is pierced
through the thickest part (between the
thigh and body). Transfer the chicken
and vegetables to a clean dish and cover
loosely with foil to keep warm.

4 Meanwhile, to make the mashed
potato, put the potatoes in a large
saucepan of salted water, bring to the
boil and cook for 20 minutes or until
very tender. Drain the potatoes, return
to the pan over low heat and stir for
1 minute or until dry. Add the cream
and butter. Using a potato masher,
mash the potatoes until smooth and
combined. Season with sea salt and
freshly ground black pepper.

5 Bring the sauce in the casserole
dish to the boil over high heat. Boil
for 10 minutes or until reduced to 250 ml
(9 fl oz/1 cup). Stir in the cream *(pic 3)*.
Transfer the sauce to a jug.

6 Carve the chicken (see page 26) and
serve with the mashed potato, vegetables
and generously drizzled with the sauce.
Garnish with the extra thyme sprigs.

Asian-style pot-roasted quails

SERVES 4 as an entrée **PREPARATION TIME** 20 minutes **COOKING TIME** 25 minutes

4 quails (about 180 g/6¼ oz each)

½ teaspoon ground cinnamon

1 tablespoon vegetable oil

250 ml (9 fl oz/1 cup) good-quality
ready-made or home-made
chicken stock (see page 30)

250 ml (9 fl oz/1 cup) Chinese
rice wine (see tip)

1 tablespoon finely julienned ginger

3 star anise

2 tablespoons sugar

200 g (7 oz) silken tofu, cut into
1.5 cm (⅝ inch) cubes

1 teaspoon light soy sauce

60 g (2¼ oz/½ cup) bean sprouts,
trimmed

¼ small red onion, very thinly sliced

⅓ cup mint leaves

⅓ cup small coriander (cilantro) sprigs

1 Preheat the oven to 180°C (350°F/
Gas 4). Briefly wash the quails under
cold running water, then pat dry with
paper towels. Truss the quails (see page
21). Rub the skin of the quails with the
cinnamon *(pic 1)*.

2 Heat the oil in a large flameproof
casserole dish over medium–low heat.
Brown the quails for 6–8 minutes,
turning occasionally to ensure they
brown evenly. Transfer to a plate.
Remove the dish from the heat and
wipe out with paper towels.

3 Add the stock, rice wine, ginger, star
anise and sugar to the casserole dish.
Return the quails to the dish *(pic 2)*,
cover and put in the oven. Cook for
12–15 minutes or until the quails are
just cooked through and the juices run
clear when they are pierced through
the thickest part (between the thigh
and body). Transfer to warmed serving
bowls and remove the string.

4 Strain the broth into a medium
saucepan. Place over low heat, add the
tofu and simmer gently for about
30 seconds (watch it the whole time as
the tofu is very delicate) or until the tofu
is just warmed through *(pic 3)*. Add the
light soy sauce.

5 Gently spoon the tofu and broth
around the quails and top with the bean
sprouts, red onion, mint and coriander.
Serve immediately.

1

2

3

TIP You can find Chinese rice
wine, also called shaoxing rice
wine, at Asian supermarkets. It is
made from a mixture of glutinous
rice, yeast and water, and the best
wines are fermented for up to
10 years. It adds depth and flavour
to Asian dishes.

Soy-braised chicken

This recipe is based on a classic Cantonese dish in which a whole chicken is simmered ever so gently in a mixture of soy sauce, sugar and Chinese rice wine. The idea translates extremely well to chicken pieces, but you do need to cook them very gently or they will be tough.

SERVES 4   **PREPARATION TIME** 30 minutes (+ 15 minutes cooling)   **COOKING TIME** 1 hour

5 cm (2 inch) piece ginger

2½ tablespoons peanut oil

1.5 kg (3 lb 5 oz) whole chicken,
    cut into 8 pieces (see page 18)

2 garlic cloves, thinly sliced

2 dried chillies

2 x 2 cm (¾ inch) wide strips
    of orange zest

1½ star anise

1 cinnamon stick

125 ml (4 fl oz/½ cup) good-quality
    ready-made or home-made chicken
    stock (see page 30)

125 ml (4 fl oz/½ cup) light soy sauce

125 ml (4 fl oz/½ cup) Chinese rice wine

65 g (2¼ oz/⅓ cup) crushed rock
    sugar (see tip)

3 teaspoons cornflour (cornstarch)

2 spring onions (scallions), thinly
    diagonally sliced

Steamed rice and baby bok choy
    (pak choy), to serve

1 Use a sharp knife to cut the ginger into very fine julienne *(pic 1)*.

2 Heat the oil in a large, heavy-based frying pan over medium heat. Cook the chicken pieces, in batches, turning once, for 5 minutes or until golden. Transfer to a medium saucepan.

3 Pour off the excess fat from the frying pan, leaving about 2 tablespoons. Add the ginger, garlic and dried chillies and cook over medium heat, stirring, for 2–3 minutes or until aromatic.

4 Add the ginger mixture, orange zest, star anise, cinnamon, stock, soy sauce, rice wine and sugar to the chicken in the saucepan. Bring slowly to a simmer over medium heat. Reduce the heat to low, cover and cook for 40 minutes or until the chicken is cooked through.

5 Transfer the chicken to a bowl and set aside, covered. Pour the cooking liquid into a bowl and set aside for about 15 minutes or until it has cooled slightly and the fat has risen to the surface.

6 Skim the fat from the surface of the cooking liquid, then strain through a sieve lined with muslin (cheesecloth) *(pic 2)*. Discard all the solids, except the star anise. Return the strained liquid and star anise to a clean medium saucepan and bring to a simmer.

7 Combine the cornflour with 1½ tablespoons of water and mix until smooth. Stirring constantly, add to the liquid in the saucepan and bring to a simmer *(pic 3)*. Cook, stirring, for 1–2 minutes or until thickened slightly.

8 Return the chicken to the pan and cook over medium heat for 4–5 minutes or until just heated through. Serve the chicken and the sauce in shallow bowls, scattered with the spring onions and accompanied by the rice and bok choy.

1

2

3

TIP Pale-yellow in colour, rock sugar is made from sugar cane and is used extensively in sweet and savoury Chinese dishes. It is available in cubes or large lumps from Asian supermarkets. Palm sugar (jaggery) can be substituted.

Chicken pizzaiola

Pizzaiola means 'pizza style'. Most of the cooking for this dish is done in the oven, so once the initial preparation is done you can forget about it until it's time to shred the chicken and cook the pasta.

SERVES 4–6 **PREPARATION TIME** 20 minutes **COOKING TIME** 1 hour 45 minutes

1.6 kg (3 lb 8 oz) whole chicken
2 tablespoons olive oil
1 large brown onion, thinly sliced
4 basil leaves
2 garlic cloves, crushed
1 tablespoon baby capers,
    drained and rinsed
4 anchovy fillets, chopped
2 x 400 g (14 oz) tins chopped tomatoes
250 ml (9 fl oz/1 cup) good-quality
    ready-made or home-made
    chicken stock (see page 30)
60 g (1¼ oz/½ cup) pitted green olives,
    chopped
400 g (14 oz) fresh or dried pappardelle
Basil leaves, shaved parmesan cheese
    and dried chilli flakes, to serve

1 Preheat the oven to 180°C (350°F/ Gas 4). Wash the chicken briefly under cold running water, then remove the neck and giblets and trim any pockets of fat. Pat the chicken dry with paper towels *(pic 1)*.

2 Heat the oil in a large flameproof casserole dish. Add the onion and basil and cook, stirring occasionally, for 5 minutes or until the onion is softened. Add the garlic, capers and anchovies. Cook, stirring, for 1 minute, or until the anchovies have dissolved. Add the tomatoes and stock *(pic 2)* and stir to combine. Add the chicken and bring to the boil. Partially cover the dish with the lid, transfer to the oven and cook for 1½ hours.

3 Remove the chicken from the casserole dish and set aside. Place the dish on the stovetop over medium heat and bring the cooking juices to the boil, then cook, stirring occasionally, for 10–15 minutes, until reduced.

4 When cool enough to handle, shred the chicken meat and discard the skin and bones. Return the chicken flesh to the casserole dish with the olives *(pic 3)*. Cook, stirring, until heated through, then season with freshly ground black pepper. You probably won't need to add salt, as the anchovies and olives are already quite salty.

5 Meanwhile, cook the pasta in a large saucepan of boiling salted water, following the packet instructions, until *al dente*. Drain well.

6 Add the pasta to the chicken pizzaiola sauce and toss to combine. Serve sprinkled with the basil and chilli flakes, and with parmesan to pass around.

1

2

3

Orecchiette with Italian sausage and tomato

Italian sausages are typically rather coarsely textured and often robustly flavoured, for example with pork and fennel. If you can't find Italian sausage, substitute any well-flavoured sausage, slipping the cases off the meat and coarsely crumbling it before cooking.

SERVES 4–6   **PREPARATION TIME** 15 minutes   **COOKING TIME** 35 minutes

400 g (14 oz) Italian sausages

2 tablespoons olive oil

2–3 garlic cloves, crushed

1 red onion, thinly sliced

6 ripe tomatoes, peeled, seeded and chopped

80 ml (2½ fl oz/⅓ cup) white wine or water

2 tablespoons tomato paste (concentrated purée)

½ teaspoon dried oregano

⅓ cup basil leaves, shredded

500 g (1 lb 2 oz) orecchiette

Whole basil leaves, to garnish

Grated pecorino cheese, to serve

1 Cut away the skin of the sausages and discard, then coarsely crumble the meat into bite-sized pieces.

2 Heat 1 tablespoon of the oil in a large frying pan. Add the sausage meat and cook over low heat, turning occasionally, for 5 minutes. Remove with a slotted spoon and drain on paper towels *(pic 1)*.

3 Add the remaining oil to the pan. Cook the garlic and onion over medium heat for 3 minutes, without letting them burn, then add the tomatoes, wine or water, tomato paste, oregano and shredded basil. Simmer for 20 minutes or until slightly thick *(pic 2)*. Season with salt and freshly ground black pepper, to taste.

4 Meanwhile, cook the pasta in a large saucepan of boiling salted water, following the packet instructions, until *al dente*. Drain.

5 Return the sausage meat to the sauce *(pic 3)* and heat through for 2 minutes.

6 Toss the sauce through the pasta and serve garnished with basil leaves and sprinkled with pecorino cheese.

1

2

3

TIP You could also use conchiglie pasta for this dish.

Pot-roasted spatchcock with olives and thyme

SERVES 2 **PREPARATION TIME** 15 minutes **COOKING TIME** 45 minutes

2 spatchcocks (500 g/1 lb 2 oz each)

½ lemon

10 thyme sprigs

2 teaspoons olive oil

15 g (½ oz) butter

250 ml (9 fl oz/1 cup) good-quality ready-made or home-made chicken stock (see page 30)

1 fresh bay leaf

300 g (10½ oz) kipfler (fingerling) potatoes, washed, cut into large chunks

50 g (1¾ oz/¼ cup) kalamata olives

½ teaspoon red wine vinegar

Mixed leaf salad, to serve

1 Preheat the oven to 200°C (400°F/ Gas 6). Wash the spatchcocks briefly under cold running water and dry with paper towels. Halve the lemon and place a lemon quarter inside the cavity of each spatchcock along with 2 sprigs of thyme. Season the spatchcocks with salt and freshly ground black pepper, then truss (see page 21).

2 Heat the oil and butter in a large flameproof casserole dish over medium heat. Brown the spatchcocks for 8 minutes, turning occasionally so they brown evenly *(pic 1)*, then transfer to a plate. Remove the dish from the heat and wipe out any oil with paper towels.

3 Pour the stock into the casserole dish. Put the spatchcocks in the middle of the dish, along with any juices. Add the bay leaf and remaining thyme sprigs and then place the potatoes and olives around the spatchcocks *(pic 2)*. Put the casserole dish over medium heat and bring the liquid to the boil.

4 Cover the dish, put in the oven and cook for 30 minutes or until the spatchcocks are cooked through, the juices run clear when the spatchcocks are pierced through the thickest part (between the thigh and body), and the potatoes are tender.

5 Remove the string from the spatchcocks *(pic 3)* and then transfer to serving plates. Add the vinegar to the sauce in the casserole dish. Taste and season with salt and freshly ground black pepper, if desired (it shouldn't need a lot of salt as the olives will provide some). Spoon the potatoes, olives and sauce around the spatchcocks and serve with a mixed leaf salad.

1

2

3

Chicken with forty cloves of garlic

SERVES 4   **PREPARATION TIME** 15 minutes   **COOKING TIME** 1 hour 20 minutes

1.6 kg (3 lb 8 oz) whole chicken
1 tablespoon olive oil
20 g (¾ oz) butter
40 garlic cloves, unpeeled (see tip)
3 thyme sprigs
1 fresh bay leaf
310 ml (10¾ fl oz/1¼ cups)
 good-quality ready-made or
 home-made chicken stock
 (see page 30)
185 ml (6 fl oz/¾ cup) white wine
Mashed potato (see page 69) and
 steamed green beans, to serve

1 Preheat the oven to 200°C (400°F/ Gas 6). Wash the chicken briefly under cold running water, remove the neck and giblets and trim any pockets of fat. Pat the chicken dry with paper towels. Season the chicken, inside and out, with salt and freshly ground black pepper. Tie the legs together with kitchen string.

2 Heat the oil in a large heavy flameproof casserole dish over high heat. Add the butter. Cook the chicken for 8 minutes or until browned on all sides. Remove the chicken and discard the oil. Return the dish to the heat, add the garlic, thyme and bay leaf and stir well. Return the chicken to the casserole dish, breast side up, with the stock and wine *(pic 1)*. Bring the liquid to a simmer.

3 Cover the dish, put in the oven and cook for 40 minutes. Remove the lid and cook for a further 15 minutes or until the chicken is cooked through, the juices run clear when the chicken is pierced through the thickest part (between the thigh and body) and the skin is golden. Remove the chicken and half the garlic cloves. Cover loosely with foil to keep warm *(pic 2)*.

4 Put the dish over medium–high heat. Press the remaining garlic with a potato masher to extract the flesh *(pic 3)*. Bring the sauce to the boil and cook for about 5 minutes or until reduced to 185 ml (6 fl oz/¾ cup). Pass through a fine sieve, pressing down on the garlic skins to extract as much flesh as possible. Stir in the reserved garlic.

5 Carve the chicken (see page 26) and drizzle with the sauce. Serve with the mashed potato and green beans.

1

2

3

TIP You will need about 4 garlic bulbs for this recipe. It is a large amount, but don't worry, the garlic has a far more subtle flavour once it's been cooked.

Braising tips

1 Braising involves cooking meat or poultry slowly in liquid, which softens the connective tissues that make meat tough. This method of cooking is particularly well suited to cuts of meat from around the shoulder, neck, breast and leg. The muscles in these parts of the animal work the hardest so they have a coarse grain and high amounts of collagen and elastin.

2 Choose a saucepan or casserole dish with a heavy base, as this will conduct heat evenly and gently. Cast-iron, either coated or not, is ideal as it is a slow conductor of heat and can easily keep the contents at a slow, gentle heat.

3 The meat or poultry is browned, sometimes lightly dusted in flour, before braising in order to seal it so that it can maintain moisture during the long cooking. Browning also forms a flavoursome crust. Make sure the meat or poultry is dry before browning and don't overcrowd the pan.

4 Braises use aromatics for flavour, such as garlic, herbs, perhaps spices such as a cinnamon stick and/or strips of citrus zest. Vegetables, such as carrots, onions and celery, add sweetness and body to the sauce. The cooking liquid is generally stock or wine or a combination of the two, and this should cover the meat or poultry and any vegetables.

5 Braises can be cooked on the stovetop or in the oven, but in either case the liquid should be held at a very gentle simmer. Do not allow it to boil or the meat will be tough and dry. Use a large spoon to skim any fat or impurities that rise to the surface of a braise during cooking.

6 Braises are ideal dishes to cook ahead of time, in fact many taste better the next day after the flavours have melded. They often freeze well, too.

7 When the meat is tender, remove it from the pan and boil the liquid to reduce it. Use a spoon to remove the excess fat from the surface. Drawing a piece of paper towel over the surface of the finished sauce will absorb any remaining fat. Return the meat to the sauce and reheat gently.

Braised rabbit with cider and apples

Farmed rabbits are available from most butchers, but they may need to be ordered in for you so allow time for this. Ask your butcher to cut the rabbit into portions for this dish.

SERVES 4–6 **PREPARATION TIME** 30 minutes **COOKING TIME** 1 hour 50 minutes–2 hours

2 tablespoons olive oil

1.4 kg (3 lb 2 oz) farmed rabbit,
 cut into 8 pieces

1 large leek, white part only, sliced into
 1 cm (½ inch) thick rounds

200 g (7 oz) button mushrooms,
 trimmed

2 green apples, peeled, cored and
 cut into 6 wedges each

600 g (1 lb 5 oz) potatoes, peeled,
 halved and cut into 5 cm
 (2 inch) pieces

3 thyme sprigs, plus extra, to garnish

3 sage leaves

3 juniper berries, crushed

500 ml (17 fl oz/2 cups) dry cider

Toasted sourdough bread and
 mixed leaf salad, to serve

1 Preheat the oven to 180°C (350°F/ Gas 4). Heat the oil in a 2 litre (70 fl oz/ 8 cup) heavy-based casserole dish over high heat and cook the rabbit, in batches, for 6–8 minutes, until browned all over. Transfer to a plate *(pic 1)* and set aside.

2 Reduce the heat to medium, add the leek and mushrooms to the casserole and cook, stirring occasionally, for 5–6 minutes, until the leeks are soft and the mushrooms are lightly browned. Add the apples *(pic 2)* and potatoes and stir to coat with the leek mixture. Stir in the herbs, juniper berries and cider and season to taste. Increase the heat to high and bring to the boil.

3 Return the rabbit to the casserole *(pic 3)*, cover and braise in the oven, turning the rabbit once, for 1½ hours or until the rabbit is tender. Taste and adjust the seasoning, if necessary.

4 Serve in shallow bowls, garnished with the extra thyme sprigs and accompanied by toasted sourdough and a mixed leaf salad, if desired.

1

2

3

TIP You can substitute chicken pieces for the rabbit in this dish, however the cooking time will need to be reduced to 1 hour.

Pea and ham soup

An oldie but a goodie, pea and ham soup is quintessential comfort food. It was originally a pauper's dish made solely of dried peas, but meat is now a mainstay and can be ham, bacon or even sausages. In Scandinavia it is commonly served with rye bread, which makes a great match.

SERVES 6   **PREPARATION TIME** 20 minutes   **COOKING TIME** 1 hour 40 minutes

1.2 kg (2 lb 11 oz) ham hock
660 g (1 lb 7 oz/3 cups) dried split
   green peas
1 onion, chopped
2 garlic cloves, chopped
1 bay leaf
⅓ cup finely chopped mint
3 teaspoons finely grated orange zest

1 Place the ham, split peas, onion, garlic and bay leaf in a large saucepan *(pic 1)*. Add 2.5 litres (87 fl oz/10 cups) water to the pan and bring to the boil over medium–high heat. Reduce the heat to low and simmer, covered, for 1½ hours or until the split peas are soft.

2 Use tongs to transfer the ham to a chopping board. Remove the bay leaf. Use a hand-held blender to purée the pea mixture until smooth *(pic 2)*.

3 When the ham hock is cool enough to handle, use a sharp knife to remove the meat from the ham bone, discarding the skin and bone, then coarsely chop the meat *(pic 3)*. Return the meat to the pan and season the soup with freshly ground black pepper.

4 Combine the mint and orange zest in a small bowl. Serve the soup sprinkled with the mint and orange zest.

1

2

3

TIP Only season with pepper, as the ham is quite salty.
   This soup will thicken upon standing. Add a little water to thin it down, if desired.
   The soup can be frozen in an airtight container for up to 1 month.

Beef braised in Guinness

Guinness, the famous Irish stout beer, is used in this rich, hearty braise to give a fantastic weight and depth to the sauce, while the long, slow cooking ensures the beef is beautifully tender.

SERVES 4–6   **PREPARATION TIME** 20 minutes   **COOKING TIME** 2 hours 55 minutes

1.3 kg (3 lb) boneless chuck steak or
   other stewing beef, cut into 4–5 cm
   (1½–2 inch) pieces
2 tablespoons vegetable oil
20 g (¾ oz) butter
250 g (9 oz) pancetta or bacon, chopped
2 brown onions, cut into 2 cm
   (¾ inch) pieces
2 carrots, peeled and cut into 1.5 cm
   (⅝ inch) pieces
2 celery stalks, cut into 1.5 cm
   (⅝ inch) pieces
2 garlic cloves, chopped
2 tablespoons plain (all-purpose) flour
435 ml (15¼ fl oz/1¾ cups) Guinness
750 ml (26 fl oz/3 cups) good-quality
   ready-made or home-made beef
   stock (see page 60)
1 tablespoon dijon mustard
1 tablespoon thyme leaves,
   plus extra, to garnish
650 g (1 lb 7 oz) new potatoes (see tip)

1 Season the beef with salt and pepper. Heat 1 tablespoon of the oil and the butter in a heavy flameproof casserole dish over medium–high heat. Add half the beef and cook, turning occasionally, for 4–5 minutes or until browned *(pic 1)*. Use a slotted spoon to transfer to a bowl and set aside. Repeat to brown the remaining beef. Add the pancetta or bacon to the casserole dish and cook, stirring often, for 2–3 minutes or until browned. Add to the beef.

2 Add the remaining oil and the onions to the casserole dish and cook, stirring often, for 4 minutes or until golden. Add the carrots and celery and cook, stirring often, for a further 2 minutes or until the onions are dark golden *(pic 2)*. Add the garlic and cook, stirring, for 1 minute more. Add the flour and cook, stirring, for 1 minute. Add half the Guinness to the casserole dish and stir, scraping any caramelisation from the base of the pan. Add the remaining Guinness *(pic 3)*, the stock, mustard and thyme. Return the beef and pancetta or bacon to the pan with any juices, increase the heat to high and bring to a simmer. Skim any fat from the surface.

3 Reduce the heat to very low (you may need to use a simmer pad) and cover. Simmer, stirring occasionally, for 1½ hours or until the beef is tender.

4 Cut the potatoes in half (or thirds, if large) and add to the casserole dish. Cook, uncovered, for a further 1 hour or until the potatoes are tender. Taste and adjust the seasoning and serve garnished with the extra thyme leaves.

1

2

3

TIP You can substitute sweet potato, peeled and cut into 3 cm (1¼ inch) chunks for the new potatoes, if desired.

Braised pork chops

Browning the pork on the stovetop and finishing it in the oven makes it wonderfully tender. Be careful not to burn yourself when finishing the sauce, it's easy to forget that the pan is hot. If you do not have a large ovenproof frying pan, you can use a large ovenproof saucepan instead.

SERVES 4   **PREPARATION TIME** 15 minutes   **COOKING TIME** 35 minutes

25 g (1 oz) butter
1 tablespoon vegetable oil
2 apples, peeled, cored and cut into
    6 wedges each
3 celery stalks, trimmed and thickly
    sliced on the diagonal (see tip)
4 pork chops (1 kg/2 lb 4 oz), excess fat
    trimmed, at room temperature
160 ml (5¼ fl oz/⅔ cup) apple cider
2 tablespoons thickened (whipping)
    cream
1 teaspoon cognac
Chives, to garnish
Mashed potato (see page 69), to serve

1 Preheat the oven to 200°C (400°F/ Gas 6). Heat the butter and half the oil in a large, deep ovenproof frying pan over medium heat. Cook the apples, turning occasionally, for 12 minutes or until browned all over and just tender *(pic 1)*. Transfer to a bowl. Add the celery to the pan and cook, stirring often, for 8 minutes, until softened. Add to the apples.

2 Heat the remaining oil in the pan and increase the heat to medium–high. Season the pork with salt and pepper. Cook the pork *(pic 2)*, in batches, for 1 minute each side, until well browned. Transfer to a plate.

3 Add the cider to the pan *(pic 3)* and bring to the boil, scraping any caramelisation from the base of the pan. Return the pork to the pan with the celery and apples, turning to coat in the sauce. Place the pan in the oven and cook for 8 minutes, until the pork is just cooked through.

4 Transfer the pork to a plate and cover loosely with foil to keep warm. Place the pan over medium–high heat and bring the sauce to the boil. Boil for 3 minutes, until the sauce thickens. Stir in the cream until combined. Remove from the heat and stir in the cognac.

5 Serve the pork drizzled with the sauce, garnished with chives and accompanied by the mashed potato.

1

2

3

TIP You could replace the celery with 1 fennel bulb, trimmed and cut into 8 thick slices, if you like.

Middle Eastern meatballs

The combination of lamb, cinnamon, cumin and fresh coriander gives these meatballs a fabulous flavour, which is complemented perfectly by a tomato sauce sweetened with honey and currants.

SERVES 4   **PREPARATION TIME** 25 minutes (+ 15 minutes chilling)   **COOKING TIME** 30 minutes

600 g (1 lb 5 oz) minced (ground) lamb
4 spring onions (scallions), trimmed
    and thinly sliced
½ teaspoon ground cinnamon,
    plus ¼ teaspoon, extra
1 teaspoon ground cumin
¼ cup chopped coriander (cilantro)
    leaves, plus whole coriander leaves,
    extra, to garnish
30 g (1 oz/½ cup, lightly packed) fresh
    white breadcrumbs
1 egg
2 tablespoons olive oil
1 onion, finely chopped
2 garlic cloves, crushed
2 x 400 g (14 oz) tins chopped tomatoes
2 teaspoons honey
2 tablespoons currants
Couscous, prepared following packet
    instructions, to serve (see tip)

1 Place the lamb, spring onions, cinnamon, cumin, 2 tablespoons of the chopped coriander, the breadcrumbs and egg in a large bowl and use your hands to mix until well combined. Roll heaped tablespoons of the mixture into meatballs *(pic 1)* and place on a baking tray. Cover with plastic wrap and refrigerate for 15 minutes.

2 Heat half the oil in a large non-stick frying pan over medium heat. Add the onion and cook, stirring occasionally, for 5 minutes. Add the garlic and extra cinnamon and cook, stirring, for 1 minute. Stir in the tomatoes and simmer for 10 minutes or until thickened. Add the honey, currants and remaining chopped coriander *(pic 2)* and stir to combine.

3 Meanwhile, heat the remaining oil in another large non-stick frying pan over medium–high heat and cook the meatballs, in batches, for 2–3 minutes, until browned all over *(pic 3)*. (The meatballs do not need to be completely cooked through at this point.) Add the meatballs to the tomato mixture in a single layer and simmer gently for 10 minutes or until cooked through.

4 Serve the meatballs and sauce on a bed of couscous, garnished with the coriander leaves.

1

2

3

TIP The couscous can be replaced with burghul (bulgur), prepared following packet instructions, if you like.
    The meatballs and sauce can be frozen, once cooled, in airtight containers for up to 1 month.

Spiced lamb shanks with saffron, cinnamon and dates

SERVES 4 **PREPARATION TIME** 25 minutes **COOKING TIME** 2 hours 25–55 minutes

2 tablespoons olive oil

4 large lamb shanks, frenched
  (see page 55)

2 onions, thinly sliced

3 garlic cloves, thinly sliced

1 tablespoon grated ginger

1 tablespoon sweet paprika

2 teaspoons ground cinnamon

¼ teaspoon saffron threads, soaked in
  2 tablespoons boiling water

500 ml (17 fl oz/2 cups) good-quality
  ready-made or home-made chicken
  or veal stock (see pages 30 or 60)

400 g (14 oz) tin chopped tomatoes

85 g (3 oz/½ cup) halved and
  pitted dates

Couscous, prepared following packet
  instructions, to serve

Coriander (cilantro) leaves, to garnish

1 Preheat the oven to 150°C (300°F/
Gas 2). Heat 1 tablespoon of the oil in a
large flameproof casserole dish over high
heat. Cook the lamb shanks, in batches
if necessary, for 8 minutes or until
browned all over *(pic 1)*. Transfer to a
plate and set aside.

2 Add the remaining oil and the onions
to the casserole dish, reduce the heat
to medium and cook, stirring, for
5 minutes or until the onion is softened.
Add the garlic, ginger, paprika and
cinnamon and cook, stirring, for
1 minute or until aromatic. Return
the lamb to the casserole dish with the
saffron liquid, stock, tomatoes and dates
(pic 2). Stir to combine, then increase
the heat to high and bring to the boil.

3 Cover the casserole dish and braise
in the oven for 2–2½ hours or until the
lamb is very tender and beginning to fall
off the bone *(pic 3)*. Use a large spoon
to skim any fat from the surface and
season with sea salt and freshly ground
black pepper, to taste. Serve the lamb
shanks and sauce on a bed of couscous,
garnished with coriander leaves.

TIP This dish can be made
up to 2 days ahead and stored
in an airtight container in the
refrigerator. Reheat in a large
saucepan over medium heat.
  It can also be frozen, once
cooled, in airtight containers for
up to 1 month.

Veal ragù with pappardelle

This dish is so easy — it's a great choice for a dinner party as you can make the ragù ahead of time, then the only thing you have to think about is cooking the pasta. The result is rustic and rewarding.

SERVES 6 **PREPARATION TIME** 10 minutes (+ 20 minutes soaking) **COOKING TIME** 2 hours 15 minutes

5 g (⅛ oz) dried porcini mushrooms

4 veal shanks (about 1.1 kg/2 lb 7 oz)

1 tablespoon plain (all-purpose) flour

2½ tablespoons olive oil

2 brown onions, chopped

3 garlic cloves, finely chopped

1 tablespoon finely chopped rosemary

250 ml (9 fl oz/1 cup) red wine

500 ml (17 fl oz/2 cups) good-quality
  ready-made or home-made beef
  stock (see page 60)

400 g (14 oz) tin chopped tomatoes

60 g (2¼ oz/¼ cup) tomato paste
  (concentrated purée)

¼ cup flat-leaf (Italian) parsley,
  chopped

500 g (1 lb 2 oz) home-made or
  ready-made herb or plain pappardelle

1

1 Preheat the oven to 200°C (400°F/ Gas 6). Cover the porcini with 80 ml (2½ fl oz/⅓ cup) boiling water and set aside for 20 minutes. Strain, reserving the soaking liquid and discarding any gritty residue.

2 Meanwhile, season the veal shanks with sea salt and freshly ground black pepper, then dust with flour *(pic 1)*.

3 Heat the oil in a large flameproof casserole dish over medium heat. Brown the shanks on each side for 2–3 minutes or until golden brown all over *(pic 2)*. Remove and set aside.

4 Reduce the heat to low, add the onions and cook, stirring often, for 3 minutes or until softened. Add the garlic and rosemary and cook, stirring,

for 2 minutes or until light golden. Add half the red wine to the dish *(pic 3)*, increase the heat to medium and bring to the boil, scraping the base of the dish to dislodge any caramelised bits.

5 Add the remaining wine, the stock, tomatoes, tomato paste, porcini and their soaking liquid and stir to combine. Return the shanks and any juices to the casserole dish. Bring to a simmer, cover and cook in the oven for 1 hour.

6 Remove the casserole dish from the oven and turn the shanks. Return to the oven for 1 hour, or until the meat is falling from the bones. Remove the shanks from the liquid, place on a chopping board and use two forks to shred the meat into chunks (discarding any fat and sinew). Remove any marrow from the bones and reserve.

7 Return the meat and marrow to the casserole dish and place over low heat. Season with salt and pepper, to taste, and stir through half the parsley.

8 Meanwhile, cook the pasta in a large saucepan of boiling salted water, following the packet instructions, until *al dente*; drain. Serve with the ragù, garnished with the remaining parsley.

2

3

TIP You might need to order the veal shanks in advance from your butcher.

Chilli con carne

Although it originated in America's southwest, with the states of Texas, New Mexico and Arizona all claiming it as their own, there's no doubt this popular dish was influenced by Mexican cuisine. This version uses minced beef, but chuck or gravy beef can be used for a chunkier result.

SERVES 6   **PREPARATION TIME** 15 minutes   **COOKING TIME** 55 minutes

2 teaspoons olive oil
1 chorizo sausage, halved lengthways, thickly sliced
100 g (3½ oz) speck or bacon, rind removed, cut into batons
1 onion, diced
1 fresh bay leaf
500 g (1 lb 2 oz) minced (ground) beef
1 tablespoon ground cumin
2 teaspoons ground coriander
1½ teaspoons dried oregano
3 garlic cloves, crushed
4 x 400 g (14 oz) tins red kidney beans, drained and rinsed
2 x 400 g (14 oz) tins chopped tomatoes
Soft tortillas, sour cream and Tabasco sauce, to serve

GUACAMOLE
2 ripe avocados, halved, stones removed
1 ripe tomato, diced
2 tablespoons finely chopped coriander (cilantro) leaves, plus whole coriander leaves, extra, to garnish
1 tablespoon lemon juice
8 dashes Tabasco sauce (or to taste)

1 To make the guacamole, place the avocado flesh in a medium bowl and use a fork to mash until smooth *(pic 1)*. Stir in the tomato, coriander and lemon juice. Add the Tabasco sauce and season with salt and freshly ground black pepper, to taste. Cover with plastic wrap until ready to serve.

2 Heat the oil in a large saucepan over medium–high heat. Cook the chorizo and speck or bacon, stirring often, for 5 minutes, until browned *(pic 2)*. Use a slotted spoon to transfer to a bowl and set aside. Reduce the heat to medium, add the onion and bay leaf to the pan and cook, stirring, for 5 minutes, until the onion is softened.

3 Increase the heat to high. Add the beef and cook, stirring to break up any lumps, for 2 minutes or until browned *(pic 3)*. Add the cumin, coriander, oregano and garlic and cook, stirring, until aromatic. Return the chorizo mixture to the pan with the kidney beans, tomatoes and 80 ml (2½ fl oz/ ⅓ cup) water. Season with salt and pepper and stir well. Bring to the boil, then reduce the heat to low and simmer, covered, for 40 minutes, until the beef is cooked through and the flavours have intensified.

4 Serve with tortillas, sour cream, Tabasco sauce and the guacamole, garnished with the extra coriander.

1

2

3

TIP The chilli con carne can be frozen, once cooled, in airtight containers for up to 1 month.

Slow-cooked lamb shoulder with chorizo and white beans

This dish can be cooked a day ahead and reheated in a casserole dish, covered, in a 180°C (350°F/Gas 4) oven for 20 minutes — the flavours will only improve and the lamb will still be wonderfully tender.

SERVES 4 **PREPARATION TIME** 25 minutes **COOKING TIME** 4 hours 10 minutes

2 tablespoons chopped rosemary

2 tablespoons chopped oregano

1 tablespoon chopped thyme

2 garlic cloves, chopped

1 teaspoon fennel seeds

60 ml (2 fl oz/¼ cup) olive oil

1 kg (2 lb 4 oz) boned shoulder of lamb (see tip)

2 chorizo sausages, cut into 1 cm (½ inch) thick slices (see tip)

125 ml (4 fl oz/½ cup) dry white wine

125 ml (4 fl oz/½ cup) good-quality ready-made or home-made chicken or veal stock (see pages 30 or 60)

2 x 400 g (14 oz) tins cannellini beans, drained and rinsed

PARSLEY PUREE

1 cup firmly-packed flat-leaf (Italian) parsley leaves

2 garlic cloves, chopped

2 tablespoons lemon juice

1 teaspoon dijon mustard

60 ml (2 fl oz/¼ cup) olive oil

1 To make the parsley purée, put all the ingredients in a food processor (*pic 1*) and process until smooth. Season with salt and pepper, to taste. Cover with plastic wrap and set aside.

2 Preheat the oven to 130°C (250°F/ Gas 1). Put the rosemary, oregano, thyme, garlic and fennel seeds in a small food processor and process until finely chopped. Add 2 tablespoons of the oil, season with salt and pepper and process until a paste forms. Place the lamb on a large plate and brush all over with the paste (*pic 2*).

3 Heat the remaining oil in a 2 litre (70 fl oz/8 cup) heavy-based flameproof casserole dish over medium heat and cook the chorizo for 2–3 minutes, until browned on both sides. Transfer to a plate, then drain the oil from the casserole dish.

4 Place the lamb in the casserole dish and pour in the wine and stock (*pic 3*). Bring to the boil over high heat, then return the chorizo to the casserole dish, cover and cook in the oven for 3 hours.

5 Remove the lamb from the oven and stir in the cannellini beans, then cover and bake for a further 1 hour. Transfer the lamb to a chopping board and carve into serving portions.

6 Place lamb in shallow serving bowls, spoon chorizo and cannellini mixture over and top with the parsley puree.

1

2

3

TIP Ask your butcher to bone a shoulder of lamb for you.
Chorizo sausages vary from mild to hot. Use whichever you prefer.

Veal goulash with herb dumplings

Goulash is a type of stew that originated in Hungary and generally contains veal, beef or lamb, seasoned with paprika. Paprika adds colour and flavour to dishes and varies from mild to hot. Sweet mild paprika is used in this dish.

SERVES 4   **PREPARATION TIME** 30 minutes   **COOKING TIME** 2 hours 30 minutes

60 ml (2 fl oz/¼ cup) olive oil

1 kg (2 lb 4 oz) veal shoulder or stewing veal, cut into 3 cm (1¼ inch) pieces

1 onion, chopped

1 red capsicum (pepper), seeded and chopped

2 garlic cloves, chopped

1 teaspoon caraway seeds, crushed

1 tablespoon sweet paprika

250 ml (9 fl oz/1 cup) dry white wine

375 ml (13 fl oz/1½ cups) good-quality ready-made or home-made chicken or veal stock (see pages 30 or 60)

400 g (14 oz) tin chopped tomatoes

2 bay leaves

4 thyme sprigs

Sour cream and rocket (arugula) salad, to serve

HERB DUMPLINGS

300 g (10½ oz/2 cups) self-raising flour

60 g (2¼ oz) butter, chopped

2 tablespoons chopped flat-leaf (Italian) parsley

2 tablespoons snipped chives

185 ml (6 fl oz/¾ cup) milk

1 Preheat the oven to 160°C (315°F/ Gas 2–3). Heat 2 tablespoons of the oil in a 2 litre (70 fl oz/8 cup) heavy-based flameproof casserole dish over high heat. Cook the veal, in batches, for 6–8 minutes or until evenly browned all over *(pic 1)*. Transfer to a bowl and set aside.

2 Heat the remaining oil in the casserole dish over low heat, add the onion and capsicum and cook, covered, for 6–8 minutes or until softened. Add the garlic, caraway seeds and paprika and cook, stirring, for 1 minute.

3 Increase the heat to high and add the wine, stock, tomatoes, bay leaves and thyme. Season with salt and pepper and bring to the boil, then reduce the heat to low and simmer for 5 minutes. Return the veal to the casserole dish, cover and braise in the oven for 1 hour.

4 Meanwhile, to make the herb dumplings, put the flour in a bowl and season with salt. Use your fingertips to rub in the butter until the mixture resembles coarse breadcrumbs. Add the herbs and milk and use a flat-bladed knife to mix *(pic 2)*, using a cutting action, to form a soft dough. Gather the dough together and shape into a smooth ball. Divide into 8 equal portions and roll each portion into a ball.

5 Place the dumplings on top of the veal goulash *(pic 3)*. Cover and bake for a further 1 hour. Serve the veal goulash and dumplings with sour cream and a rocket salad.

1

2

3

> **TIP** Instead of dumplings, you can serve veal goulash with buttered noodles or mashed potato (see page 69).
>
> These dumplings can be placed on a lamb or beef casserole for the final hour of cooking.

Corned beef with parsley sauce

SERVES 6 **PREPARATION TIME** 15 minutes **COOKING TIME** 1 hour 40 minutes

1 kg (2 lb 4 oz) piece corned beef
1 tablespoon light brown sugar
1 tablespoon red wine vinegar
5 whole cloves
2 fresh bay leaves
Stems from 1 bunch parsley
½ teaspoon black peppercorns
1 kg (2 lb 4 oz) new potatoes
2 bunches baby carrots, stems trimmed
　(pic 1)
450 g (1 lb) green beans, trimmed

PARSLEY SAUCE
50 g (1¾ oz) butter
2 tablespoons plain (all-purpose) flour
435 ml (15¼ fl oz/1¾ cups) milk,
　warmed
2 tablespoons finely chopped flat-leaf
　(Italian) parsley
Pinch of freshly grated nutmeg
White pepper, to taste (see tip)

1 Rinse the beef and place in a large saucepan with the sugar, vinegar, cloves, bay leaves, parsley stems and peppercorns *(pic 2)*. Add enough water to cover the beef completely.

2 Bring to the boil over high heat, then reduce the heat to low and gently simmer, covered, for 1½ hours or until a skewer inserted into the beef is easily removed (see tip). Remove the saucepan from the heat and leave the beef in the hot liquid until ready to serve.

3 Meanwhile, cook the potatoes in a steamer basket over a saucepan of boiling water for 12 minutes, until cooked through. Cook the carrots and beans in a metal steamer basket over a saucepan of boiling water for 5 minutes or until just tender.

4 To make the parsley sauce, melt the butter in a medium saucepan over medium heat. Add the flour and cook, stirring, for 1 minute, until pale and bubbling. Gradually whisk in the milk *(pic 3)* until the sauce is smooth. Cook, stirring constantly, for 2–3 minutes, until the sauce boils and thickens. Remove from the heat. Stir in the parsley and nutmeg and season with salt and white pepper.

5 Thinly carve the beef and serve with the parsley sauce and vegetables.

1

2

3

TIP White pepper is preferable for aesthetic purposes, to keep the sauce clear of black specks. However, black pepper can be substituted, if desired.
　The cooking time will vary according to the cut and age of the meat, so begin testing after 1 hour of cooking. Ensure the bubbles are barely breaking the surface when simmering, as boiling will make the beef tough.

Slow-braised goat with rosemary and fennel

Goat is a very lean meat that needs to be cooked gently for a long time or it tends to dry out and become tough. Adding stock and wine to the pan and then covering it helps ensure the goat remains moist, as the meat steams while it is roasting.

SERVES 4–6   **PREPARATION TIME** 15 minutes (+ 10 minutes resting)   **COOKING TIME** 4 hours 30 minutes

1 tablespoon fennel seeds

1 tablespoon chopped rosemary, plus
  rosemary sprigs, extra, to garnish

1 teaspoon sea salt

2 kg (4 lb 8 oz) goat shoulder
  (on the bone), jointed (ask your
  butcher to do this)

2 tablespoons olive oil

1 lemon, juiced

250 ml (9 fl oz/1 cup) good-quality
  ready-made or home-made chicken
  stock (see page 30)

125 ml (4 fl oz/½ cup) white wine

700 g (1 lb 9 oz) all-purpose potatoes,
  peeled and quartered

8 garlic cloves, unpeeled

1 Preheat the oven to 150°C (300°F/ Gas 2). Use a mortar and pestle to pound the fennel seeds, chopped rosemary and salt until crushed. Place the goat in a large roasting pan and rub with the fennel mixture, then drizzle with the oil *(pic 1)*. Pour the lemon juice, stock and wine into the pan.

2 Cover the pan with non-stick baking paper and then foil *(pic 2)*. This is important to help keep the goat moist. Braise in the oven for 3½ hours, then add the potatoes and garlic cloves to the pan *(pic 3)*, cover with the baking paper and foil again and cook for a further 1 hour or until the meat is very tender and the potatoes are cooked through.

3 Remove the pan from the oven, cover loosely with foil and set aside for 10 minutes to rest. Carve the goat (the meat should be so tender that it can be flaked with a fork). Serve with the potatoes, garlic to squeeze out of the cloves, any pan juices spooned over and rosemary sprigs, to garnish.

1

2

3

Beef cheeks braised in red wine

This is a great dish for winter entertaining, as it's guaranteed to impress and is easy to make in larger quantities. Beef is often braised in red wine, but using beef cheeks for the cut of meat gives an exceptionally tender result. You may need to order the beef cheeks in advance from your butcher.

SERVES 4–6   **PREPARATION TIME** 30 minutes (+ overnight marinating)   **COOKING TIME** 4–4½ hours

6 untrimmed beef cheeks (about 2 kg/
   4 lb 8 oz), fat and sinew trimmed
330 ml (11¼ fl oz/1⅓ cups) full-bodied
   red wine (see tip)
6 garlic cloves, peeled
12 thyme sprigs
1 orange, quartered
10 black peppercorns
6 juniper berries
1½ tablespoons vegetable oil
200 g (7 oz) pancetta or thickly sliced
   bacon, cut into lardons
2 large brown onions, cut into wedges
1.16 litres (40¼ fl oz/4⅔ cups)
   good-quality ready-made or
   home-made beef stock (see page 60)
1½ tablespoons tomato paste
   (concentrated purée)
3 carrots, peeled and quartered
1½ tablespoons finely chopped parsley
1 kg (2 lb 4 oz) sweet potato,
   peeled and chopped
50 g (1¾ oz) butter
60 ml (2 fl oz/¼ cup) thin
   (pouring/whipping) cream
Steamed greens, to serve

1 Combine the beef cheeks, wine, garlic, thyme, orange and spices in a glass or ceramic bowl *(pic 1)*. Cover with plastic wrap and refrigerate overnight.

2 Preheat the oven to 160°C (315°F/Gas 2–3). Drain the beef cheeks in a colander set over a bowl. Reserve the liquid and solids. Tie the peppercorns and juniper berries in a piece of muslin. Pat the beef dry with paper towels and season with salt and pepper. Heat half the oil in a flameproof casserole dish over medium–high heat. Cook half the beef for 1–2 minutes each side or until well browned *(pic 2)*. Transfer to a plate. Add the remaining oil and repeat to brown the remaining beef. Set aside.

3 Add the pancetta or bacon and the onions to the casserole dish and cook, stirring occasionally, for 3 minutes or until golden. Add the reserved marinade liquid *(pic 3)*, bring to the boil and boil, scraping any caramelisation from the base of the pan, for 1 minute. Add the stock, tomato paste, beef cheeks and any juices and stir well. Add the carrots, reserved marinade solids and muslin parcel. Cover and bake for 3½ hours. Insert a skewer into the beef cheeks; if it comes out easily, they are cooked. If not, return to the oven for 30 minutes more.

4 Remove and discard the muslin parcel, orange pieces and thyme stems. Use a slotted spoon to carefully transfer the beef cheeks, carrots, onion, pancetta or bacon and garlic to a warmed serving dish. Cover and set aside.

5 Place the casserole dish over medium heat and bring the cooking liquid to the boil. Boil rapidly for 20–25 minutes or until reduced to about 500 ml (17 fl oz/ 2 cups). Stir through the parsley.

6 Meanwhile, cook the sweet potato in a saucepan of salted simmering water for 12–15 minutes or until tender. Drain, then return to the pan with the butter. Use a hand-held blender to blend until smooth. Stir in the cream and season. Serve the beef cheeks with the sauce, sweet potato mash and steamed greens.

TIP Use a good-quality red wine for this dish, one that you would be happy to drink with the meal.

Twice-cooked pork belly

This dish does require double the effort of most braises, as there are two separate cooking stages for the pork, but there's a good reason for this. The slow simmering in the stock imparts the flavours, while the deep-frying gives the pork an unbeatable crunch.

SERVES 4   **PREPARATION TIME** 25 minutes (+ 45 minutes cooling and overnight chilling)
COOKING TIME 2 hours 15 minutes

80 g (2¾ oz) snow peas (mangetout),
  trimmed
1 Lebanese (short) cucumber
30 g (1 oz/1 cup) watercress leaves
Vegetable oil, for deep-frying
Steamed rice, to serve

PORK BELLY STOCK

375 ml (13 fl oz/1½ cups) soy sauce
375 ml (13 fl oz/1½ cups) Chinese
  rice wine
175 g (6 oz/¾ cup) yellow rock sugar
  (see tip)
10 cm (4 inch) piece ginger
4 garlic cloves, sliced
6 star anise
4 cinnamon sticks
4 pieces dried mandarin peel (see tip)
1 kg (2 lb 4 oz) piece boneless pork belly
  (from the thicker part of the belly)

DRESSING

60 ml (2 fl oz/¼ cup) kecap manis
60 ml (2 fl oz/¼ cup) light soy sauce
60 ml (2 fl oz/¼ cup) rice wine vinegar
1 spring onion (scallion), thinly sliced

1 To make the pork belly stock, put 2.25 litres (79 fl oz/9 cups) water in a saucepan that will be wide enough to fit the pork belly. Add the soy sauce, rice wine, sugar, ginger, garlic, star anise, cinnamon and mandarin peel. Bring to the boil over high heat, then reduce the heat to low and simmer gently for 30 minutes.

2 Carefully add the pork belly to the pan, skin side up *(pic 1)*, and simmer gently for 1½ hours. Remove from the heat and set aside for 45 minutes, until

the pork belly is cool enough to handle. Remove the pork belly from the stock and place, skin side down, on a baking tray lined with plastic wrap. Place another tray on top and weigh down with a heavy object such as a granite mortar *(pic 2)* or even a couple of bricks. Cool to room temperature, then refrigerate overnight.

3 To make the dressing, combine all the ingredients in a small bowl. Set aside.

4 Cook the snow peas in a saucepan of boiling salted water for 30 seconds, then refresh in iced water, drain and shred. Halve the cucumber lengthways and scrape out the seeds with a teaspoon, then cut in half again and thinly slice. Toss the watercress, cucumber and snow peas together. Refrigerate until required.

5 Use paper towels to wipe away any jelly or moisture from the pork belly, then cut in half. Cut each portion into 4 thick slices *(pic 3)*. Fill a large, deep heavy-based saucepan one-third full of oil and heat to 180°C (350°F) or until a cube of bread dropped into the oil turns golden brown in 15 seconds. Deep-fry the pork belly, in batches, for 3 minutes or until golden and crisp. Be careful, as the oil will spit when you first add the pork — cover with a metal wire shield if you have one or stand well clear of the pan. Transfer the pork to paper towels to drain.

6 Serve the pork belly with steamed rice, topped with the salad and drizzled with the dressing.

1

2

3

> **TIP** Rock sugar and dried mandarin peel are both available from Asian supermarkets. White sugar and fresh mandarin peel, respectively, can be substituted if necessary.

Stewing, Casseroling and Curries

Orange and mint chicken

SERVES 4   **PREPARATION TIME** 20 minutes   **COOKING TIME** 1 hour

1.8 kg (4 lb) whole chicken, cut
   into 8 pieces (see page 18)
1 tablespoon olive oil
50 g (1¾ oz) butter, cubed
1 brown onion, diced
2 garlic cloves, crushed
250 ml (9 fl oz/1 cup) good-quality
   ready-made or home-made
   chicken stock (see tip)
125 ml (4 fl oz/½ cup) strained
   freshly squeezed orange juice
1 cup finely chopped mint
¼ cup finely chopped coriander
   (cilantro) leaves
¼ cup finely chopped flat-leaf
   (Italian) parsley
2 teaspoons finely grated
   orange zest
Couscous, prepared following
   packet directions, to serve

1 Season the chicken with salt and pepper. Heat the oil and 20 g (¾ oz) of the butter in a large heavy-based flameproof casserole dish over high heat. Cook the chicken, in batches, for 8 minutes or until browned all over. Remove the chicken from the dish.

2 Add the onion to the casserole dish and cook over medium heat, stirring, for 8 minutes or until softened. Stir in the garlic and cook for 1 minute or until aromatic. Return the chicken to the casserole dish and add the stock *(pic 1)*. Stir well and bring to the boil. Reduce the heat to medium–low, cover and cook for 20 minutes or until the breast cuts are just cooked through.

3 Transfer the breast cuts to a plate, cover and set aside. Cook the remaining chicken pieces for a further 5 minutes or until cooked through.

4 Transfer the remaining chicken to the plate with the breast cuts *(pic 2)* and cover loosely with foil to keep warm.

5 Bring the sauce in the casserole dish to the boil over high heat and boil until reduced to 185 ml (6 fl oz/¾ cup). Add the orange juice and return to the boil. Gradually whisk in the remaining butter until it melts and the sauce thickens slightly *(pic 3)*. Remove from the heat.

6 Return the chicken to the pan with the herbs and zest, and toss to coat. Serve the chicken with couscous.

1

2

3

TIP Brown chicken stock (see page 30) would work really well in this recipe.

Coq au vin

It's hard to improve on this classic French dish, however the use of prosciutto, sage, anchovies, a good pinot noir and interesting mushrooms updates it perfectly. Cook the meat at a very gentle simmer — vigorous simmering or boiling will cause the meat to be tough and dry, no matter how long you cook it.

SERVES 4   **PREPARATION TIME** 30 minutes (+ 1 hour soaking)   **COOKING TIME** 1 hour 20 minutes

20 g (¾ oz/½ cup) dried porcini
    mushrooms
100 ml (3½ fl oz) extra virgin olive oil
3 garlic cloves, very thinly sliced
2 tablespoons chopped anchovy fillets
200 g (7 oz) prosciutto, in one piece,
    skin trimmed, cut into 2.5 cm
    (1 inch) long strips
2½ tablespoons tomato paste
    (concentrated purée)
¼ teaspoon ground cloves
1 fresh bay leaf
Small handful of sage leaves
1.5 kg (3 lb 5 oz) whole chicken, cut into
    8 pieces (see page 18)
50 g (1¾ oz/⅓ cup) plain (all-purpose)
    flour, seasoned, for dusting
500 ml (17 fl oz/2 cups) pinot noir or
    other soft red wine
250 ml (9 fl oz/1 cup) chicken stock
300 g (10½ oz) French shallots, peeled,
    large ones halved lengthways
150 g (5½ oz) king brown mushrooms,
    cleaned and sliced lengthways
150 g (5½ oz) chestnut mushrooms
Soft polenta or mashed potato (see
    page 69) and rocket (arugula) salad,
    to serve

1 Cover the porcini with 250 ml (9 fl oz/ 1 cup) of boiling water and set aside for 1 hour. Strain, reserving the soaking liquid and discarding any grit.

2 Heat 1 tablespoon of the oil in a large heavy-based ovenproof saucepan or flameproof casserole dish over medium heat. Cook the garlic, anchovies and prosciutto, stirring, for 4–5 minutes or until aromatic. Add the tomato paste and cloves and stir for 2 minutes *(pic 1)*. Add the bay leaf and sage.

3 Dust the chicken with the seasoned flour. Heat another 1 tablespoon of the oil in a large frying pan over medium heat and cook half the chicken pieces, turning once, for 5 minutes or until golden *(pic 2)*. Add to the prosciutto mixture in the saucepan. Repeat with the remaining chicken.

4 Add half the red wine to the frying pan and bring to the boil, scraping any caramelisation from the base of the pan *(pic 3)*. Add the remaining wine and bring to the boil, then add to the saucepan with the stock, porcini and soaking liquid. Bring to a simmer. Partially cover and cook over low heat for 45–50 minutes or until the chicken is very tender.

5 Meanwhile, preheat the oven to 190°C (375°F/Gas 5). Toss the shallots in 2 tablespoons of the oil. Put in a roasting pan and roast for 40 minutes or until deep golden and tender.

6 Skim the surface of the liquid in the pan to remove any excess fat and discard the bay leaf. Simmer for a further 10 minutes or until reduced slightly.

7 Heat the remaining 1 tablespoon of oil in a large frying pan over medium–high heat and cook the mushrooms, shaking the pan often, for 8 minutes or until golden and tender. Serve with the chicken, shallots and polenta or mashed potato, with the sauce generously drizzled over and accompanied by the rocket salad.

Creamy chicken casserole

This is real winter comfort food — flavoursome and filling. Use your favourite full-flavoured beer to personalise this dish and buy good-quality chicken thigh fillets.

SERVES 4–6   **PREPARATION TIME** 15 minutes   **COOKING TIME** 55 minutes

1 kg (2 lb 4 oz) skinless chicken thigh
   fillets, halved
75 g (2¾ oz/½ cup) plain (all-purpose)
   flour, seasoned, for dusting
80 ml (2½ fl oz/⅓ cup) vegetable oil
200 g (7 oz) Swiss brown mushrooms,
   cleaned and sliced
1 brown onion, finely diced
2 carrots, sliced
1 tablespoon gin
125 ml (4 fl oz/½ cup) beer
   (such as a pale ale)
350 ml (12 fl oz) white chicken stock
   (see page 30)
1 tablespoon thyme leaves
2 fresh bay leaves
65 g (2¼ oz/¼ cup) crème fraîche or
   sour light cream
1 tablespoon verjuice or riesling
1½ teaspoons wholegrain mustard
1 tablespoon chopped tarragon
Boiled potatoes, to serve

1 Dust the chicken with seasoned flour to lightly coat *(pic 1)*. Heat 1 tablespoon of the oil in a flameproof casserole dish over medium heat and cook half the chicken, turning once, for 5–8 minutes or until golden *(pic 2)*. Set aside. Repeat with the remaining chicken.

2 Heat another tablespoon of the oil and cook the mushrooms for 4 minutes or until golden. Set aside with the chicken. Heat the remaining oil and cook the onion and carrots for 5 minutes or until the onion is soft and translucent. Add the gin and flambé (see tip) *(pic 3)*.

3 Add the beer, stock, thyme and bay leaves to the dish, along with the chicken and mushrooms, and bring to a simmer. Partially cover and cook over low heat for 30 minutes or until the chicken is cooked through.

4 Stir through the crème fraîche, verjuice and mustard. Taste and adjust the seasoning, if necessary. Stir through the tarragon. Serve with boiled potatoes.

1

2

3

TIP When you flambé a dish, you ignite the alcohol to burn it off and give the dish a slightly singed flavour.

Chicken, apricot, pumpkin and chickpea tagine

SERVES 4   **PREPARATION TIME** 30 minutes   **COOKING TIME** 1 hour

2 tablespoons olive oil

1.7 kg (3 lb 12 oz) whole chicken,
cut into 8 pieces (see page 18)

3 garlic cloves, crushed

½ teaspoon saffron threads

1 teaspoon ground cumin

1 teaspoon ground ginger

6 cardamom pods, bruised

1 cinnamon stick

6 baby onions, peeled, leaving the root
end intact, halved lengthways

155 g (5½ oz/1 cup) dried apricots

1½ tablespoons honey

1½ tablespoons lemon juice

400 g (14 oz) tin chickpeas,
drained and rinsed

875 ml (30 fl oz/3½ cups) good-quality
ready-made or home-made chicken
stock (see page 30)

750 g (1 lb 10 oz) jap pumpkin (winter
squash), peeled, seeded and cut into
5 cm (2 inch) pieces

Chopped pistachios and coriander
(cilantro) leaves, to garnish

Couscous, prepared following packet
directions, and harissa, to serve

1 Heat 1 tablespoon of the oil in a large heavy-based saucepan over medium–high heat and cook the chicken pieces, in batches, for 4 minutes each side or until well browned. Transfer to a plate and set aside.

2 Add the remaining oil, the garlic and the spices to the saucepan and cook over medium heat, stirring, for 2–3 minutes or until the spices are aromatic and the garlic has softened slightly *(pic 1)*.

3 Return the chicken to the pan with the onions, apricots, honey, lemon juice and chickpeas. Add the stock *(pic 2)* — the mixture should only just be covered; add a little more stock or water if necessary. Season with sea salt and freshly ground black pepper. Place the pumpkin on top of the mixture *(pic 3)*, then bring to a gentle simmer. Reduce the heat to low, cover the pan and cook the tagine for 35–45 minutes or until the chicken and pumpkin are tender.

4 Serve sprinkled with the pistachios and coriander and accompanied by the couscous, with harissa passed separately.

1

2

3

Duck maryland, potato and vegetable stew

SERVES 4 **PREPARATION TIME** 15 minutes **COOKING TIME** 2 hours

4 x 280 g (10 oz) duck marylands

1 tablespoon olive oil

1½ brown onions, roughly chopped

2 carrots, cut into 2 cm (¾ inch) pieces

3 celery stalks, trimmed, cut into 2 cm (¾ inch) pieces

3 garlic cloves, chopped

1 tablespoon plain (all-purpose) flour

500 ml (17 fl oz/2 cups) good-quality ready-made or home-made chicken stock (see page 30)

1 tablespoon tomato paste (concentrated purée)

2 tablespoons thyme leaves

1 bay leaf

450 g (1 lb) desiree potatoes, peeled and cut into 2–3 cm (¾–1¼ inch) pieces

3 teaspoons cornflour (cornstarch)

155 g (5½ oz/1 cup) fresh peas

2–3 tablespoons redcurrant jelly

1 Wash the duck marylands briefly under cold running water and pat dry with paper towels. Season with sea salt and freshly ground black pepper. Heat the oil in a large flameproof casserole dish over medium heat. Cook the marylands, skin side down, for 10 minutes or until golden brown. Turn and cook for a further 4 minutes *(pic 1)*. (You really want to get some good colour on the skin at this stage as it will impart flavour into the stew.) Remove the duck and set aside. Pour off almost all the fat, leaving 1½ tablespoons.

2 Return the dish to medium–low heat, add the onions and cook, stirring occasionally, for 4 minutes or until golden. Add the carrots and celery and cook, stirring occasionally, for 2 minutes. Add the garlic and cook for 2 minutes more, stirring frequently. Sprinkle over the flour and cook for a further 1 minute, stirring frequently. Add the stock and use a wooden spoon to scrape any caramelisation from the base of the casserole dish *(pic 2)*.

3 Bring to a simmer and add the tomato paste, thyme, bay leaf and potatoes *(pic 3)*, then the duck and any juices. Cover, reduce the heat to very low and simmer for 1½ hours or until the duck is cooked and tender. Remove the marylands from the casserole dish and set aside in a warm place.

4 Skim off any fat from the cooking liquid. Combine the cornflour with 1½ tablespoons of water and then stir into the stew. Bring to the boil, add the peas and simmer for 5 minutes or until the peas are just cooked. Stir through the redcurrant jelly, season to taste and then spoon the stew into four deep bowls. Top with the duck and serve.

Allspice quail tagine with tabouleh

SERVES 4   **PREPARATION TIME** 15 minutes (+ 30 minutes soaking)   **COOKING TIME** 45 minutes

8 quails (about 180 g/6¼ oz each)
2 tablespoons olive oil
1 tablespoon allspice
2 tablespoons sea salt
40 g (1½ oz) butter
4 red onions, cut into thin wedges
2 x 400 g (14 oz) tins chopped tomatoes
2 cinnamon sticks
2 tablespoons honey
40 g (1½ oz/¼ cup) pine nuts,
    toasted
Coriander (cilantro) sprigs, to serve

TABOULEH
175 g (6 oz/1 cup) burghul (bulgur)
1 bunch flat-leaf (Italian) parsley,
    chopped
1 vine-ripened tomato, chopped
80 ml (2½ fl oz/⅓ cup) extra virgin
    olive oil
2 tablespoons lemon juice
1 garlic clove, crushed

1 To make the tabouleh, put the burghul in a bowl and cover with warm water. Soak for 30 minutes or until the burghul has softened. Drain *(pic 1)* and then squeeze with your hands to remove the excess water. Place in a bowl and toss with the parsley. Set aside.

2 Meanwhile, wash the quails briefly under cold running water. Dry well with paper towels and then truss (see page 21). (You need to do this so that all the quails will fit in the casserole dish.) Brush the quails with half the oil. Combine the allspice and sea salt and sprinkle over the quails *(pic 2)*.

3 Melt half the butter in a flameproof casserole dish over medium–low heat. Add half the quails and cook for 4 minutes, turning every minute. (You are aiming to cook the quails just so they change colour, not to brown them.) Remove and set aside. Repeat with the remaining butter and quails.

4 Add the remaining oil to the casserole dish with the onions and cook, stirring occasionally, over medium–low heat for 8–10 minutes, until the onions are soft but still holding their shape. Stir in the tomatoes and cinnamon. Return the quails and any cooking juices to the dish — they should fit snugly in one layer *(pic 3)*. Reduce the heat to low, cover and simmer for 15–20 minutes or until the quails are just cooked through and the juices run clear when they are pierced with a skewer through the thickest part (between the thigh and body).

5 Meanwhile, to finish the tabouleh, add the tomato to the burghul and parsley. Combine the oil, lemon juice and garlic and season well with salt and freshly ground black pepper. Add to the tabouleh and toss to combine.

6 Transfer the quails to a serving platter, remove the string and cover loosely to keep warm. Add the honey to the casserole dish and cook, stirring occasionally, for 5 minutes or until the sauce reduces slightly. Season with salt and pepper. Spoon the sauce around the quails, sprinkle with the pine nuts and coriander and serve with the tabouleh.

2

3

1

Indian-style chicken curry

This dish is all about the spices — aromatic cumin, coriander and cloves, spicy chillies and ginger, warming turmeric and earthy curry leaves all combine in this divine curry.

SERVES 4   **PREPARATION TIME** 15 minutes (+ 1½ hours marinating)   **COOKING TIME** 1 hour 5 minutes

200 g (7 oz/¾ cup) plain yoghurt
2 tablespoons chilli flakes
1 teaspoon ground cloves
3 tablespoons ground cumin
2 tablespoons ground coriander
1 teaspoon sea salt
1.8 kg (4 lb) whole chicken, cut into
    8 pieces (see page 18)
10 cm (4 inch) piece ginger
9 garlic cloves
1 large brown onion, roughly chopped
1 tablespoon vegetable oil
1 teaspoon ground turmeric
1 kg (2 lb 4 oz) desiree potatoes, peeled
    and cut into 1 cm (½ inch) pieces
600 g (1 lb 5 oz) roma (plum) tomatoes,
    chopped
200 ml (7 fl oz) white chicken stock
    (see page 30)
80 ml (2½ fl oz/⅓ cup) vegetable oil,
    extra
16 curry leaves
Steamed basmati rice and naan bread,
    to serve

1 Combine the yoghurt, chilli, cloves, cumin, coriander and salt in a large glass or ceramic bowl. Add the chicken pieces and turn to coat in the marinade *(pic 1)*. Cover and refrigerate for 1½ hours.

2 Coarsely chop the ginger and garlic, then put in a food processor and pulse until finely chopped. Remove from the food processor and set aside. Finely chop the onion in the food processor and set

aside. Heat the oil in a large heavy-based saucepan over medium heat. Add the ginger and garlic and cook, stirring, for 2 minutes or until golden. Add the chopped onion and turmeric and cook, stirring occasionally, for 3 minutes or until the onion is soft. Add the potatoes to the pan, reduce the heat to low and cook, stirring regularly and scraping any caramelisation from the base of the pan, for 5 minutes *(pic 2)*.

3 Purée the tomatoes in the food processor and add to the pan with the marinated chicken pieces and any remaining marinade left in the bowl. Add the stock, increase the heat to high and bring to the boil.

4 Reduce the heat, cover and simmer, stirring regularly, for 45 minutes, until the chicken is tender and cooked through. Season with salt, to taste.

5 Heat the extra oil and curry leaves in a small saucepan over medium heat. When the leaves begin to sizzle and crisp, remove them using a slotted spoon *(pic 3)* and drain on paper towels.

6 Serve the curry scattered with the fried curry leaves and accompanied by steamed rice and naan bread.

Creamy chicken and corn pies

This recipe begins with a simple method for poaching a chicken. If you are pressed for time, you could bypass this step and use leftover chicken from another recipe or a purchased cooked chicken, such as a barbecued chicken, and good-quality ready-made chicken stock.

SERVES 6 **PREPARATION TIME** 40 minutes (+ 1 hour cooling and 2 hours chilling) **COOKING TIME** 1 hour 45 minutes

1.8 kg (4 lb) whole chicken
1 carrot, chopped
1 brown onion, halved
1 celery stalk, chopped
6 parsley stalks
50 g (1¾ oz) butter
6 spring onions (scallions), trimmed
   and chopped
1 fennel bulb, trimmed and cut into
   1 cm (½ inch) pieces
200 g (7 oz) button mushrooms,
   cleaned, thickly sliced
35 g (1¼ oz/¼ cup) plain
   (all-purpose) flour
2 corn cobs, kernels removed
⅓ cup chopped flat-leaf (Italian) parsley
250 g (9 oz) sour light cream
2 sheets frozen butter puff pastry,
   thawed
1 egg, lightly whisked
Dressed salad leaves, to serve

1 Wash the chicken briefly under cold running water, remove the neck and giblets and trim any pockets of fat. Pat the chicken dry with paper towels, put in a large stockpot and add the carrot, onion, celery and parsley stalks. Cover with cold water (about 6 litres/ 210 fl oz/24 cups), bring slowly to the boil and simmer gently for 40 minutes, occasionally skimming any scum from the surface. Turn off the heat, cover and cool the chicken in the stock for at least 1 hour.

2 Remove the chicken from the stock, then strain and reserve the stock. Refrigerate the stock for 1 hour or until chilled, then use a spoon to skim the fat from the surface.

3 When cool enough to handle, remove the skin and bones from the chicken and shred the flesh *(pic 1)*.

4 Heat the butter in a large saucepan over low heat and cook the spring onions and fennel, covered, for 10 minutes or until soft. Add the mushrooms and stir over medium heat for about 5 minutes, until soft. Add the flour and stir for 2 minutes. Gradually stir in 500 ml (17 fl oz/ 2 cups) of the reserved stock (freeze the remaining stock for another use). Bring to a simmer over medium heat, stirring constantly. Simmer for 2 minutes. Remove from the heat. Stir in the chicken, corn, parsley and sour cream and season to taste *(pic 2)*. Refrigerate for 1 hour or until the mixture has cooled to room temperature.

5 Preheat the oven to 180°C (350°F/ Gas 4). Spoon the filling into six 250 ml (9 fl oz/1 cup) pie dishes. Cut each pastry sheet into 4 squares (you will only need to use 6 squares, reserve the remaining squares for another use). Brush the edge of each dish with egg, then drape a pastry square over each dish *(pic 3)*, pressing around the edge to seal. Cut a few slits in the top of the pastry to allow the steam to escape and brush with the remaining egg.

6 Place the pies on a baking tray and bake for 30 minutes or until the pastry is puffed and golden and the filling is hot. Serve with the dressed salad leaves.

Green chicken curry

SERVES 4   **PREPARATION TIME** 20 minutes   **COOKING TIME** 35 minutes

2 teaspoons coriander seeds
1 teaspoon whole black peppercorns
3 long green chillies, seeded and
    chopped
1 tablespoon finely grated ginger
¼ cup firmly packed chopped coriander
    (cilantro) leaves, roots and stems
2 large garlic cloves
5 spring onions (scallions), white and
    firm green parts, chopped
3 cm (1¼ inch) piece lemongrass
    stem, white part only, roughly
    chopped (pic 1)
2 tablespoons vegetable oil
4 kaffir lime leaves
400 ml (14 fl oz) tin coconut cream
1 kg (2 lb 4 oz) skinless chicken thigh
    fillets, trimmed, cut into 2 cm
    (¾ inch) pieces
1 small bunch basil, leaves picked
1 tablespoon fish sauce
Steamed rice and lime wedges,
    to serve

1 Grind the coriander seeds and peppercorns in a food processor, spice grinder *(pic 2)* or using a mortar and pestle until finely ground. Add the chillies, ginger, coriander, garlic, spring onions and lemongrass and continue to grind to form a paste.

2 Heat the oil in a medium saucepan, add the curry paste and cook, stirring, for 3–4 minutes or until aromatic. Add the kaffir lime leaves and coconut cream *(pic 3)* and simmer for 10 minutes.

3 Add the chicken and 250 ml (9 fl oz/ 1 cup) water to the sauce and bring to a simmer over medium–low heat. Simmer gently for 15–20 minutes or until the chicken is tender.

4 Add the basil leaves and fish sauce to the curry and stir through. Serve with the steamed rice and lime wedges.

1

2

3

TIP You can make double or triple quantities of the curry paste and refrigerate it for future use. It will keep in an airtight container in the refrigerator for up to 1 week. It can also be frozen in ice-cube trays for up to 3 months and added straight to the pan from the freezer.

Navarin of lamb

This traditional French stew makes the most of spring vegetables, such as baby carrots, beans, peas and small turnips, which is why it is often referred to as 'navarin printanier' which means spring stew. It can be made with lamb neck or shoulder, or a combination of both cuts.

SERVES 6   **PREPARATION TIME** 20 minutes   **COOKING TIME** 2½ hours

1 kg (2 lb 4 oz) boned shoulder
   of lamb (ask your butcher to bone
   the lamb for you)
1 tablespoon olive oil
20 g (¾ oz) butter
1 brown onion, finely chopped
3 garlic cloves, crushed
125 ml (4 fl oz/½ cup) white wine
2 x 400 g (14 oz) tins chopped tomatoes
Bouquet garni *(pic 1)* (see tip)
600 g (1 lb 5 oz) new potatoes
2 bunches baby carrots, peeled,
   stems trimmed
2 bunches bulb spring onions
   (scallions), tops trimmed and
   halved if large
235 g (8½ oz) frozen peas, defrosted
   and blanched in boiling water
Flat-leaf (Italian) parsley leaves,
   to garnish

1 Trim the lamb and cut into 4 cm (1½ inch) pieces. Heat the oil and butter in a large saucepan over medium–high heat. Cook the lamb, in batches, for 4 minutes or until browned all over *(pic 2)*. Transfer to a plate. Reduce the heat to medium and cook the onion, stirring, for 5 minutes, until softened. Add the garlic and cook, stirring, until aromatic. Add the wine, scraping any caramelisation from the base of the pan, and bring to the boil. Stir in the tomatoes and bouquet garni.

2 Return the lamb to the pan, season with salt and freshly ground black pepper and stir well. Bring to the boil, then reduce the heat to low and simmer, covered, for 1½ hours.

3 Add the potatoes to the pan and simmer, covered, for 25 minutes. Add the carrots and spring onions *(pic 3)* and simmer, covered, for a further 15 minutes or until the lamb and vegetables are tender. Remove the bouquet garni, then stir in the peas. Taste and adjust the seasoning, if necessary. Serve sprinkled with parsley.

1

2

3

TIP You can buy ready-made bouquet garni or make your own with a bay leaf, parsley stems and thyme sprigs tied up with kitchen string, or rolled up in an 8 cm (3¼ inch) piece of green, outer leek leaf and then tied with string.

Individual meat pies

MAKES 4   **PREPARATION TIME** 45 minutes (+ cooling)   **COOKING TIME** 3 hours 10 minutes

2 tablespoons plain (all-purpose) flour

600 g (1 lb 5 oz) chuck steak, cut into
   1 cm (½ inch) pieces

60 ml (2 fl oz/¼ cup) olive oil

4 brown onions, thinly sliced

1 medium carrot, finely chopped

1 celery stalk, finely chopped

2 garlic cloves, crushed

1 teaspoon caster (superfine) sugar

125 ml (4 fl oz/½ cup) red wine

500 ml (17 fl oz/2 cups) good-quality
   ready-made or home-made beef
   stock (see page 60)

200 g (7 oz) Swiss brown mushrooms,
   trimmed and quartered

900 g (2 lb) home-made or ready-made
   shortcrust pastry

1 egg, lightly whisked

1 Place the flour in a large bowl and season with sea salt and freshly ground black pepper. Add the beef, toss to coat in the flour and shake off any excess.

2 Heat 1 tablespoon of the oil in a large heavy-based flameproof casserole dish. Add half the beef and cook, turning often, for 5 minutes or until browned all over. Transfer to a plate and repeat with the remaining beef, adding a little extra oil if necessary.

3 Heat half the remaining oil in the casserole dish. Add the onions, carrot and celery and cook, stirring occasionally, for 10–12 minutes or until the vegetables are soft. Add the garlic and sugar and cook, stirring, for 30 seconds.

4 Add the wine and bring to the boil. Reduce the heat to low and simmer, uncovered, for 2 minutes or until slightly reduced. Return the beef to the casserole dish with the stock. Bring to the boil, then reduce the heat and simmer, covered, for 1 hour. Uncover

and cook for a further 1 hour or until the meat is very tender and the liquid has thickened.

5 Meanwhile, heat the remaining oil in a frying pan over medium–high heat. Add the mushrooms and cook, stirring, for about 5 minutes or until browned all over. Add to the beef mixture and stir to combine. Transfer to a bowl and cool to room temperature.

6 Preheat the oven to 180°C (350°F/ Gas 4). Divide the pastry into 2 portions, one twice as big as the other *(pic 1)*. Use a lightly floured rolling pin to roll out the smaller portion of pastry on a lightly floured work surface until 3 mm (⅛ inch) thick. Use the top of an 11 cm (4¼ inch) (top diameter), 7.5 cm (3 inch) (base diameter) pie tin to cut 4 rounds from the pastry *(pic 2)*.

7 Divide the larger portion of pastry into 4 equal portions and roll each out on a lightly floured work surface, taking care not to overwork the dough or it will become too soft, into a 15 cm (6 inch) diameter round. Carefully ease each round into a pie tin, using your fingertips to press them into the base and side. Roll the rolling pin over the tops of the tins to trim the excess pastry.

8 Divide the beef mixture among the pastry-lined tins *(pic 3)*. Brush the top edges of the pastry with a little egg. Place the smaller pastry rounds on top to cover the beef mixture and use a lightly floured fork to press the edges together. Use a small sharp knife to make 2 slits in the top of each pastry lid. Brush the tops lightly with egg and bake for 40 minutes or until golden. Set aside for 10 minutes to cool slightly, then remove from the tins. Serve hot.

TIP These pies are best eaten on the day they are made. If you have more pies than you need, freeze them in sealed freezer bags for up to 2 months. Thaw overnight in the refrigerator and reheat in an oven preheated to 180°C (350°F/ Gas 4) for 20–25 minutes.

Steak and kidney pudding

Steak and kidney pudding is a traditional British dish that utilises cheap cuts of meat to great effect — long cooking renders the meat rich and incredibly tender. Traditionally, ratios are equal quantities of kidneys to steak but if you find this too strong you can reduce the kidneys and increase the steak.

SERVES 6   **PREPARATION TIME** 40 minutes (+ 20 minutes chilling and 20 minutes cooling)   **COOKING TIME** 3 hours

2½ tablespoons plain (all-purpose) flour
350 g (12 oz) chuck steak, fat trimmed and cut into 1.5 cm (⅝ inch) pieces
350 g (12 oz) beef kidney, trimmed and cut into 1.5 cm (⅝ inch) pieces
150 ml (5 fl oz) good-quality ready-made or home-made beef stock (see page 60), warmed
1 tablespoon Vegemite or other yeast spread
2½ tablespoons worcestershire sauce
2 tablespoons hot English mustard
1 onion, finely chopped
1 tablespoon thyme leaves
1 egg yolk, whisked
Steamed green vegetables, to serve

SUET PASTRY
350 g (12 oz/2⅓ cups) self-raising flour
2 teaspoons salt
1 teaspoon freshly ground pepper
135 g (4¾ oz) suet mix (see tip)
250 ml (9 fl oz/1 cup) iced water, approximately

1 To make the suet pastry, combine the flour, salt and pepper in a large bowl. Add the suet and toss to combine well. Using your hands to mix, add enough iced water to form a firm dough; you may need a little extra water *(pic 1)*. Turn out onto a lightly floured surface and knead very briefly until smooth. Shape into a disc, wrap in plastic wrap and refrigerate for 20 minutes.

2 Grease a 2 litre (70 fl oz/8 cup) pudding basin or heatproof bowl well with butter. Place the flour in a bowl, add the steak and kidney and toss to coat. Combine the stock, Vegemite,

worcestershire and mustard in a separate bowl. Mix in the onion, thyme, salt and pepper. Add to the meat and mix well.

3 Half-fill a large saucepan with water and bring to the boil over medium heat. Reduce the heat and keep at a simmer.

4 Meanwhile, remove about a third of the pastry and set aside. Roll the remaining pastry out on a lightly floured surface to a 27 cm (10¾ inch) round, about 5–7 mm (¼ inch) thick. It needs to be large enough to cover the inside of the pudding basin, coming near the top of the basin but with room to fit the pastry lid and allow for expansion. Place the pastry in the basin, then press it over the surface to cover the inside surface *(pic 2)*.

5 Place the meat mixture in the pastry-lined basin. Roll the remaining portion of pastry out to form a round large enough to fit over the surface of the bowl. Brush egg yolk over the top edge of the pastry in the basin, then place the round of dough on top to cover the meat mixture. Press firmly to seal the edges well *(pic 3)*. Cover the pudding with a tight-fitting lid or a double layer of foil or non-stick baking paper secured firmly with kitchen string.

6 Place the pudding basin in the saucepan of simmering water — the water should come halfway up the side of the basin. Cover the saucepan and simmer over medium heat for 3 hours. Cool the pudding in the basin for about 20 minutes, then carefully turn out and serve with steamed vegetables.

1

2

3

TIP Suet is derived from the fat around beef kidneys. Suet mix is available from the baking section of the supermarket.

Pork vindaloo

This curry comes from the region of Goa in southern India. Goa was a Portuguese colony until 1961 and this recipe was created by the Portuguese Christian community, hence the use of pork. It is usually made with fenni, a local alcohol made from cashews or coconut, however vodka is a good substitute.

SERVES 6   **PREPARATION TIME** 20 minutes (+ overnight marinating)   **COOKING TIME** 2 hours

4 long red chillies, chopped

8 garlic cloves, chopped

50 g (1¾ oz) piece ginger, peeled and finely grated

125 ml (4 fl oz/½ cup) coconut vinegar (see tip)

1 kg (2 lb 4 oz) pork belly, rind removed and fat trimmed *(pic 1)*, cut into 3 cm (1¼ inch) pieces

3 brown onions, coarsely grated

8 whole cloves

2 cinnamon sticks

2 teaspoons ground cumin

1 teaspoon ground turmeric

1 teaspoon freshly ground black pepper

3 ripe tomatoes, chopped

60 ml (2 fl oz/¼ cup) vodka

Steamed rice and naan bread or chapatti, to serve

1 Put the chillies, garlic, ginger and vinegar in a small food processor and process to a coarse paste *(pic 2)*. Transfer to a large bowl and add the pork, onions and spices. Cover with plastic wrap and refrigerate overnight.

2 Transfer the pork and marinade to a large saucepan over medium–high heat. Stir in the tomatoes and bring to the boil *(pic 3)*. Reduce the heat to medium–low and simmer, covered, for 2 hours or until the pork is tender. Stir in the vodka and taste and adjust the seasoning, if necessary.

3 Serve the curry with steamed rice and warmed naan bread or chapatti.

1

2

3

TIP Coconut vinegar is available from Indian and Asian supermarkets, as it's also used widely in Thai cuisine.
This dish can be frozen in airtight containers for up to 1 month.

Massaman beef curry

The beauty of making your own curry paste is the freshness of the flavours and the fact that you can adjust the heat to your preference, so don't let the thought of a little extra effort put you off. Beef brisket is an ideal cut to use in a curry, as it is robust and can hold its own with the strong flavours.

SERVES 4   **PREPARATION TIME** 40 minutes   **COOKING TIME** 4 hours 15 minutes

2 tablespoons vegetable oil

2 onions, thinly sliced

750 g (1 lb 10 oz) beef brisket, cut into
    3 cm (1¼ inch) pieces

400 ml (14 fl oz) tin coconut milk

250 ml (9 fl oz/1 cup) good-quality
    ready-made or home-made beef
    stock (see page 60)

1 cinnamon stick

2 bay leaves

400 g (14 oz) boiling potatoes, peeled
    and cut into chunks

2 teaspoons tamarind paste (see tip)

1 tablespoon fish sauce

2 teaspoons grated palm sugar
    (jaggery) or brown sugar

Steamed jasmine rice, to serve

Chopped roasted peanuts and coriander
    (cilantro) leaves, to garnish

CURRY PASTE

1 tablespoon coriander seeds

1 tablespoon cumin seeds

1 tablespoon black peppercorns

1 teaspoon ground nutmeg

6 (10 cm/4 inch) dried red chillies,
    soaked in 250 ml (9 fl oz/1 cup)
    hot water for 20 minutes (see tip)

4 garlic cloves, chopped

3 cm (1¼ inch) piece ginger,
    peeled and chopped

1 large red onion, chopped

1 lemongrass stem, white part only,
    chopped

3 teaspoons shrimp paste

1 To make the curry paste, put the coriander seeds, cumin seeds, peppercorns and nutmeg in a small frying pan over medium heat. Cook, stirring, for 1–2 minutes or until aromatic *(pic 1)*. Transfer to a bowl and set aside to cool, then use a mortar and pestle or spice grinder to grind to a powder. Drain the chillies, discard the seeds and coarsely chop. Place in a food processor with the ground spices and the remaining ingredients *(pic 2)* and process to a paste. Measure out 130 g (4½ oz/½ cup) and set aside. (Put the remaining curry paste in an airtight container in the refrigerator to reserve for another use. Keep for up to 1 week.)

2 Heat the oil in a large heavy-based saucepan over medium–high heat. Cook the onions, stirring occasionally, for 5 minutes or until golden. Add the beef, increase the heat to high and cook, stirring, for 3 minutes or until browned. Scoop the cream off the top of the coconut milk *(pic 3)*, add to the pan with the curry paste and cook, stirring, for 3–4 minutes or until aromatic.

3 Add the remaining coconut milk, the stock, cinnamon stick and bay leaves to the pan. Bring to the boil, then reduce the heat, cover and simmer gently for 3½ hours. Add the potatoes and simmer for a further 30 minutes or until the potatoes are cooked through and the meat is very tender. Season the curry with the tamarind paste, fish sauce and palm sugar, to taste.

4 Serve the curry with steamed rice, garnished with the chopped peanuts and coriander leaves.

> **TIP** Tamarind paste is a tart, sour paste available from supermarkets and Asian food stores.
> If your dried chillies are the small variety, you will only need 3.
> You can use 55 g (2 oz/¼ cup) ready-made massaman curry paste if you are short of time.

Roman lamb stew

Lamb shoulder is ideal for slow-cooked stews such as this. When it's finished cooking, the meat should be just about falling apart. Diced boneless lamb leg would also work well. Although this stew is traditionally served with soft polenta, creamy mashed potato would be just as good.

SERVES 4   **PREPARATION TIME** 25 minutes   **COOKING TIME** 2 hours 20 minutes

2 tablespoons olive oil
1 kg (2 lb 4 oz) boned lamb shoulder, cut into 3 cm (1¼ inch) pieces
1 large onion, diced
2 celery stalks, diced
1 large carrot, diced
2 garlic cloves, thinly sliced
2 teaspoons chopped rosemary
4 anchovy fillets, chopped
250 ml (9 fl oz/1 cup) white wine
500 g (1 lb 2 oz) vine-ripened tomatoes, chopped
375 ml (13 fl oz/1½ cups) good-quality ready-made or home-made chicken or veal stock (see pages 30 or 60)
Soft polenta, to serve

GREMOLATA
1 cup flat-leaf (Italian) parsley leaves
2 teaspoons finely grated lemon zest
1 garlic clove, finely chopped

1 Preheat the oven to 160°C (315°F/ Gas 2–3). Heat half the oil in a large flameproof casserole dish over high heat. Cook the lamb, in batches, for 2–3 minutes or until browned all over *(pic 1)*. Transfer to a plate and set aside.

2 Add the remaining oil to the casserole dish and cook the onion, celery and carrot over medium heat, stirring often, for 6–7 minutes or until softened. Add the garlic, rosemary and anchovies *(pic 2)* and cook, stirring, for 2 minutes. Return the lamb to the dish, add the wine and simmer until the wine has reduced by half. Stir in the tomatoes and stock and bring to the boil.

3 Cover the casserole dish and bake for 2 hours or until the lamb is very tender.

4 Meanwhile, to make the gremolata, finely chop the parsley *(pic 3)* and combine with the zest and garlic.

5 Season the casserole with sea salt and freshly ground black pepper, to taste. Serve on soft polenta, garnished with the gremolata.

1

2

3

TIP Gremolata is an Italian accompaniment of chopped parsley, lemon and garlic that is traditionally served with osso buco but is delicious with most slow-cooked casseroles.

Pork meatball curry

This dish gives the traditional meatball an Asian twist, using pork and a Thai-style green curry sauce. The home-made curry paste has a wonderfully fresh, light flavour and you only need to use half of it, so the rest can be frozen for the next time you make these more-ish meatballs.

SERVES 4   **PREPARATION TIME** 25 minutes   **COOKING TIME** 25 minutes

500 g (1 lb 2 oz) minced (ground) pork
3 teaspoons finely grated ginger
2 tablespoons finely chopped
    water chestnuts
1½ tablespoons thinly sliced
    garlic chives
¼ teaspoon salt
3 teaspoons peanut oil
560 ml (19¼ fl oz) tin coconut cream
250 ml (9 fl oz/1 cup) good-quality
    ready-made or home-made
    chicken stock (see page 30)
4 kaffir lime leaves, finely shredded
1 tablespoon fish sauce
1 tablespoon lime juice
2 teaspoons palm sugar (jaggery)
    or brown sugar
Lime wedges, steamed rice and
    steamed Asian greens, to serve
Coriander (cilantro) sprigs, to garnish

GREEN CURRY PASTE
1 teaspoon cumin seeds
1 teaspoon coriander seeds
1 lemongrass stem, white part only,
    finely chopped
3 cm (1¼ inch) piece ginger,
    peeled and chopped
90 g (3¼ oz) red Asian shallots,
    finely chopped
3 garlic cloves, chopped
2 long green chillies, chopped
1 teaspoon shrimp paste
5 coriander (cilantro) roots,
    cleaned and chopped
Finely grated zest of 1 lime
2 tablespoons lime juice

1 To make the green curry paste, put the cumin and coriander seeds in a small heavy-based frying pan over medium heat and cook, stirring, for 1 minute or until aromatic. Use a mortar and pestle to grind to a fine powder. Add the lemongrass and pound until incorporated. Add the ginger, shallots and garlic and pound until a paste is starting to form *(pic 1)*. Add the chilli, shrimp paste, coriander root and lime zest and pound to combine. Add the lime juice and pound to incorporate. Measure out half the paste (3½ tablespoons) and set aside. (Put the remaining curry paste in a small airtight container and freeze to use at a later date. Keep for up to 1 month.)

2 Combine the minced pork, ginger, water chestnuts, garlic chives and salt in a bowl. Use damp hands to shape tablespoons of the mixture into balls.

3 Meanwhile, heat the oil in a wok over low heat, add the curry paste and fry for 1 minute or until aromatic *(pic 2)*. Add the coconut cream, stock and kaffir lime leaves and bring to a gentle simmer.

4 Add half the meatballs to the wok *(pic 3)* and simmer for 8 minutes, stirring occasionally, until just cooked through. Use a slotted spoon to transfer to a warm dish. Cook the remaining meatballs, then return all the meatballs to the wok and heat for 2 minutes. Season with fish sauce, lime juice and sugar and gently stir to combine.

5 Serve with lime wedges, steamed rice and steamed Asian greens, and garnished with coriander sprigs.

TIP You can use a small food processor to make the curry paste if you prefer.

Oxtail stew

Oxtail is, as the name suggests, taken from the tail of a cow (the older the cow, the meatier the tail will be). Most butchers will stock it, although they may need to order it in for you so ask ahead. When cooked slowly, oxtail becomes meltingly tender and produces a rich, gelatinous sauce.

SERVES 6   **PREPARATION TIME** 30 minutes   **COOKING TIME** 3 hours 50 minutes – 4 hours 25 minutes

35 g (1¼ oz/¼ cup) plain
  (all-purpose) flour
2 teaspoons sweet paprika
1.25 kg (2 lb 12 oz) oxtail pieces
  (see tip)
2 tablespoons olive oil
2 large onions, sliced
2 large carrots, peeled and diced
2 celery stalks, diced
100 g (3½ oz) pancetta, diced
3 garlic cloves, thinly sliced
250 ml (9 fl oz/1 cup) white wine
2 x 400 g (14 oz) tins chopped tomatoes
2 fresh bay leaves
Soft polenta, steamed greens or
  rocket (arugula) salad and
  crusty bread, to serve

1 Combine the flour and paprika on a large plate and season with sea salt and freshly ground black pepper. Toss the oxtail in the seasoned flour, shaking off any excess. Heat half the oil in a large flameproof casserole dish over high heat. Cook the oxtail, in batches, for 2–3 minutes, until browned all over *(pic 1)*. Transfer to a clean plate.

2 Preheat the oven to 160°C (315°F/ Gas 2–3). Return the pan to medium heat and add the remaining oil, the onion, carrot, celery, pancetta and garlic. Cook, stirring occasionally, for 6–7 minutes or until the vegetables are softened *(pic 2)*.

3 Add the wine and simmer, stirring often, for 5 minutes or until reduced by half. Add the tomatoes, bay leaves and 250 ml (9 fl oz/1 cup) water, increase the heat to high and bring to the boil. Return the oxtail to the pan *(pic 3)*, cover and bake for 3½–4 hours or until the meat is tender and falling off the bone. Remove from the oven and use a large spoon to skim any excess fat from the surface.

4 Serve the oxtail on the polenta with steamed greens or salad and bread.

1

2

3

TIP If you are unable to find oxtail, you can make this dish using beef shin instead.

Lamb, spinach and cashew korma curry

When time is of the essence, this quick and easy Indian curry is just what you need. Thanks to ready-made curry paste and lamb leg steaks, which require little cooking, it can be on the table in just over half an hour. The cashew nuts make the sauce particularly rich and creamy.

SERVES 4   **PREPARATION TIME** 15 minutes   **COOKING TIME** 25 minutes

2 tablespoons olive oil
700 g (1 lb 9 oz) lamb leg steaks,
    cut into 1.5 cm (⅝ inch) dice
1 large red onion, cut into thin wedges
1½ tablespoons ready-made korma
    curry paste
270 ml (9½ fl oz) coconut milk
3 vine-ripened tomatoes, diced
105 g (3½ oz/⅔ cup) cashew nuts,
    finely chopped (see tip)
150 g (5½ oz) green beans, trimmed
    and cut into 3 cm (1¼ inch) lengths
1 bunch (250 g/9 oz) English spinach,
    trimmed and leaves shredded
Lime juice, to taste
Naan bread, to serve
Coriander (cilantro) leaves, to garnish
    (optional)

1 Heat half the oil in a large frying pan or wok over high heat. Cook the lamb, in batches, for 1–2 minutes or until browned all over *(pic 1)*. Transfer to a plate and set aside.

2 Heat the remaining oil in the pan over medium–high heat, add the onion and cook, stirring occasionally, for 2–3 minutes or until golden. Add the curry paste and cook, stirring, for a further 1–2 minutes or until aromatic *(pic 2)*. Add the coconut milk, tomatoes and 125 ml (4 fl oz/½ cup) water and bring to the boil, then reduce the heat and simmer for 10 minutes.

3 Add the cashew nuts and beans to the pan and simmer for 2–3 minutes, until the beans are tender crisp. Return the lamb to the pan *(pic 3)*, add the spinach and stir until the lamb is heated through and the spinach is just wilted. Remove from the heat and add lime juice, to taste. Serve with warm naan bread and garnish with coriander leaves, if desired.

1

2

3

TIP The cashews can be finely chopped using a food processor, but pulse briefly just until chopped or they will begin to form a paste.
    This curry can be frozen, once cooled, in airtight containers for up to 3 months.

Veal, artichoke and broad bean casserole

SERVES 6 **PREPARATION TIME** 20 minutes **COOKING TIME** 1 hour 40 minutes

1.8 kg (4 lb) veal shin, boned and
  trimmed (ask your butcher to
  do this)
35 g (1¼ oz/¼ cup) plain
  (all-purpose) flour
1½ tablespoons olive oil
40 g (1½ oz) butter
100 g (3½ oz) piece pancetta,
  cut into 1 cm (½ inch) dice
3 garlic cloves, crushed
125 ml (4 fl oz/½ cup) white wine
350 g (12 oz) frozen broad beans,
  defrosted (see tip)
6 small globe artichokes (see tip)
1 lemon
140 g (5 oz/1 cup) frozen peas,
  defrosted
Steamed potatoes, to serve

LEMON GREMOLATA
½ cup finely chopped flat-leaf
  (Italian) parsley
Finely grated zest of 1 lemon
1 teaspoon finely chopped thyme
2 anchovy fillets, finely chopped

1 Preheat the oven to 190°C (375°F/ Gas 5). Cut the veal into 5 cm (2 inch) pieces. Place the flour on a large plate and season with salt and freshly ground black pepper. Roll the veal in the flour to coat, then tap to remove any excess.

2 Heat 1 tablespoon of the oil and half the butter in a large flameproof casserole dish over medium–high heat. Cook the veal, in batches, for about 5 minutes or until browned all over. Add the remaining butter to the pan when you've browned about half the veal. Transfer to a plate and set aside.

3 Heat the remaining oil in the casserole dish and cook the pancetta over medium heat, stirring often, for 2 minutes, until browned. Add the garlic and cook, stirring, until aromatic. Add the wine and cook, scraping any caramelisation from the base of the casserole dish. Bring to the boil, then add 250 ml (9 fl oz/1 cup) water and return the veal to the casserole dish. Return to the boil, then cover and bake for 1 hour, until the veal is just tender.

4 Blanch the broad beans in a small saucepan of boiling salted water for 3 minutes. Drain and cool in iced water. Drain again and remove the tough outer skin *(pic 1)*.

5 To make the lemon gremolata, combine all the ingredients in a bowl.

6 To prepare the artichokes, squeeze half a lemon into a bowl of cold water (see tip). Trim the artichokes, cutting off the stalks to within 5 cm (2 inches) of the base and remove the tough outer leaves *(pic 2)*. Cut off the top quarter of each. Remove the small, furry chokes with a small knife *(pic 3)*, then put each artichoke in the lemon water to prevent them discolouring.

7 Add the artichokes to the veal and bake, covered, for a further 20 minutes or until the veal and artichokes are tender. Stir in the broad beans and peas and cook, uncovered, on the stovetop over medium heat until heated through.

8 Serve the veal with the lemon gremolata and steamed potatoes.

1

2

3

TIP You can use fresh broad beans if you like. You'll need 1 kg (2 lb 4 oz), podded. Cook them as in step 4.
  Use the remaining lemon half to brush over the artichokes as you trim them. Work quickly as they don't take long to discolour.

Cassoulet

Cassoulet is a rich slow-cooked casserole that originated in the south of France and has come to be a source of great national pride. It typically contains pork sausage, pork, duck and white beans.

SERVES 4   **PREPARATION TIME** 30 minutes   **COOKING TIME** 3 hours

1 tablespoon olive oil
400 g (14 oz) pork belly, skin removed,
    cut into 2 cm (¾ inch) dice
4 duck marylands
2 pork sausages
2 onions, finely chopped
100 g (3½ oz) pancetta, cut into
    lardons (see tip)
3 garlic cloves, thinly sliced
2 thyme sprigs
1 tablespoon tomato paste
    (concentrated purée)
400 g (14 oz) tin chopped tomatoes
400 g (14 oz) tin cannellini beans,
    drained and rinsed (see tip)
500 ml (17 fl oz/2 cups) good-quality
    ready-made or home-made chicken or
    beef stock (see pages 30 or 60)
80 g (2¾ oz/1⅓ cups, lightly packed)
    fresh white breadcrumbs
2 tablespoons chopped flat-leaf
    (Italian) parsley
2 tablespoons melted butter
Mixed leaf salad, to serve

1 Heat the oil in a large flameproof casserole dish over high heat and cook the pork belly, in batches, stirring often, for 3–4 minutes or until browned *(pic 1)*. Transfer to a large plate and set aside.

2 Add the duck marylands to the casserole dish and cook for 2 minutes each side or until browned *(pic 2)*. Add to the plate with the pork belly. Reduce the heat to medium–high, add the sausages to the casserole dish and cook, turning often, for 5 minutes or until golden. Remove from the dish, cut into thick slices and add to the plate.

3 Preheat the oven to 160°C (315°F/ Gas 2–3). Add the onions, pancetta, garlic and thyme to the casserole dish, reduce the heat to medium and cook, stirring, for 5 minutes or until softened. Add the tomato paste and cook, stirring, for 1 minute. Add the tomatoes, beans and stock and bring to the boil. Return all the meats to the dish, ensuring they are covered in the tomato mixture.

4 Cover the casserole dish and bake for 2 hours, until the duck and pork belly are tender. Meanwhile, combine the breadcrumbs, parsley and melted butter in a bowl. Remove the cassoulet from the oven and use a large spoon to skim any excess fat from the surface. Sprinkle the cassoulet with the breadcrumb mixture *(pic 3)*, then bake, uncovered, for a further 20–25 minutes or until the breadcrumbs are golden. Transfer to a serving dish and serve with the salad.

1

2

3

TIP If pancetta is not available, substitute thickly cut bacon.
    You can try using different white beans, such as butterbeans (lima beans), if desired.

Boeuf bourguignon

This immensely popular French beef stew comes from the Burgundy region in France which is renowned for its wine, one of the main ingredients in this dish. Although it began as peasant fare, using slow cooking to tenderise a very cheap cut of meat, it's now on the menu of every bistro in France.

SERVES 6　**PREPARATION TIME** 30 minutes (+ overnight marinating)　**COOKING TIME** 2 hours 20 minutes

1.2 kg (2 lb 11 oz) gravy beef, cut into
　4 cm (1½ inch) pieces
375 ml (13 fl oz/1½ cups) red wine
　(see tip)
2 fresh bay leaves
2 tablespoons olive oil
50 g (1¾ oz) butter
100 g (3½ oz) speck or bacon, rind
　removed and cut into lardons
1 onion, finely chopped
1 teaspoon thyme leaves
3 garlic cloves, crushed
185 ml (6 fl oz/¾ cup) good-quality
　ready-made or home-made beef
　stock (see page 60)
12 baby onions, peeled leaving the
　roots intact
400 g (14 oz) button mushrooms
Mashed potato (see page 69), to serve
Parsley leaves, to garnish

1 Put the beef, wine and bay leaves in a large glass or ceramic bowl, cover with plastic wrap and refrigerate overnight.

2 Strain the beef, reserving the wine and bay leaves. Put the wine in a small saucepan, bring to the boil and remove from the heat. You should have about 250 ml (9 fl oz/1 cup) of wine.

3 Preheat the oven to 200°C (400°F/ Gas 6). Pat the beef dry with paper towels, then season with salt and freshly ground black pepper. Heat half each of the oil and butter in a large flameproof casserole dish over medium–high heat. Cook the beef, in 2 batches, for 2–3 minutes or until well browned all over (*pic 1*). Transfer to a plate.

4 Add the speck, chopped onion and reserved bay leaves to the casserole dish (*pic 2*) and cook over medium heat, stirring, for 8 minutes, until the speck is crisp and the fat has melted, and the onion has softened. Discard the fat, leaving about 1 tablespoon. Add the thyme and garlic and cook, stirring, for 30 seconds. Return the beef to the casserole dish with any juices and stir well. Add the reserved wine. Bring to the boil over high heat, then stir in the stock and return to the boil. Cover the casserole dish and bake for 1½ hours or until the beef is just tender.

5 Meanwhile, heat the remaining oil in a large frying pan over medium–high heat. Cook the baby onions, stirring, for 10 minutes or until golden (*pic 3*). Use tongs to transfer the onions to a plate, then discard the oil. Heat the remaining butter in the pan and cook the mushrooms, turning often, for 6 minutes or until well browned.

6 Add the baby onions and mushrooms to the beef, gently pushing them into the meat and sauce. Bake, covered, for a further 30 minutes or until the beef and vegetables are tender.

7 Serve with mashed potato and garnished with parsley.

TIP Use a good-quality, full-bodied red wine such as a merlot.
　If you don't have time to marinate the beef, reduce the wine to 250 ml (9 fl oz/1 cup) and do not boil it as there will be no impurities from the meat.

Lamb, carrot and apricot tagine

A tagine is a slow-cooked Berber stew from northern Africa. It is named after the earthenware vessel it is traditionally cooked in, which has a high, domed lid that is designed to send all the condensation back down onto the meat. This version is cooked slowly in a regular saucepan.

SERVES 6–8   **PREPARATION TIME** 20 minutes (+ 30 minutes soaking)   **COOKING TIME** 2 hours 40 minutes

200 g (7 oz/1¼ cups) dried apricot
  halves
375 ml (13 fl oz/1½ cups) boiling water
Large pinch of saffron threads
1½ teaspoons ground ginger
1½ teaspoons sweet paprika
½ teaspoon ground cardamom
2 garlic cloves, crushed
1 teaspoon freshly ground black pepper
80 ml (2½ fl oz/⅓ cup) olive oil
2 kg (4 lb 8 oz) piece lamb shoulder,
  cut through the bone into 4 cm
  (1½ inch) pieces (ask your butcher
  to do this) (see tip)
600 g (1 lb 5 oz) carrots (about 4 large),
  cut into 5 mm (¼ inch) thick slices
90 g (3¼ oz/¼ cup) honey
750 ml (26 fl oz/3 cups) good-quality
  ready-made or home-made chicken
  or veal stock (see pages 30 or 60),
  approximately
80 g (2¾ oz/½ cup) blanched almonds,
  toasted, to garnish (optional)
Coriander (cilantro) leaves, to garnish
Couscous and harissa, to serve

1 Place the apricots and boiling water in a heatproof bowl and set aside for 30 minutes or until softened. Drain the apricots, reserving the liquid.

2 Meanwhile, combine the saffron, ginger, paprika, cardamom, garlic, pepper and half the oil in a large glass or ceramic bowl. Add the lamb and toss to coat well (*pic 1*).

3 Heat the remaining oil in a large heavy-based saucepan over medium–low heat. Add the lamb mixture, season with sea salt and cook, stirring often, for 5–6 minutes or until the meat has changed colour (*pic 2*). Add the carrots, honey, stock and reserved apricot liquid. Bring to a simmer, then reduce the heat to low, cover and cook for 2 hours.

4 Add the soaked apricots (*pic 3*) and cook, uncovered, for a further 30 minutes or until the meat and apricots are very tender.

5 Use a large spoon to skim any excess fat from the surface. Serve the tagine scattered with almonds, if desired, and coriander, and accompanied by couscous and harissa.

1

2

3

TIP This recipe can be halved. You do not have to use lamb on the bone, but it will give a better flavour to the tagine and the bones will contribute body to the cooking liquid.

Tagliatelle bolognese

Perhaps the best-known and best-loved of all pasta sauces, bolognese is made with a meat-rich mixture of minced beef and pork, plus pancetta. Long, slow cooking makes the sauce intensely flavoursome. Long pastas such as tagliatelle, spaghetti and linguine suit this sauce best.

SERVES 4–6 **PREPARATION TIME** 15 minutes **COOKING TIME** 2 hours 15 minutes

60 ml (2 fl oz/¼ cup) olive oil
1 large brown onion, finely chopped
2 garlic cloves, crushed
1 celery stalk, finely chopped
1 large carrot, finely chopped
¼ cup flat-leaf (Italian)
    parsley, chopped
500 g (1 lb 2 oz) minced (ground) beef
250 g (9 oz) minced (ground) pork
50 g (1¾ oz) sliced pancetta,
    finely chopped
2 x 400 g (14 oz) tins chopped tomatoes
50 g (1¾ oz) tomato paste
    (concentrated purée)
125 ml (4 fl oz/½ cup) red or white wine
250 ml (9 fl oz/1 cup) good-quality
    ready-made or home-made
    beef stock (see page 60)
500 g (1 lb 2 oz) tagliatelle
Shaved parmesan cheese, to serve

1 Heat the oil in a large frying pan. Add the onion and garlic and cook over medium–low heat for 3 minutes or until soft. Add the celery, carrot and parsley *(pic 1)*. Cook, stirring, for 3 minutes.

2 Add the minced beef and pork and break up any lumps with a wooden spoon *(pic 2)*. Cook, stirring, for a further 4–5 minutes or until the meat starts to brown.

3 Add the pancetta, tomatoes, tomato paste, wine and stock *(pic 3)*. Season with salt and freshly ground black pepper. Simmer, partially covered, for 2 hours. Add a little stock or water if the sauce becomes too dry.

4 When the sauce is almost ready, cook the pasta in a large saucepan of boiling salted water, following the packet instructions, until *al dente*. Drain.

5 Serve with the meat sauce and parmesan cheese.

1

2

3

Lamb shank tagine
with Persian couscous

This is a really easy dish — it just ticks away on the stovetop, filling the house with enticing aromas from the spices. It's packed with flavour even though you don't brown the shanks or the onions. Play around and change the spices to suit your taste.

SERVES 4 **PREPARATION TIME** 15 minutes **COOKING TIME** 2 hours 15 minutes

1 teaspoon coriander seeds
1 teaspoon fennel seeds
70 g (2½ oz) unsalted butter, chopped
1 teaspoon ground ginger
½ teaspoon cayenne pepper
2 brown onions, chopped
2 garlic cloves, chopped
4 lamb shanks, frenched (see page 55)
750 ml (26 fl oz/3 cups) good-quality
   ready-made or home-made
   chicken stock (see page 30)
1 cinnamon stick
200 g (7 oz/1 cup) Persian
   (moghrabieh) couscous
50 g (1¾ oz/¼ cup) pitted dates
1 pomegranate
1 tablespoon honey
Steamed green beans, to serve
½ preserved lemon, rind only,
   rinsed and thinly sliced
¼ cup flat-leaf (Italian) parsley leaves

1 Toast the coriander and fennel seeds in a small frying pan over medium heat until aromatic. Use a mortar and pestle or spice grinder to grind to a powder.

2 Heat the butter in a flameproof casserole dish over medium–low heat, add the ground coriander and fennel, ginger and cayenne pepper and stir. Add the onions and garlic and cook for 1 minute just to coat them in the butter mixture. Season the lamb shanks with sea salt and add to the dish, turning them to coat in the butter (*pic 1*).

3 Add the chicken stock and cinnamon stick, increase the heat to high and bring to a simmer. Cover and reduce the heat to low so that the liquid gently simmers (you may need to use a simmer pad). Cook for 1 hour.

4 Meanwhile, boil the couscous in boiling salted water for 5 minutes, drain and set aside.

5 Remove the lid and turn the shanks so that they cook evenly. Add the couscous and dates (*pic 2*), ensuring that the couscous is covered by the liquid. Cover and cook for 1 hour or until the lamb shanks and couscous are tender. Remove from the heat, cover and leave to rest while you prepare the garnish.

6 Remove the seeds from the pomegranate, measure out ⅓ cup and set aside. Place the remaining seeds in a fine sieve over a bowl and use the back of a large kitchen spoon to extract the juice from them (*pic 3*).

7 Remove the shanks from the casserole. Stir through the honey and add 2 tablespoons of the pomegranate juice. Taste for seasoning, adding sea salt if desired.

8 Spoon the couscous into shallow bowls and place the beans and lamb shanks on top. Garnish with the preserved lemon, parsley and pomegranate seeds.

TIP Persian (moghrabieh) couscous has large grains about the size of a pea. Buy it from large supermarkets, delis or Middle Eastern grocery stores.

Veal osso buco with parsnip purée

This classic Italian dish is sure to become a family favourite, if it isn't already. Veal osso buco vary in tenderness, so the cooking time will also vary. Test for doneness a few times during the braising — when the meat is just falling off the bone it is ready.

SERVES 4 **PREPARATION TIME** 45 minutes **COOKING TIME** 2 hours 20 minutes

1.5 kg (3 lb 5 oz) veal osso buco, cut about 4 cm (1½ inch) thick (ask your butcher to cut evenly sized pieces)
2 tablespoons plain (all-purpose) flour
60 ml (2 fl oz/¼ cup) olive oil
1 onion, finely chopped
1 celery stalk, finely chopped
1 carrot, finely chopped
4 garlic cloves, finely chopped
250 ml (9 fl oz/1 cup) dry white wine
400 g (14 oz) tin chopped tomatoes
2 teaspoons tomato paste (concentrated purée)
250 ml (9 fl oz/1 cup) good-quality ready-made or home-made chicken or veal stock (see pages 30 or 60)
2 x 1 cm (½ inch) wide strips of lemon zest
1 tablespoon chopped oregano

GREMOLATA
2 garlic cloves, finely chopped
⅓ cup finely chopped flat-leaf (Italian) parsley
1 tablespoon finely grated lemon zest

PARSNIP PUREE
900 g (2 lb) parsnips, peeled and chopped
50 g (1¾ oz) butter
60 ml (2 fl oz/¼ cup) thin (pouring/whipping) cream

1 Preheat the oven to 180°C (350°F/Gas 4). Toss the veal in the flour to coat and shake off any excess. Heat 2 tablespoons of the oil in a 2 litre (70 fl oz/8 cup) heavy-based flameproof casserole dish over medium heat. Cook the veal, in 2 batches, for 5 minutes, turning once, until browned (*pic 1*). Transfer to a plate and set aside.

2 Heat the remaining oil in the casserole dish, add the onion, celery and carrot and cook, covered, over low heat for 5–7 minutes or until soft (*pic 2*). Add the garlic, wine, tomatoes, tomato paste, stock, lemon zest and oregano and bring to the boil.

3 Return the veal to the casserole dish, cover and bake for 2 hours or until the meat is very tender.

4 Meanwhile, to make the parsnip purée, add the parsnips to a saucepan of salted simmering water and cook over medium heat for 10–15 minutes, until tender. Drain, then return to the pan and add the butter. Use a hand-held blender to blend until smooth. Stir in the cream and season with salt and pepper, to taste.

5 To make the gremolata, put all the ingredients in a small bowl and mix until well combined (*pic 3*).

6 Spoon the parsnip purée into shallow bowls, spoon over the osso buco and sprinkle with the gremolata.

TIP To vary the flavour, you could try using dry red wine instead of white wine for a slightly richer sauce; adding cooked peas to the osso buco just before serving; or adding finely chopped anchovies to the gremolata.

Poaching and Steaming

Chicken laksa

Laksa spice pastes are available from supermarkets and Asian food stores, but a home-made paste is superior in flavour and gives you more control over the seasoning, especially the heat. If you like your laksa really hot, add more dried chillies to the paste, or more red chilli at the end.

SERVES 6   **PREPARATION TIME** 30 minutes (+ 4 hours 45 minutes standing/chilling)   **COOKING TIME** 1 hour 45 minutes

1.8 kg (4 lb) whole chicken
4 cm (1½ inch) piece ginger, sliced
4 garlic cloves
1 brown onion, halved
60 ml (2 fl oz/¼ cup) vegetable oil
400 ml (14 fl oz) tin coconut milk
60 ml (2 fl oz/¼ cup) fish sauce
3 teaspoons grated palm sugar (jaggery)
220 g (7¾ oz) dried flat rice noodles
150 g (5½ oz) bean sprouts, trimmed
1 Lebanese (short) cucumber, halved,
    seeded and diagonally sliced
3 spring onions (scallions),
    diagonally sliced
20 g (¾ oz/¼ cup) crispy fried shallots
¼ cup mint leaves
¼ cup coriander (cilantro) leaves
Lime wedges and sliced red chilli,
    to serve

SPICE PASTE
10 g (¼ oz/1½ tablespoons) dried
    shrimp (see tip)
5 dried small red chillies, seeded
    and chopped
2 teaspoons shrimp paste (see tip)
1 lemongrass stem, pale part only,
    chopped
30 g (1 oz) macadamia nuts
3 garlic cloves, chopped
1 tablespoon chopped ginger
1 teaspoon ground turmeric
2 French shallots, chopped
2 teaspoons coriander seeds
60 ml (2 fl oz/¼ cup) vegetable oil

1 Wash the chicken briefly under cold running water and pat dry with paper towels. Half-fill a large stockpot with water, add the ginger, garlic, onion and 1 teaspoon salt and bring to the boil.

2 Lower the chicken into the pot and add more water to cover the chicken if necessary. Poach gently for 25 minutes *(pic 1)*. Remove from the heat, cover and stand for 45 minutes. Remove chicken.

3 Transfer the stock to a bowl or jug, cover and refrigerate for 4 hours or overnight. Use a spoon to skim off the fat, then put in a large saucepan, bring to the boil and boil for 1 hour or until reduced to 1.5 litres (52 fl oz/6 cups). Strain through a fine sieve; discard solids.

4 Meanwhile, to make the spice paste, soak the shrimp and chillies in hot water for 30 minutes. Drain and process in a small food processor with the remaining ingredients to a smooth paste *(pic 2)*.

5 Heat the oil in a large saucepan over medium heat and cook the spice paste, stirring, for 3 minutes *(pic 3)*. Add the stock and bring to the boil. Add the coconut milk, fish sauce and palm sugar. Simmer over medium heat for 5 minutes. Add more sugar and/or salt, to taste.

6 Put the noodles in a heatproof bowl, cover with boiling water and set aside for 3–4 minutes, until tender. Drain.

7 Meanwhile, remove the skin and bones from the chicken and shred the flesh. Add to the soup and heat through.

8 Divide the noodles among six deep bowls and ladle over the soup. Top with the bean sprouts, cucumber, spring onions, fried shallots and herbs. Serve with lime wedges and sliced chilli.

TIP Shrimp paste is made from salted, fermented prawns (shrimp). It is pungent and needs to be dry-roasted before use.
  Shrimp paste and dried shrimp are available from supermarkets and Asian grocery stores.

Turkey and cabbage salad

A single turkey breast needs careful cooking to prevent it becoming dry. Steaming is a very gentle method of cooking and therefore a perfect choice for turkey breast, especially if the breast is cooked wrapped in plastic wrap to retain its juices.

SERVES 4–6   **PREPARATION TIME** 50 minutes (+ 2 hours marinating and 1 hour cooling)   **COOKING TIME** 45 minutes

500 g (1 lb 2 oz) skinless single
   turkey breast fillet
125 ml (4 fl oz/½ cup) dry cider or
   white wine
1 cup coarsely chopped mint leaves,
   plus ½ cup firmly packed leaves
1 cup coarsely chopped coriander
   (cilantro) leaves, plus ½ cup firmly
   packed leaves, plus extra, to serve
300 g (10½ oz) savoy cabbage,
   very thinly sliced
200 g (7 oz) red cabbage, very
   thinly sliced
40 g (1½ oz/¼ cup) currants, soaked
   in hot water for 10 minutes, drained
45 g (1¾ oz/¼ cup) drained baby
   capers in brine
70 g (2½ oz) walnut halves, toasted,
   coarsely chopped

MAYONNAISE

1 egg yolk
1 tablespoon lemon juice
½ teaspoon dijon mustard
100 ml (3½ fl oz) olive oil

1 Place the turkey breast in a dish just large enough to hold it. Pour over the cider or wine and sprinkle with the chopped herbs. Cover and refrigerate for 2 hours to marinate.

2 Remove the turkey breast from the marinade and place on a large piece of plastic wrap. Use a sharp knife to slash the flesh four times across the breast (this allows the flavours to be infused

easily) *(pic 1)*. Place half the herbs from the marinade over the breast, then season with salt and pepper. Wrap the plastic wrap tightly around the turkey breast to enclose *(pic 2)*.

3 Place a double steamer or bamboo steaming basket over a saucepan or wok of simmering water (make sure the base of the basket doesn't touch the water). Place the turkey parcel in the basket and steam for 45 minutes or until the turkey is just cooked *(pic 3)*. Remove the turkey from the steamer and set aside to cool in the plastic wrap.

4 To make the mayonnaise, combine the egg yolk, lemon juice and mustard in the bowl of a small food processor and process until combined. Add the oil, drop by drop for the first 2 tablespoons and then in a slow steady stream, processing constantly until it is thick. Season with salt and freshly ground black pepper, to taste. (See tip.)

5 Combine the cabbage, currants, capers and walnuts in a large bowl. Stir in the mayonnaise and mix well.

6 Use a sharp knife to cut the turkey breast into very thin slices. Add the turkey and whole mint and coriander leaves to the cabbage mixture and toss gently to combine. Divide among serving plates and serve sprinkled with the extra coriander leaves.

1

2

3

TIP You can replace the mayonnaise with 120 g (4¼ oz/ ½ cup) good-quality ready-made whole egg mayonnaise. Stir through 1 tablespoon lemon juice before adding it to the salad.

Oven-steamed Asian chicken parcels

SERVES 4 **PREPARATION TIME** 15 minutes **COOKING TIME** 20 minutes

4 x 150 g (5½ oz) skinless chicken
   breast fillets
3 cm (1¼ inch) piece ginger,
   cut into thin matchsticks
2 spring onions (scallions),
   thinly sliced diagonally
1 small red capsicum (pepper),
   seeded and cut into thin strips
115 g (4 oz) baby corn, halved
   lengthways
2 tablespoons soy sauce
1 tablespoon fish sauce
2 teaspoons sesame oil
2 teaspoons finely grated lime zest
1 tablespoon lime juice
½ cup coriander (cilantro) leaves
Steamed rice, to serve

1 Preheat the oven to 200°C (400°F/
Gas 6).

2 Place four 30 cm (12 inch) squares
of non-stick baking paper on a work
surface. Place a chicken fillet in the
centre of each square. Combine the
ginger, spring onions, capsicum and
corn in a bowl. Divide the vegetable
mixture among the chicken fillets.
Combine the sauces, oil, lime zest and
juice in a small bowl. Spoon the sauce
over the vegetables *(pic 1)*.

3 Working with one square of baking
paper at a time, bring two sides of the
paper up to the centre and fold the ends
together *(pic 2)*. Roll up the ends to
enclose the chicken and seal. Place the
parcels on a baking tray *(pic 3)*.

4 Bake for 18–20 minutes or until
the chicken is just cooked through.
Serve the chicken parcels opened,
sprinkled with the coriander leaves and
accompanied by steamed rice.

1

2

3

Creamy chicken and corn soup

SERVES 4   **PREPARATION TIME** 15 minutes   **COOKING TIME** 2 hours

1 litre (35 fl oz/4 cups) water
1 litre (35 fl oz/4 cups) good-quality
   ready-made or home-made
   chicken stock (see page 30)
1 small carrot, coarsely chopped
1 celery stalk, trimmed, coarsely
   chopped
1 small brown onion, coarsely chopped
1.5 kg (3 lb 5 oz) whole chicken
25 g (1 oz) butter
35 g (1¼ oz/¼ cup) plain
   (all-purpose) flour
2 tablespoons lemon juice
310 g (11 oz) tin creamed corn
150 g (5½ oz/1 cup) frozen corn kernels
125 ml (4 fl oz/½ cup) thin
   (pouring/whipping) cream
¼ cup snipped chives

1 Combine the water, stock, carrot, celery and onion in a large saucepan over medium–high heat. Bring to the boil, then reduce the heat to a simmer. Add the chicken, cover and simmer for 1 hour or until the chicken is cooked and the juices run clear when it is pierced through the thickest part (between the thigh and body). Remove the chicken from the pan. Simmer the broth, covered, for a further 30 minutes. Strain through a sieve or colander lined with muslin (cheesecloth) into a large heatproof bowl *(pic 1)*. Discard the vegetables. Clean the pan.

2 Melt the butter in the cleaned saucepan over medium heat. Add the flour and cook, stirring, for 1 minute. Gradually stir in the strained broth and lemon juice. Stir until the mixture boils and thickens slightly *(pic 2)*. Stir in the creamed corn, corn kernels and cream. Reduce the heat and simmer for 20 minutes.

3 Meanwhile, carve the chicken (see page 26, and *pic 3),* then remove and discard the skin and bones. Shred the meat coarsely, add to the soup and stir until heated through. Serve sprinkled with the chives.

1

2

3

TIP This soup can be stored in an airtight container in the freezer for up to 2 months. Thaw in the refrigerator.

Chicken dumplings

Intensifying and infusing the chicken stock that these dumplings are simmered in adds a great depth of flavour to these irresistible morsels. Use the broth as a base for soup, if desired.

MAKES 40   **PREPARATION TIME** 30 minutes (+ 10 minutes cooling)   **COOKING TIME** 45 minutes

300 g (10½ oz) minced (ground) skinless chicken thigh fillets (see page 25)
1½ teaspoons finely grated ginger
1 tablespoon hoisin sauce
2 tablespoons finely snipped garlic chives
1 teaspoon dark soy sauce
1 teaspoon black vinegar (see tip)
40 round gow gee (egg) dumpling wrappers
2 teaspoons cornflour (cornstarch)
Light soy sauce, to serve

POACHING BROTH

3 litres (105 fl oz/12 cups) white chicken stock (see page 30)
1 dried shiitake mushroom (see tip)
1 piece dried mandarin peel (see tip)
2 spring onions (scallions), white part only, split in half lengthways
2 star anise
1 cm (½ inch) piece ginger, sliced
1 piece cassia bark
1 tablespoon light soy sauce

1 To make the poaching broth, place the stock in a large saucepan and bring to the boil. Boil for 15 minutes or until reduced by a third. Add the dried shiitake mushroom, mandarin peel, spring onions, star anise, ginger and cassia, reduce the heat and simmer for 10 minutes to allow the flavours to infuse. Set aside to cool for 10 minutes. Strain the broth into a clean saucepan and place over medium heat. Stir in the light soy sauce and bring to a simmer.

2 Meanwhile, place the chicken, ginger, hoisin sauce, garlic chives, dark soy sauce and black vinegar in a bowl and mix with your hands to combine. Lay out a few gow gee wrappers on a clean, dry work surface. Place a heaped teaspoon of the chicken mixture in the centre of each wrapper *(pic 1)*. Combine the cornflour with 2 tablespoons water in a small bowl and use your finger to spread some around the edge of a wrapper *(pic 2)*. Holding the wrapper in your hand, fold it over to form a half-moon shape. Pleat and press the edges to enclose the filling, forming a dumpling *(pic 3)*. Repeat with the remaining wrappers and filling.

3 Add the dumplings to the simmering broth in batches, cooking them for 3–4 minutes or until just cooked through. Remove with a slotted spoon and serve immediately with soy sauce.

TIP Black vinegar is either dark brown or black in colour and has an intense flavour, with the aged vinegars being highly prized.
Black vinegar, dried shiitake mushrooms and dried mandarin peel are all available from Asian supermarkets.

Chicken ravioli with mushroom sauce

SERVES 8 as an entrée   **PREPARATION TIME** 40 minutes (+ 1 hour chilling)   **COOKING TIME** 25 minutes

250 g (9 oz) skinless chicken breast fillets, trimmed

2 spring onions (scallions), finely chopped

1 egg white

185 ml (6 fl oz/¾ cup) thin (pouring/whipping) cream

64 square won ton wrappers

1 egg yolk, lightly whisked

Freshly grated or shaved parmesan cheese (optional), to serve

MUSHROOM SAUCE

40 g (1½ oz) butter

1 tablespoon olive oil

500 g (1 lb 2 oz) button mushrooms, cleaned, thinly sliced

80 ml (2½ fl oz/⅓ cup) brandy

500 ml (17 fl oz/2 cups) thin (pouring/whipping) cream

250 ml (9 fl oz/1 cup) good-quality ready-made or home-made chicken stock (see page 30)

2 tablespoons lemon juice

⅓ cup finely snipped chives

1 Coarsely chop the chicken and put in a food processor with the spring onions, then process until finely minced (ground) *(pic 1)*. Add the egg white and process until smooth. Transfer the mixture to a medium bowl, cover with plastic wrap and refrigerate for 1 hour.

2 Use a wooden spoon to gradually stir the cream into the chicken mixture until evenly incorporated. Season well with salt and pepper.

3 Working quickly and in batches, place 5–6 won ton wrappers on a work surface and place 2 teaspoons of mixture on the centre of each. Brush the edges of the wrappers lightly with a little of the egg yolk *(pic 2)*, cover each with another wrapper, then firmly press the edges together to enclose the filling. Repeat with the remaining wrappers and filling. Use a round 7 cm (2¾ inch) cutter to cut the ravioli into discs *(pic 3)*. Place on a tray lined with non-stick baking paper, with baking paper separating each layer. Cover with plastic wrap and refrigerate until needed.

4 To make the mushroom sauce, melt the butter and oil in a large frying pan over high heat until foaming. Add the mushrooms and cook, stirring often, for 3–4 minutes or until tender and browned. Stir in the brandy and cook for 30 seconds. Stir in the cream, stock, lemon juice and chives and bring to a simmer. Simmer for 2 minutes or until thickened slightly. Taste and season with salt and pepper. Remove from the heat, cover and set aside.

5 Bring a large saucepan of salted water to the boil. Add a third of the ravioli and simmer for 4–5 minutes or until the wrappers are tender, the filling is cooked and they rise to the surface. Use a slotted spoon to remove the ravioli from the water and drain, then place them in the sauce, stirring gently to coat. Cook the remaining ravioli in 2 more batches and place in the sauce, adding a little cooking water to the sauce if it has thickened too much on standing. Serve sprinkled with parmesan, if desired.

1

2

3

Vietnamese chicken and noodle salad

SERVES 6   **PREPARATION TIME** 20 minutes (+ 10 minutes standing)   **COOKING TIME** 15 minutes

2 kaffir lime leaves

600 g (1 lb 5 oz) skinless chicken breast
   fillets, halved lengthways

150 g (5½ oz) rice vermicelli noodles

1 small red capsicum (pepper), seeded
   and thinly sliced

1 large carrot, cut into thin matchsticks

100 g (3½ oz) snow peas (mangetout),
   trimmed, thinly sliced

½ small Chinese cabbage (wong bok),
   finely shredded (see tip)

2 spring onions (scallions), thinly sliced

60 g (2¼ oz/½ cup) bean sprouts,
   trimmed

½ cup mint leaves

½ cup coriander (cilantro) leaves

60 g (2¼ oz) roasted unsalted peanuts,
   coarsely chopped

CHILLI DRESSING

80 ml (2½ fl oz/⅓ cup) sweet
   chilli sauce

2 tablespoons fish sauce

60 ml (2 fl oz/¼ cup) lime juice

3 teaspoons sesame oil

1 large garlic clove, crushed

1 Put 1 litre (35 fl oz/4 cups) water
and the kaffir lime leaves in a medium
saucepan over medium–high heat. Bring
to the boil, then reduce the heat to a
simmer. Add the chicken, cover and
simmer for 8–10 minutes or until just
cooked through. Remove from the heat
and leave the chicken in the poaching
liquid for 10 minutes. Drain, then
coarsely shred the chicken *(pic 1)*.

2 Put the noodles in a heatproof bowl.
Cover with boiling water and set aside
for 2–3 minutes or until tender. Drain.
Rinse under cold water, and drain.

3 To make the chilli dressing, put
the sauces, lime juice, oil and garlic
in a small bowl and whisk until well
combined *(pic 2)*.

4 Combine the capsicum, carrot, snow
peas, Chinese cabbage, spring onions,
bean sprouts, half the herbs, the noodles
and chicken in a large bowl *(pic 3)*.
Drizzle with the dressing and toss to
combine. Serve the salad sprinkled with
the remaining herbs and the nuts.

1

2

3

TIP Chinese cabbage is
elongated in shape with a crisp,
crinkly, pale-green leaf.

Hainan chicken rice with ginger and spring onion sauce

SERVES 4–6 **PREPARATION TIME** 10 minutes (+ 2 hours standing) **COOKING TIME** 1 hour 15 minutes

5 cm (2 inch) piece ginger, sliced

2 spring onions (scallions), trimmed

1 teaspoon sesame oil

2 litres (70 fl oz/8 cups) white chicken stock (see page 30), approximately

4 pandan leaves, knotted (optional, see tip)

1.8 kg (4 lb) whole chicken

Seeded and sliced Lebanese (short) cucumber, coriander (cilantro) sprigs, sliced red chillies and soy sauce, to serve

RICE

3 teaspoons peanut oil

1 garlic clove, crushed

300 g (10½ oz/1½ cups) jasmine rice

SAUCE

2 tablespoons peanut oil

1 tablespoon finely chopped ginger

2 garlic cloves, crushed

6 spring onions (scallions), trimmed and finely chopped

1 teaspoon sesame oil

1 Combine the ginger, spring onions, sesame oil, stock and pandan leaves, if using, in a large saucepan over high heat. Bring to the boil, then carefully add the chicken, breast side down *(pic 1)*. Bring the liquid to just below a simmer (the surface should be trembling but small bubbles should not be breaking the surface). Cover and cook over a very low heat for 40 minutes; do not allow the stock to come to a full simmer or the chicken will be tough. Without lifting the lid, remove the pan from the heat and set aside at room temperature for 2 hours to allow the chicken to finish cooking. When the chicken has cooled, remove it carefully *(pic 2)*, reserving and straining the cooking liquid.

2 To make the rice, measure 625 ml (21½ fl oz/2½ cups) of the reserved stock. Heat the oil in a medium saucepan, add the garlic and rice and cook, stirring, for 2–3 minutes or until aromatic. Add the stock and bring to a simmer, then cover the pan tightly, reduce the heat to low and cook for about 15 minutes or until the liquid is absorbed. Remove from the heat and stand, covered, for 5 minutes.

3 Meanwhile, to make the sauce, heat the oil over medium–low heat in a small saucepan. Add the ginger and garlic and cook, stirring, for 2 minutes or until slightly softened and aromatic. Add the spring onions *(pic 3)* and stir to combine, then remove from the heat. Stir in the sesame oil and 80 ml (2½ fl oz/⅓ cup) reserved stock or enough to form a thick sauce. Season with sea salt and freshly ground black pepper, to taste.

4 Cut the chicken Chinese-style (see page 28) and place on a platter with the cucumber slices. Scatter with the coriander and chillies, drizzle with a little of the reserved chicken stock and spoon over the sauce. Serve with the rice and soy sauce passed separately.

1

2

3

TIP Pandan leaves are narrow and elongated with a subtle, yet distinctive, aroma and flavour. They are available from Asian supermarkets.

Chicken and vegetable soup with parsley pistou

This hearty soup is a complete meal in itself, loaded with vegetables, rice and pasta and sublime flavours that hail from the Mediterranean. If you don't have time to poach a chicken, use leftover chicken and home-made stock from the freezer or a good-quality ready-made one.

SERVES 8   **PREPARATION TIME** 35 minutes (+ 1 hour cooling)   **COOKING TIME** 1 hour 10 minutes

60 ml (2 fl oz/¼ cup) olive oil
2 brown onions, chopped
1 celery stalk, finely chopped
2 carrots, cut into 1 cm (½ inch) pieces
1 small fennel bulb, trimmed, chopped
    into 1 cm (½ inch) pieces
4 garlic cloves, chopped
3 sprigs each thyme, oregano and
    flat-leaf (Italian) parsley
75 g (2¾ oz/⅓ cup) arborio rice
100 g (3½ oz) baby orecchiette pasta
100 g (3½ oz) baby spinach leaves
75 g (2¾ oz/½ cup) frozen peas
Extra virgin olive oil, shaved Parmigiano
    Reggiano cheese and crusty bread,
    to serve

POACHED CHICKEN

1.8 kg (4 lb) whole chicken
1 carrot, chopped
1 brown onion, halved
1 celery stalk, chopped
6 flat-leaf (Italian) parsley stalks

PARSLEY PISTOU

4 garlic cloves, chopped
1 cup firmly packed flat-leaf
    (Italian) parsley leaves
80 ml (2½ fl oz/⅓ cup) extra virgin
    olive oil

1 To make the poached chicken, wash the chicken briefly under cold running water, remove the neck and giblets and trim any pockets of fat, then pat dry with paper towels. Put the chicken in a large stockpot, add the carrot, onion, celery and parsley stalks. Cover with cold water, bring slowly to the boil and simmer gently for 40 minutes,

skimming any scum from the surface occasionally. Turn off the heat and cool the chicken in the stock for at least 1 hour. Remove the chicken, then strain and reserve the stock. Cool, then skim the fat from the surface. When the chicken is cool enough to handle, remove the skin and bones and shred the flesh into bite-sized pieces.

2 To make the parsley pistou, crush the garlic and parsley to a paste using a mortar and pestle. Season to taste and gradually incorporate the oil *(pic 1)*.

3 Meanwhile, heat the olive oil in a large saucepan over low heat, add the onions, celery, carrots and fennel, cover and cook for about 15 minutes or until the vegetables are soft *(pic 2)*. Add the garlic and herbs and stir for 2 minutes.

4 Add 3 litres (105 fl oz/12 cups) of the reserved stock, the rice and pasta to the pan. Bring to the boil over high heat, then reduce the heat to low and simmer, covered, for 8 minutes.

5 Remove the herb sprigs from the soup *(pic 3)*. Add 3 cups of shredded chicken (reserve the remaining chicken for another use), the spinach and peas and simmer, uncovered, for 5 minutes or until the rice and pasta are just cooked.

6 Ladle the soup into bowls, stir in a spoonful of parsley pistou, drizzle with extra virgin olive oil, sprinkle with Parmigiano Reggiano and serve with crusty bread.

1

2

3

TIP The parsley pistou can also be made in a small food processor.

Coconut-poached chicken

SERVES 4   **PREPARATION TIME** 15 minutes (+ 10 minutes standing)   **COOKING TIME** 20 minutes

400 ml (14 fl oz) tin coconut milk

250 ml (9 fl oz/1 cup) good-quality ready-made or home-made chicken stock (see page 30)

1 tablespoon grated palm sugar (jaggery)

1 lemongrass stem, pale part only, trimmed and chopped

2 garlic cloves, thinly sliced

4 cm (1½ inch) piece ginger, cut into matchsticks

2 tablespoons chopped coriander (cilantro) root (see tip)

1 long red chilli, thinly sliced

4 x 150 g (5½ oz) skinless chicken breast fillets

2 tablespoons fish sauce

2 tablespoons lime juice

1 large carrot, shredded

115 g (4 oz/1 cup) bean sprouts, trimmed

2 spring onions (scallions), thinly sliced

¾ cup coriander (cilantro) leaves

½ cup mint leaves

Steamed jasmine rice, to serve

1 Combine the coconut milk, stock, palm sugar, lemongrass, garlic, ginger, coriander root and chilli in a large saucepan over medium–high heat *(pic 1)* and bring just to a simmer. Reduce the heat, add the chicken, cover and simmer very gently for 5 minutes. Uncover and very gently simmer for a further 5 minutes or until the chicken is just cooked through.

2 Remove the pan from the heat and set aside for 5 minutes. Remove the chicken from the pan *(pic 2)* and set aside for 5 minutes before slicing thinly. Set aside, covered to keep warm.

3 Meanwhile, return the poaching liquid to the boil. Boil for 5–7 minutes or until the liquid has reduced by half. Strain and discard the solids *(pic 3)*, then stir in the fish sauce and lime juice.

4 Meanwhile, combine the carrot, bean sprouts, spring onions and herbs in a bowl. Spoon the rice onto serving plates. Top with the sliced chicken, drizzle with the poaching liquid and finish with the herb mixture.

1

2

3

TIP Coriander roots are a great way to add an intense coriander flavour to a dish. Wash them well before chopping to remove any grit.

Chicken, quinoa and corn soup

Quinoa has a nutty flavour and a high protein content. Most quinoa comes pre-rinsed but just in case, it's a good habit to rinse it under cold water until the water runs clear, then drain it. This removes any bitter-tasting outer coating.

SERVES 6 **PREPARATION TIME** 20 minutes **COOKING TIME** 30 minutes

1 tablespoon olive oil

1 brown onion, diced

2 celery stalks, trimmed and diced

2 skinless chicken breast fillets
(500 g/1 lb 2 oz)

150 g (5½ oz/¾ cup) white quinoa,
rinsed and drained

3 corn cobs

⅓ cup flat-leaf (Italian) parsley leaves,
roughly chopped

1 Heat the oil in a large saucepan over medium heat, add the onion and celery and cook, stirring, for 5 minutes or until softened. Add 2 litres (70 fl oz/8 cups) water and the chicken, season with salt and freshly ground black pepper and bring to the boil over medium heat. Reduce the heat to a slow simmer and cook for 2 minutes or until the chicken is just cooked through *(pic 1)*. Remove the chicken from the pan and set aside to cool slightly.

2 Stir the quinoa into the poaching liquid *(pic 2)* and gently boil, covered, for 15 minutes or until the quinoa starts to soften. Meanwhile, shred the chicken into bite-sized pieces.

3 Cut the kernels from the corn cobs. To do this, place each cob upright on a chopping board and cut down the sides of the cob to remove the kernels *(pic 3)*. Halving the cobs crossways beforehand makes them easier to handle.

4 Add the corn kernels to the soup and simmer for a further 5 minutes or until the quinoa is tender but the corn is only just tender.

5 Return the chicken to the soup and simmer for 1 minute, or until heated through. Check the seasoning and stir in the parsley.

1

2

3

TIP If you're in a hurry you can make this soup using good-quality chicken stock and some shredded barbecued chicken.

Chargrilling and Barbecuing

Barbecued Tuscan chicken

SERVES 4   **PREPARATION TIME** 25 minutes (+ 4 hours marinating)   **COOKING TIME** 40 minutes

1.2 kg (2 lb 10 oz) whole chicken
1 lemon, zest finely grated and juiced
2 garlic cloves, crushed
2 tablespoons finely chopped sage or
  rosemary leaves
80 ml (2½ fl oz/⅓ cup) extra virgin
  olive oil
2 teaspoons sea salt flakes

BEAN SALAD
400 g (14 oz) green beans, topped
400 g (14 oz) tin borlotti (cranberry)
  beans, drained and rinsed
1 bunch rocket (arugula), washed
  and dried
2 tablespoons lemon juice
60 ml (2 fl oz/¼ cup) extra virgin
  olive oil

1 Wash the chicken briefly under cold running water, remove the neck and giblets and trim any pockets of fat. Pat the chicken dry with paper towels and place, breast side up, on a chopping board. Use kitchen scissors to cut through the chicken on either side of the backbone *(pic 1)*. Remove the backbone and discard or reserve for stock. Flatten the chicken, skin side up, using your hand to press down hard on the breastbone to break it *(pic 2)*.

2 Whisk together the lemon zest, 2½ tablespoons of lemon juice, the garlic, sage or rosemary, olive oil, salt and some freshly ground black pepper

until combined. Add the chicken, turning to coat. Cover with plastic wrap and refrigerate for 4 hours to marinate.

3 Drain the chicken, reserving the marinade. Heat a barbecue grill to medium–low heat. Put the chicken on the grill, skin side down, then weight the chicken to flatten it. The easiest way to do this is to place a roasting pan or frying pan holding 2–3 kg (4 lb 8 oz– 6 lb 12 oz) of tinned food on top of the chicken *(pic 3)*. Cook the chicken for 40 minutes or until it is just cooked through and the juices run clear when the chicken is pierced through the thickest part (between the thigh and body). Set aside for 5 minutes to rest.

4 Meanwhile for the bean salad, cook the green beans in a saucepan of boiling salted water for 3–4 minutes or until tender-crisp and bright green. Drain well and refresh under cold running water. Combine with the remaining ingredients in a large bowl.

5 Transfer the chicken to a chopping board. Cut it in half lengthways through the breast, then cut each half into four pieces. Serve with bean salad.

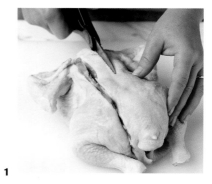

1

2

3

> **Tip** You can also add some black olives to the bean salad and serve with the chicken, along with boiled new potatoes, if you wish.

Lebanese chicken skewers

SERVES 4   **PREPARATION TIME** 20 minutes (+ 15 minutes standing/marinating)   **COOKING TIME** 20 minutes

600 g (1 lb 5 oz) skinless chicken thigh
   fillets, cut into 3 cm (1¼ inch) cubes
2 garlic cloves, smashed
1 tablespoon olive oil
1 teaspoon allspice
1 small brown onion, cut into 8 wedges
Hummus and pitta bread, to serve

TABOULEH
45 g (1¾ oz/¼ cup) burghul (bulgur)
2 large tomatoes, diced
1½ cups finely chopped flat-leaf
   (Italian) parsley
½ cup finely chopped mint
2 spring onions (scallions), trimmed,
   finely chopped
2 tablespoons extra virgin olive oil
1 tablespoon lemon juice

1 Start by making the tabouleh. Put the burghul in a medium saucepan with 250 ml (9 fl oz/1 cup) water. Bring to the boil over high heat. Reduce the heat and simmer for 5 minutes, until the burghul starts to soften. Set aside for 15 minutes or until it is just tender.

2 Meanwhile, combine the chicken, garlic, oil and allspice in a medium bowl. Season generously with freshly ground black pepper and toss to coat *(pic 1)*. Cover and put in the refrigerator for 15 minutes to marinate.

3 Drain the burghul and put in a medium bowl. When it has cooled to room temperature, add the remaining ingredients and toss to combine. Season with salt and freshly ground black pepper. Set aside.

4 Season the chicken with salt. Thread the chicken and onion alternately onto 4 long metal skewers *(pic 2)*. Heat a chargrill pan over medium heat and cook the skewers *(pic 3)*, turning occasionally, for 10–12 minutes or until lightly charred and cooked through.

5 Serve the chicken skewers with the tabouleh, hummus and pitta bread.

Chargrilled caesar salad

SERVES 4   **PREPARATION TIME** 15 minutes (+ 5 minutes resting)   **COOKING TIME** 20 minutes

60 ml (2 fl oz/¼ cup) olive oil
½ loaf rustic bread (such as sourdough
   or ciabatta), crust removed
12 thin slices pancetta or 4 thin
   bacon rashers
4 skinless chicken breast fillets,
   trimmed
2 baby cos (romaine) lettuces, leaves
   separated and washed
2 tablespoons finely grated
   parmesan cheese
Anchovy fillets, to serve (optional)
Shaved parmesan cheese, to serve

DRESSING
1 garlic clove
4 anchovy fillets
½ teaspoon sea salt flakes
1 egg yolk
1½ tablespoons white wine vinegar
1 teaspoon dijon mustard
125 ml (4 fl oz/½ cup) olive oil

1 Preheat the oven to 180°C (350°F/
Gas 4). Put 1½ tablespoons of the oil
in a bowl and season with salt. Tear the
bread into pieces, approximately 3 cm
(1¼ inches), add to the bowl *(pic 1)*
and toss to coat in the oil. Spread on
a baking tray. Place the pancetta on a

separate baking tray and brush with
2 teaspoons of the remaining oil.
Cook the pancetta for 6–8 minutes
or until crisp. Cook the croutons for
8–10 minutes or until light golden.
Remove both trays from the oven
and set aside.

2 To make the dressing, pound the
garlic, anchovies and sea salt using a
mortar and pestle until a paste forms.
Whisk in the egg yolk, vinegar and
mustard. Gradually whisk in the oil
until incorporated *(pic 2)*.

3 Preheat the barbecue grill to medium.
Brush the chicken with the remaining
oil and season with sea salt and freshly
ground black pepper. Cook for
5 minutes each side, until just cooked
through. Set aside for 5 minutes to rest.

4 Put the lettuce leaves in a large bowl.
Drizzle over the dressing, add the grated
parmesan, season with salt and pepper
and toss well. Slice the chicken across
the grain *(pic 3)*, add to the bowl with
the croutons and pancetta and toss
gently. Serve the salad topped with
anchovies and shaved parmesan.

1

2

3

Barbecued chicken wings

These chicken wings are cooked using two different methods. Poaching them adds flavour and helps them remain succulent inside, while barbecuing makes the outside deliciously crisp and charred.

SERVES 4 as an entrée   **PREPARATION TIME** 1 hour (+ 2 hours chilling, 1 hour marinating, and cooling)
COOKING TIME 50 minutes

1.2 kg (2 lb 10 oz) chicken wings
5 cm (2 inch) piece galangal, thinly
    sliced (optional)
5 kaffir lime leaves
5 cm (2 inch) lemongrass stem,
    pale part only, sliced
5 cm (2 inch) piece ginger, thinly sliced
4 garlic cloves, halved
4 French shallots, peeled and sliced
3 small red chillies, halved lengthways
12 coriander (cilantro) sprigs
1 teaspoon salt

MARINADE
2 tablespoons sesame oil
2 garlic cloves, peeled and halved
90 ml (3 fl oz) dark soy sauce
90 ml (3 fl oz) light soy sauce
200 g (7 oz) caster (superfine) sugar
125 ml (4 fl oz/½ cup) rice wine vinegar
2 long red chillies, thinly sliced
10 cm (4 inch) piece ginger, peeled
    and finely grated

1 Put the chicken, galangal (if using), kaffir lime leaves, lemongrass, ginger, garlic, shallots, chillies, coriander and salt in a large saucepan *(pic 1)*. Add enough water to cover. Place over high heat and bring to the boil, then reduce the heat and simmer for 20 minutes. Cool, then cover and refrigerate for 2 hours.

2 To make the marinade, heat the sesame oil in a small saucepan over medium heat and cook the garlic cloves for 2 minutes, until light golden. Add the soy sauces, sugar and vinegar. Increase the heat and bring to the boil, then reduce the heat and simmer for 10 minutes. Add the chillies and ginger and set aside to cool to room temperature. Reserve 80 ml (2½ fl oz/⅓ cup) of the marinade to serve. Place the remaining marinade in a large snap-lock bag or glass or ceramic bowl.

3 Use a pair of tongs to transfer the chicken wings from the stock to the marinade *(pic 2)*. Discard the stock. Coat the chicken in the marinade (see tip). Cover and refrigerate for 1 hour to marinate.

4 Preheat the barbecue grill to medium–high. Drain the chicken from the marinade and cook for 8–10 minutes, turning once *(pic 3)*, until nicely charred and heated through. Drizzle the chicken wings with the reserved marinade and serve.

1

2

3

TIP When marinating chicken, it's a good idea to seal the chicken and marinade in a strong snap-lock bag. This helps it become well and evenly coated with the marinade, and makes it easier to turn too.

Barbecued chicken with salsa verde

SERVES 4   **PREPARATION TIME** 20 minutes   **COOKING TIME** 12 minutes

4 (about 650 g/1 lb 7 oz) skinless
   chicken breast fillets
1 tablespoon olive oil
2 garlic cloves, smashed
4 large strips lemon zest (see tip)
Steamed potatoes, to serve

SALSA VERDE
80 ml (2½ fl oz/⅓ cup) extra virgin
   olive oil
1 cup basil leaves
1 cup flat-leaf (Italian) parsley leaves
2 anchovy fillets
1 garlic clove, crushed
1 tablespoon lemon juice
1 teaspoon drained capers, rinsed

TOMATO AND RED ONION SALAD
500 g (1 lb 2 oz) ripe tomatoes,
   sliced *(pic 3)*
¼ small red onion, thinly sliced
2 tablespoons extra virgin olive oil
1½ tablespoons balsamic vinegar

1 Combine the chicken, oil, garlic and lemon zest in a medium bowl. Season with pepper *(pic 1)* and toss to coat. Set aside to marinate while you prepare the salsa verde and salad.

2 To make the salsa verde, process all the ingredients in a small food processor until a chunky sauce forms *(pic 2)*.

3 To make the tomato and red onion salad, arrange the tomatoes and onion on a serving plate. Drizzle with the oil and vinegar and season with sea salt and freshly ground black pepper.

4 Preheat a chargrill pan over medium heat. Season the chicken with salt and then chargrill, turning once, for 10–12 minutes or until lightly charred and just cooked through.

5 Serve the chicken with the tomato salad and steamed potatoes, and with the salsa verde spooned over.

1

2

3

Tip As the lemon zest for the chicken marinade will be discarded, simply peel a few strips with a vegetable peeler.

Tandoori chicken

SERVES 4   **PREPARATION TIME** 20 minutes (+ 4 hours marinating)   **COOKING TIME** 30 minutes

60 ml (2 fl oz/¼ cup) malt vinegar
or lemon juice

2½ teaspoons ground chilli

2½ teaspoons sweet paprika

3 teaspoons ground coriander

3 teaspoons ground cumin

1½ teaspoons garam masala

1½ tablespoons finely grated ginger

6 garlic cloves, crushed

1½ teaspoons salt

95 g (3¼ oz/⅓ cup) plain yoghurt

1.4 kg (3 lb 2 oz) whole chicken,
spatchcocked (see page 22)

60 ml (2 fl oz/¼ cup) melted ghee or
vegetable oil

Cooked basmati rice and/or naan bread
or chapattis, and lemon wedges,
to serve

1 Combine the vinegar, chilli, paprika, coriander, cumin, garam masala, ginger, garlic, salt and yoghurt in a medium glass or ceramic bowl.

2 Place the chicken, skin side up, on a chopping board. Use a sharp knife to make 6 slashes, about 5 mm (¼ inch) deep, in the fleshy part of the chicken *(pic 1)*. Place the chicken on a tray and use your fingertips to spread the marinade over until well coated, rubbing it into the flesh. Cover with plastic wrap and refrigerate for 4 hours or overnight to marinate.

3 Preheat a barbecue plate or grill to medium. Brush with the ghee or oil, then put the chicken on the preheated barbecue, skin side up, and cook, brushing occasionally with any marinade remaining in the bowl *(pic 2)* and turning halfway through cooking, for 30 minutes or until charred and just cooked through.

4 Use a sharp knife to cut the chicken into 8 portions *(pic 3)* (see page 18). Serve with rice and/or bread, and lemon wedges on the side.

1

2

3

Tip You can use 1 kg (2 lb 4 oz) chicken drumsticks instead of the whole chicken. Reduce the cooking time to 20 minutes and turn them frequently during cooking.

Barbecued quail with peach and asparagus salad

SERVES 4 **PREPARATION TIME** 40 minutes (+ 2 hours marinating and 30 minutes standing) **COOKING TIME** 20 minutes

1 teaspoon ground ginger
1 teaspoon ground cinnamon
Large pinch of saffron threads
60 ml (2 fl oz/¼ cup) olive oil
2 tablespoons lemon juice
4 quails, spatchcocked (see page 22)
8 quail eggs (see tip)
16 asparagus spears, trimmed
1 tablespoon olive oil, extra
150 g (5½ oz) bacon rashers or
    sliced speck, trimmed, cut into
    1 cm (½ inch) strips
2 witlof (chicory/Belgian endive),
    leaves separated
75 g (2¾ oz) trimmed watercress sprigs
2 peaches, cut into thin wedges
35 g (1¼ oz/¼ cup) coarsely chopped
    roasted and skinned hazelnuts

DRESSING
1½ tablespoons red wine vinegar
    or caramelised balsamic vinegar
    (see tip)
1 tablespoon maple syrup
60 ml (2 fl oz/¼ cup) extra virgin
    olive oil

1 Combine the ginger, cinnamon, saffron, olive oil and lemon juice in a medium glass or ceramic bowl and season with salt and pepper. Add the quails, turn to coat, cover and refrigerate for 2 hours or overnight to marinate *(pic 1)*.

2 Remove the quails from the refrigerator and set aside, still in the marinade, at room temperature for 30 minutes. Preheat the barbecue plate or chargrill to high. Remove the quails from the marinade and barbecue, skin side down, for 5–6 minutes or until well browned. Turn *(pic 2)* and barbecue for

another 5–6 minutes for medium or until cooked to your liking. Transfer to a baking tray, cover loosely with foil and set aside for 10 minutes to rest.

3 Meanwhile, bring a small saucepan of water to the boil, then reduce the heat to low, carefully add the quail eggs and simmer for 3 minutes. Use a slotted spoon to remove *(pic 3)* and rinse under cold running water. Peel the eggs when they are cool enough to handle, then cut in half lengthways and set aside.

4 Bring a saucepan of salted water to the boil over medium heat, add the asparagus and cook for 1 minute or until tender-crisp and bright green. Drain, rinse under cold running water and pat dry with paper towels. Set aside.

5 Heat the extra olive oil in a frying pan over medium heat and cook the bacon, tossing often, for 3–4 minutes or until crisp. Drain on paper towels.

6 To make the dressing, combine all the ingredients in a screw-top jar, season with salt and freshly ground black pepper and shake well to combine.

7 Put the asparagus on serving plates. Toss the witlof and watercress with half the dressing and place over the asparagus. Top with the quail eggs, bacon, peach wedges and barbecued quails. Drizzle with the remaining dressing and sprinkle with hazelnuts.

1

2

3

TIP Caramelised balsamic vinegar is available from speciality food stores and some delicatessens.
  Peaches are ideal in this salad, but if you would like to make it in autumn or winter, 2 small pears will make a good substitute.
  If quail eggs are not available, just leave them out rather than substituting boiled hen eggs.

Piri piri spatchcock

Piri piri is a classic Portuguese marinade for chicken, although here we use it for spatchcock. It varies in heat and this recipe is 'medium' hot. If you want more fire, use hot instead of sweet paprika.

SERVES 4   **PREPARATION TIME** 25 minutes (+ 2 hours marinating and 40 minutes standing)   **COOKING TIME** 20 minutes

4 large red chillies, seeded and chopped
3 garlic cloves, chopped
1 teaspoon salt
1 teaspoon dried oregano
½ teaspoon sweet paprika
60 ml (2 fl oz/¼ cup) cider vinegar
60 ml (2 fl oz/¼ cup) extra virgin olive oil
2 x 500 g (1 lb 2 oz) spatchcocks
2 egg yolks
200 ml (7 fl oz) light olive oil
2 tablespoons lemon juice
Crunchy roasted potato wedges, green salad and lemon wedges, to serve

1 Combine the chillies, garlic, salt, oregano, paprika, vinegar and extra virgin olive oil in a small saucepan and cook over medium heat for 3 minutes. Cool, then blend in a small food processor until smooth, or use a hand-held stick blender.

2 Halve the spatchcocks. Use poultry scissors to cut down either side of the backbones (*pic 1*) and discard. Cut between both breasts. Make several cuts into the flesh of the spatchcocks.

3 Place the spatchcocks in a large bowl and add all but 2 tablespoons of the piri piri sauce, rubbing it into the birds with your hands. Cover with plastic wrap and refrigerate for 2 hours or overnight if possible. Reserve the remaining sauce. Stand the spatchcocks at room temperature for 30 minutes before cooking.

4 Meanwhile, combine the egg yolks and reserved sauce in a bowl using a hand-held stick blender. With the stick blender running, gradually add the oil in a thin stream until the aïoli is thick (*pic 2*). Add the lemon juice and process until smooth. Season to taste, cover and refrigerate until ready to use.

5 Preheat the barbecue or chargrill to medium–high. Remove the spatchcocks from the marinade and cook, skin side down, for about 8 minutes, until well browned (*pic 3*). Turn and barbecue for a further 8 minutes or until cooked through. Transfer to a baking tray, cover loosely with foil and rest for 10 minutes.

6 Use a knife to separate the leg and breast meat of each spatchcock half. Serve the spatchcock portions on a bed of green salad with crunchy potato wedges, aïoli and lemon wedges.

1

2

3

TIP A whole chicken can also be used for this recipe. For best results, cut the chicken into 8 pieces (see page 18) and slash the flesh before marinating.

Chicken burgers

SERVES 4   **PREPARATION TIME** 15 minutes   **COOKING TIME** 10 minutes

500 g (1 lb 2 oz) minced (ground)
skinless chicken thighs (see page 25)
40 g (1½ oz/⅓ cup) dry breadcrumbs
1 egg
1 spring onion (scallion), finely chopped
2 teaspoons thyme leaves
1 teaspoon finely grated lemon zest
4 burger buns, split
Olive oil, to drizzle
85 g (3 oz/⅓ cup) whole egg
mayonnaise
1 Lebanese (short) cucumber
180 g (6¼ oz/4 cups, loosely packed)
baby rocket (arugula)
Perfect fries (see page 68), to serve

1 Put the chicken, breadcrumbs, egg,
spring onion, thyme and lemon zest
in a medium bowl and mix until well
combined. Season with salt and pepper.
Shape the mixture into 4 large patties
(about 10 cm/4 inches wide) *(pic 1)*.

2 Heat a chargrill pan over medium–high
heat. Chargrill the burger buns, cut
side down, for 1 minute or until lightly
charred *(pic 2)*.

3 Drizzle the chicken patties with a
little oil. Reduce the heat to medium
and cook the patties for 3–4 minutes
each side or until lightly charred and
cooked through.

4 Meanwhile, spread the buns with
mayonnaise and use a wide vegetable
peeler to cut the cucumber into thin
ribbons *(pic 3)*. Sandwich the rocket,
patties and cucumber between buns.
Serve the burgers with the fries.

1

2

3

Tip You can vary the size of the
patties according to the size of
your buns, but bear in mind that
the thicker they are, the longer
they will take to cook.

Bay leaf and lemon skewers with parsley sauce

SERVES 4 **PREPARATION TIME** 20 minutes (+ 30 minutes soaking/marinating) **COOKING TIME** 8 minutes

700 g (1 lb 9 oz) skinless chicken breast
    fillets, cut into 2.5 cm (1 inch) chunks
60 ml (2 fl oz/¼ cup) olive oil
2 lemons, zest removed in strips with
    a vegetable peeler, and juiced
16 fresh bay leaves
1 teaspoon dried oregano
4 large garlic cloves, thinly sliced
Tomato salad and lemon wedges,
    to serve

PARSLEY SAUCE
1 cup, firmly packed, flat-leaf (Italian)
    parsley leaves
1 tablespoon oregano leaves
2 spring onions (scallions)
2 garlic cloves
Pinch of ground cinnamon
Pinch of ground cumin
60 ml (2 fl oz/¼ cup) olive oil
2 tablespoons lemon juice

1 Soak 8 wooden skewers in water for 30 minutes to prevent scorching during cooking.

2 Combine the chicken, olive oil, lemon zest and juice, bay leaves, oregano and garlic in a medium glass or ceramic bowl, season with salt and freshly ground black pepper and mix well *(pic 1)*. Refrigerate while the skewers are soaking.

3 Meanwhile, to make the parsley sauce, put all the ingredients in a food processor *(pic 2)* and process until well combined and smooth. Season well with salt and freshly ground black pepper. Transfer to a serving dish, cover with plastic wrap and set aside.

4 Preheat a barbecue grill or chargrill to high. Thread the chicken, lemon zest, bay leaves and garlic slices alternately onto the skewers *(pic 3)*.

5 Cook the skewers for 6–8 minutes, turning occasionally, or until just cooked through. Serve with the parsley sauce, tomato salad and lemon wedges.

1

2

3

Chargrilling and barbecuing tips

1 When chargrilling or barbecuing meat, a very high heat is required to produce an appealingly charred surface and succulent, full-flavoured juicy interior. Poultry, on the other hand, generally requires a medium heat. Position the poultry about 10 cm (4 inches) from the heat source — too much heat applied to the outside will char the meat before it is cooked, while too low a heat will dry the meat before it is cooked.

2 Choose similar-sized pieces of poultry to barbecue. Dark meat (thighs and legs) will take longer to cook than white meat (breasts or wings). If using boneless thighs, use a rolling pin or meat mallet to flatten the pieces and give them a uniform thickness. Chicken breasts are difficult to keep moist during cooking, so try cutting them into smaller pieces, suitable for kebabs, for example.

3 If barbecuing a whole bird, such as a chicken, spatchcock or quail, flatten it to produce a compact shape that cooks evenly. To do this, use poultry shears to cut down either side of the backbone and remove it completely. Open the bird out as much as possible and place it, breast side up, on a flat surface. Using the heel of your hand, press down firmly on the breast to flatten it (see page 23 for a step-by-step guide). Cook the underside first, for about two-thirds of the cooking time, then turn for the remaining cooking time.

4 Lightly brush the meat or poultry with butter or oil before cooking. Do not brush the grill bars of a barbecue with oil as this will cause it to flare up.

5 Cook meat on one side until it is well coloured and half cooked, then turn it over. Avoid turning meat more than once as this results in a loss of temperature and juices, and can dry the meat out. If the cut of meat is thick, you may need to move it away from the hottest part of the chargrill or barbecue towards the end of cooking so it can finish cooking without the outside burning. Barbecues are generally cooler around the sides.

6 Additional flavours can be added during cooking. Use a brush made from sprigs of fresh bay leaves, thyme or rosemary to apply marinade.

7 Keep a bottle of water with a spray attachment nearby to spray the barbecue coals if they catch fire when a marinade is brushed over meat or poultry.

8 Never place cooked barbecue poultry on the same platter that held the raw poultry, as this could lead to contamination and food poisoning.

9 Do not pierce meat to check for doneness while it is barbecuing, as you will lose juices. Use an instant-read meat thermometer to judge when it is cooked. Also, turn the meat using tongs, don't use a sharp implement such as a meat fork.

10 Thinner cuts of meat should be served immediately to avoid drying out, but thicker steaks will benefit from a 5-minute rest before serving.

Steak sandwich with beetroot relish

Making a steak sandwich at home means you can customise it to include your favourite ingredients. Here we have used mushrooms and a beetroot relish to give an earthy, wintry version. We have used sourdough bread as it will hold its form despite the juices from the steak and mushrooms.

SERVES 4   **PREPARATION TIME** 15 minutes   **COOKING TIME** 20 minutes

4 x 120 g (4¼ oz) thin beef sirloin steaks (about 1 cm/½ inch thick), at room temperature
4 field mushrooms, cut into 1 cm (½ inch) thick slices
Olive oil, to drizzle
8 slices sourdough
Softened butter, for spreading
30 g (1 oz) baby spinach leaves

BEETROOT RELISH

1 tablespoon olive oil
1 large beetroot (about 260 g/9¼ oz), peeled and coarsely grated
60 ml (2 fl oz/¼ cup) red wine vinegar
½ teaspoon thyme leaves
80 ml (2½ fl oz/⅓ cup) water
2 tablespoons light brown sugar

1 To make the beetroot relish, put all the ingredients in a small saucepan and cook over low heat, stirring occasionally, for 15 minutes, until most of the liquid has evaporated *(pic 1)*. The beetroot should still have a tiny bit of resistance when you bite it. Season with salt and pepper, to taste, and set aside.

2 Preheat a barbecue or chargrill to high. Trim the fat from the steaks *(pic 2)* and use a meat mallet or rolling pin to beat them lightly until an even thickness. Place on a greased baking tray with the mushrooms and season with sea salt and freshly ground black pepper *(pic 3)*. Drizzle with the oil.

3 Grill (broil) the sourdough slices on one side. Cook the steaks and mushrooms for 1–2 minutes each side, until the meat is cooked to your liking. Spread the ungrilled sides of the sourdough with butter. Divide the spinach, steaks, mushrooms and beetroot relish among half the sourdough slices, then top with the remaining slices of sourdough. Serve immediately.

1

2

3

TIP It is important to use good-quality sirloin, even though it is being used for a sandwich. Ask your butcher to cut the steaks for you so they are all at the required thickness.

Veal cutlets with lemon thyme and pepper

A veal cutlet is a beautiful piece of meat that looks impressive and, when cooked and rested properly, is succulent and flavoursome. This recipe uses lemon thyme and a citrus-flavoured salt, which give a refreshing lift to the finished dish.

SERVES 4   **PREPARATION TIME** 10 minutes (+ 8 hours standing and 5 minutes resting)   **COOKING TIME** 8 minutes

4 x 230 g (8 oz) veal cutlets, trimmed, at room temperature
80 ml (2½ fl oz/⅓ cup) extra virgin olive oil
⅓ cup lemon thyme leaves
Lemon wedges, to serve

LEMON SALT
1 tablespoon sea salt
Finely grated zest of ½ lemon

1 To make the lemon salt, pound the sea salt and lemon zest using a mortar and pestle until well combined *(pic 1)*. Transfer to a small baking tray and leave in a warm place for 8 hours or overnight for the mixture to dry out a little. Use your fingers to crumble the mixture and remove any clumps.

2 Preheat a barbecue or chargrill on high. Season the cutlets lightly with sea salt and drizzle with half the oil. Cook for 2–3 minutes each side, then turn on their side, with the fat facing down *(pic 2)*, and cook for 1–2 minutes.

3 Meanwhile, finely chop the lemon thyme leaves on a chopping board. Transfer half the thyme to a small bowl. Grind black pepper over the thyme on the board and sprinkle with a little of the lemon salt. Place the veal cutlets on top *(pic 3)*, then season with a little more lemon salt and black pepper and sprinkle with the remaining chopped thyme. Set aside for 5 minutes to rest.

4 Carve each cutlet into 3 or 4 slices, leaving some meat on the bone as well. Serve on the board as part of a barbecue lunch, or plate each portion (including the bone) and drizzle over any juices and remaining thyme. Finish with a drizzle of the remaining olive oil and serve with lemon wedges.

1

2

3

TIP You can substitute orange or lime zest for the lemon zest to give a different flavour. The flavoured salt can be kept in an airtight container for up to 1 week.

Spice-marinated barbecued lamb

There's a twist to this marinade, as it is applied to the leg of lamb after barbecuing rather than before. This helps the meat absorb the flavours as it rests, making it exceptionally tasty and tender. As always, don't cut the resting time short — in this case, both flavour and tenderness depend on it.

SERVES 6 **PREPARATION TIME** 20 minutes (+ 10 minutes resting) **COOKING TIME** 35 minutes

1.25 kg (2 lb 12 oz) boned leg of lamb, butterflied (see page 53), trimmed of excess fat, at room temperature
2 garlic cloves, thinly sliced
80 ml (2½ fl oz/⅓ cup) olive oil
2 tablespoons red wine vinegar
2 tablespoons chopped coriander (cilantro) leaves
2 teaspoons ground coriander
2 teaspoons ground cumin
2 teaspoons finely grated lemon zest
Quinoa or couscous, prepared following packet instructions, to serve

1 Use a sharp knife to cut 10–12 small slits into the surface of the lamb and place a slice of garlic in each slit *(pic 1)*. Drizzle 1 tablespoon of the olive oil over the lamb and season with sea salt and freshly ground black pepper.

2 Put the remaining olive oil, the vinegar, chopped and ground coriander, cumin and lemon zest in a jug and use a fork to whisk until combined. Set aside.

3 Preheat the barbecue to high. Reduce the heat to medium and place the lamb, skin side down, on the barbecue. Cook, with the hood up, for 12–15 minutes, then turn *(pic 2)* and cook for a further 15–20 minutes or until a meat thermometer inserted into the thickest part of the lamb reads 60°C (140°F), for medium-rare lamb, or until cooked to your liking. Transfer to a large shallow dish, pour over the coriander mixture, cover loosely with foil *(pic 3)* and set aside to rest for 10 minutes, turning the lamb occasionally.

4 Thinly slice the lamb and arrange on a large serving platter. Drizzle over some of the juices in the dish. Serve with quinoa or couscous.

1

2

3

Barbecued pork ribs

This is a lip-smacking, finger-licking kind of dish that will appeal to adults and children alike. You can make the sauce and marinate the ribs the night before, leaving little to do on the day other than barbecue the ribs until they are nicely charred, juicy and loaded with flavour.

SERVES 4 **PREPARATION TIME** 15 minutes (+ cooling and 4 hours or overnight marinating)
COOKING TIME 1 hour 5 minutes

1.1 kg (2 lb 7 oz) American-style
   pork ribs

BARBECUE SAUCE
2 tablespoons vegetable oil
2 onions, chopped
2 garlic cloves, crushed
1 teaspoon chilli powder
400 g (14 oz) tin chopped tomatoes
100 g (3½ oz/½ cup, lightly packed)
   light brown sugar
125 ml (4 fl oz/½ cup) tomato sauce
   (ketchup)
1 tablespoon red wine vinegar
½ teaspoon salt

1 To make the barbecue sauce, put the oil and onions in a small saucepan over low heat and cook, stirring often, for 10–12 minutes or until golden and starting to caramelise *(pic 1)*. Add the garlic and chilli powder and cook, stirring, for 1 minute. Add the tomatoes, increase the heat to high and bring to the boil. Reduce the heat and simmer for 5 minutes, stirring occasionally. Set aside for 10 minutes to cool slightly. Add the remaining

ingredients and use a stick blender to blend until smooth. (A blender or small food processor would also do the job well.) Cool to room temperature.

2 Cut the racks of ribs in half and place in a large glass or ceramic bowl. Pour over one-third of the barbecue sauce and turn the ribs to coat *(pic 2)*. Cover with plastic wrap and refrigerate for 4 hours, or ideally overnight, to marinate.

3 Preheat a barbecue to medium–high heat. Transfer the ribs to disposable foil baking trays, meaty side up *(pic 3)*. Place the trays on the flat plate, cover with the hood and cook, using one-third of the remaining barbecue sauce to baste the ribs every 15 minutes, for 45 minutes, until the ribs are cooked and lightly charred.

4 Meanwhile, heat the remaining sauce in a small saucepan on the barbecue and serve with the ribs.

1

2

3

TIP Make a double quantity of the sauce and serve it with other barbecued meats. Refrigerate in an airtight container for up to 1 week.

Lamb, lentil, dukkah and roasted pumpkin salad with labne

The Middle Eastern flavours of this warm salad are a perfect match for lamb. If you are unable to find labne, a dollop of Greek-style yoghurt is the next best thing.

SERVES 4 **PREPARATION TIME** 25 minutes **COOKING TIME** 35 minutes

800 g (1 lb 12 oz) pumpkin (winter squash), peeled, seeded and cut into 2 cm (¾ inch) pieces
3 teaspoons ground cumin
60 ml (2 fl oz/¼ cup) olive oil, plus extra, for drizzling
200 g (7 oz) green beans, topped and halved
35 g (1¼ oz/¼ cup) dukkah, plus 1 tablespoon, extra, to garnish (see tip)
600 g (1 lb 5 oz) lamb tenderloin, at room temperature
125 ml (4 fl oz/½ cup) orange juice
2 tablespoons white wine vinegar
400 g (14 oz) tin brown lentils, drained and rinsed
½ cup parsley leaves
½ red onion, thinly sliced
100 g (3½ oz) labne in oil (see tip), to serve
Grilled (broiled) flatbread, to serve (optional)

1 Preheat the oven to 200°C (400°F/Gas 6). Spread the pumpkin over a large roasting pan lined with non-stick baking paper, sprinkle with 2 teaspoons of the cumin, season with salt and pepper and drizzle with extra oil *(pic 1)*. Roast the pumpkin for 25 minutes or until is tender and golden.

2 Blanch the beans in a saucepan of boiling water for 2 minutes, until bright green and tender crisp. Drain and rinse under cold running water.

3 Place the dukkah on a large plate, add the lamb and turn to coat *(pic 2)*. Drizzle with 1 tablespoon of the oil. Heat a large chargrill pan or barbecue chargrill to high and cook the lamb for 2–3 minutes each side for medium lamb, or until cooked to your liking. Transfer to a plate, cover loosely with foil and set aside for 3 minutes to rest.

4 Meanwhile, put the orange juice, remaining cumin and oil, and the vinegar in a small bowl and whisk to combine. Place the pumpkin, beans, lentils, parsley and onion in a large bowl. Cut the lamb into 1.5 cm (⅝ inch) thick slices *(pic 3)* and add to the salad with the dressing. Toss to combine.

5 Serve immediately, sprinkled with the extra dukkah and accompanied by the labne and grilled flatbread, if desired.

1

2

3

TIP Dukkah is an Egyptian mixture of herbs, nuts and spices. Labne is strained plain yoghurt. Both are available from selected supermarkets and delicatessens.

T-bone steak with roasted garlic butter

This succulent and flavoursome cut of meat is best cooked over a fast, dry heat so it is particularly suited to barbecuing. For added flavour, you could sprinkle chopped mixed fresh herbs such as oregano, rosemary and sage over the meat before drizzling with oil and cooking.

SERVES 4   **PREPARATION TIME** 10 minutes (+ cooling and 5 minutes resting)   **COOKING TIME** 15–20 minutes

4 beef T-bone steaks (about 550 g/
   1 lb 4 oz each), at room temperature
2 teaspoons olive oil
Barbecued potatoes and green salad
   (optional), to serve

GARLIC BUTTER
2 tablespoons rock salt
1 garlic bulb
2 teaspoons olive oil
150 g (5½ oz) butter, softened
2 tablespoons finely chopped
   flat-leaf (Italian) parsley
Freshly ground white pepper

1 To make the garlic butter, preheat the barbecue grill to medium–high. Place the rock salt on a square 30 cm (12 in) double sheet of foil. Break up the garlic into single cloves and place on the rock salt, drizzle with the olive oil *(pic 1)* and seal tightly. Place on the barbecue grill and cook for 10–15 minutes or until

the garlic is soft. Remove the foil parcel and set aside to cool slightly. Increase the barbecue heat to high. When the garlic is cool enough to handle, put the butter, parsley, pepper and salt in a bowl and squeeze in the flesh from the garlic cloves *(pic 2)*. Mix to combine.

2 Make sure the barbecue grill is very hot. Season the steaks generously with sea salt and freshly ground black pepper *(pic 2)* and drizzle with the oil, then cook on the grill for 2–3 minutes each side for medium-rare or until cooked to your liking. Transfer to a plate, cover loosely with foil and set aside in a warm place for 5 minutes to rest. Serve the steaks with the garlic butter spooned on top and accompanied by the potatoes and salad, if desired.

TIP You can vary the butter flavouring by using different herbs, or omitting the garlic and adding finely grated lemon or orange zest, or adding 1–2 mashed anchovy fillets for a stronger flavour.

Greek lamb chops

This simple dish is a staple at Greek barbecues. The lamb chops are quite rich, so the fresh Greek salad is a good accompaniment — use the best olives and feta cheese you can find.

SERVES 4–6 **PREPARATION TIME** 20 minutes (+ 4 hours or overnight marinating) **COOKING TIME** 10–12 minutes

8 large lamb forequarter chops (about 185 g/6½ oz each), trimmed of excess fat *(pic 1)*
2 tablespoons dried oregano
4 garlic cloves
Finely grated zest and juice of 1 lemon
125 ml (4 fl oz/½ cup) olive oil
Lemon wedges, to serve

GREEK SALAD
1 Lebanese (short) cucumber
½ red capsicum (pepper), seeds and membrane removed
150 g (5½ oz) cherry tomatoes, halved
¼ red onion, thinly sliced
60 g (2¼ oz/⅓ cup) kalamata olives
150 g (5½ oz) feta cheese, crumbled
2 tablespoons parsley leaves
2 tablespoons extra virgin olive oil
1 tablespoon red wine vinegar

1 Place the lamb chops in a large glass or ceramic dish and season with sea salt. Crush the oregano using a mortar and pestle until finely ground. Add the garlic and a pinch of sea salt and pound to a rough paste, then stir through the lemon zest and juice, and oil. Pour over the chops *(pic 2)* and turn to coat. Cover with plastic wrap and refrigerate for at least 4 hours, or ideally overnight, to marinate. Remove from the refrigerator an hour before cooking.

2 To make the Greek salad, cut the cucumber and capsicum into pieces about the same size as the halved tomatoes *(pic 3)*. Combine in a bowl with the remaining ingredients, season with sea salt and toss to combine.

3 Preheat a barbecue or chargrill to medium heat. Cook the lamb chops for 5–6 minutes each side or until cooked to your liking. Serve with the Greek salad and lemon wedges.

1

2

3

TIP You could dice a boned leg of lamb and substitute it for the chops. Soak bamboo skewers in water to prevent burning, then thread the meat onto the skewers and cook on a chargrill.

Korean beef skewers

Marinated and chargrilled meats are very popular in Korean cuisine and this delicious marinade would also work well with strips of pork or skinless chicken breast fillet. If you have time, marinate the beef overnight for maximum tenderness and flavour. Partially freezing the beef will make it easier to slice.

SERVES 4   **PREPARATION TIME** 20 minutes (+ 1 hour marinating)   **COOKING TIME** 10 minutes

40 g (1½ oz/¼ cup) sesame seeds, lightly toasted
2 tablespoons soy sauce
2 tablespoons rice wine or mirin
¼ teaspoon mustard powder
2 garlic cloves, crushed
2 teaspoons sesame oil
500 g (1 lb 2 oz) beef rump steak, thinly sliced across the grain into long strips (pic 1)
Steamed rice, to serve

CABBAGE SALAD
¼ small red cabbage, trimmed and shredded
2 large carrots, grated
4 spring onions (scallions), trimmed and sliced diagonally
1 tablespoon sesame oil
1 tablespoon rice vinegar
½ teaspoon caster (superfine) sugar

1 Use a mortar and pestle to pound 2 tablespoons of the sesame seeds until crushed. Add the soy sauce, rice wine or mirin, mustard, garlic and sesame oil and stir to combine. Place the beef strips in a glass or ceramic bowl, add the marinade (pic 2) and stir to coat. Cover with plastic wrap and refrigerate for at least 1 hour to marinate.

2 Meanwhile, to make the cabbage salad, put the cabbage, carrots and spring onions in a large bowl and toss to combine. Combine the sesame oil, rice vinegar and sugar in a small bowl and stir gently until the sugar dissolves. Set aside. Soak 12 bamboo skewers in cold water for 30 minutes (see tip).

3 Preheat a chargrill pan or barbecue to high. Weave the strips of meat onto the skewers (pic 3). Cook the skewers, in batches if necessary, for 1–2 minutes each side or until lightly charred.

4 Serve the beef skewers accompanied by steamed rice and the cabbage salad, dressed with the sesame oil mixture and sprinkled with the remaining sesame seeds.

1

2

3

TIP Metal skewers can be used instead of bamboo ones. They will not need to be soaked.

Thai beef salad

This irresistible salad of grilled beef and salad vegetables is tossed with a spicy fish sauce, lime and chilli dressing. If you like things really spicy, add a small red chilli as well as the long one (the smaller ones are hotter). Scotch fillet, rump or fillet steak would also work well in this recipe.

SERVES 4   **PREPARATION TIME** 25 minutes   **COOKING TIME** 10 minutes

2 x 250 g (9 oz) beef sirloin steaks, trimmed, at room temperature
Olive oil, for brushing
250 g (9 oz) cherry tomatoes, halved
2 red Asian shallots, thinly sliced
2 Lebanese (short) cucumbers, halved and sliced diagonally
¼ small white cabbage, trimmed and shredded
½ cup coriander (cilantro) leaves
½ cup mint leaves

DRESSING
1 tablespoon chopped coriander (cilantro) root
1 garlic clove, chopped
1 long red chilli, chopped
60 ml (2 fl oz/¼ cup) lime juice
60 ml (2 fl oz/¼ cup) fish sauce
1 tablespoon light brown sugar

1 To make the dressing, use a mortar and pestle to pound the coriander root, garlic and chilli to a paste *(pic 1)*. Add the lime juice, fish sauce and sugar and stir until the sugar dissolves. Set aside.

2 Heat a large chargrill pan or barbecue grill to high heat. Brush the steaks with oil, then cook for 2–3 minutes each side for medium-rare beef, or until cooked to your liking *(pic 2)*. Transfer to a plate, cover loosely with foil and set aside for 2–3 minutes to rest.

3 Meanwhile, place the tomatoes, shallots, cucumbers, cabbage and herbs in a large bowl. Thinly slice the beef *(pic 3)*, add to the salad with the dressing and gently toss to combine. Serve immediately.

1

2

3

TIP You can remove the seeds from the chilli if you prefer a little less heat in the salad.

Pork loin with fig and pecan stuffing

The sweetness of the dried figs and the crunch of the pecan nuts make this a truly memorable dish. You will need a barbecue with a hood in order to 'roast' the pork loin.

SERVES 4–6 **PREPARATION TIME** 25 minutes (+ 15 minutes resting) **COOKING TIME** 1 hour 25 minutes

50 g (1¾ oz) butter
1 small brown onion, finely chopped
35 g (1¼ oz/⅓ cup) pecans,
    finely chopped
30 g (1 oz/½ cup, lightly packed) fresh
    breadcrumbs
100 g (3½ oz) dried figs, finely chopped
2 tablespoons finely chopped flat-leaf
    (Italian) parsley
1 teaspoon finely grated lemon zest
1.5 kg (3 lb 5 oz) boneless rolled pork
    loin with rind, at room temperature
2 teaspoons olive oil, plus extra,
    for drizzling
1 tablespoon sea salt flakes
1 teaspoon freshly ground black pepper
750 g (1 lb 10 oz) new potatoes
8 garlic cloves, unpeeled
Apple sauce (see tip) and green salad,
    to serve

1 Preheat the barbecue (it will need to have a hood) to high heat, until the temperature reaches 220°C (425°F).

2 Heat the butter in a medium saucepan over medium heat. Add the onion and cook, stirring, for 4–5 minutes or until soft. Add the pecans and cook for 1–2 minutes or until lightly toasted. Remove from the heat, then stir in the breadcrumbs, figs, parsley and lemon zest.

3 Unroll the pork and place on a chopping board, rind down. Starting at the centre, cut through the thickest part of the meat to butterfly *(pic 1)*. Press the stuffing mixture onto the pork *(pic 2)*. Roll up the pork to enclose the stuffing and secure with kitchen string at 2 cm (¾ inch) intervals.

4 Place the rolled pork on a rack in a roasting pan and add enough water to the pan to come 2 cm (¾ inch) up the side. Rub the pork with the oil, then rub the sea salt and pepper into the rind *(pic 3)*. Place the pan on the barbecue flatplate and lower the hood. Cook for 25–30 minutes, then reduce the heat to 180°C (350°F) and cook for a further 40–45 minutes, adding extra water to the pan as it evaporates, if necessary. Remove the pork from the barbecue, cover loosely with foil and set aside in a warm place for 15 minutes to rest.

5 Meanwhile, preheat the oven to 200°C (400°F/Gas 6). Cook the potatoes in a large saucepan of boiling water for 10 minutes, until just tender. Drain, pat dry with paper towels and transfer to a roasting pan. Scatter over the garlic cloves, drizzle with the extra oil and season well with sea salt and pepper. Bake for 20 minutes, until light golden brown. Remove from the oven and use the back of a spoon to gently flatten them a little.

6 Serve the pork with the potatoes, roasted garlic cloves, apple sauce and a green salad.

1

2

3

TIP To make apple sauce, peel, core and chop 4 green apples. Put the apples, 125 ml (4 fl oz/ ½ cup) water, 1 tablespoon caster (superfine) sugar, 2 cloves and 1 cinnamon stick in a saucepan. Cook, covered, over medium–low heat for 10 minutes, until softened.

Gourmet beef burgers

The secret to these superb burgers is in the minced meat — it needs to be a bit fatty. If it is too lean, it will dry out when cooked and it won't be as flavoursome. The toppings you choose are another way to elevate a burger beyond the ordinary. We have used a spicy tomato relish and gruyère cheese.

SERVES 4   **PREPARATION TIME** 20 minutes (+ 10 minutes chilling)   **COOKING TIME** 30 minutes

600 g (1 lb 5 oz) minced (ground) beef
    chuck steak (see tip)
½ red onion, finely grated
1 tablespoon HP sauce (see tip)
2 teaspoons dijon mustard
40 g (1½ oz/⅔ cup, lightly packed)
    fresh breadcrumbs
1 egg
4 slices gruyère cheese
Pickled bread and butter cucumbers,
    thinly sliced
Baby cos (romaine) lettuce leaves
4 bread rolls, split

TOMATO RELISH

1 tablespoon olive oil
1 red onion, finely diced
1 garlic clove, crushed
½ teaspoon dried chilli flakes
1 teaspoon brown mustard seeds
400 g (14 oz) tin chopped tomatoes
2 teaspoons balsamic vinegar
2 teaspoons light brown sugar

1 To make the tomato relish, heat the oil in a medium saucepan over medium heat. Add the onion and cook, stirring occasionally, for 5 minutes. Add the garlic, chilli and mustard seeds and cook, stirring, for 1–2 minutes. Add the tomatoes, vinegar and sugar and stir to combine. Reduce the heat to low and simmer for 15 minutes or until thick (*pic 1*). Remove from the heat and set aside to cool.

2 Place the beef, onion, HP sauce, mustard, breadcrumbs and egg in a large bowl and season with salt and pepper (*pic 2*). Use clean hands to mix until well combined, then divide into 4 equal portions. Shape each portion into a round patty, place on a baking tray, cover with plastic wrap and refrigerate for 10 minutes.

3 Preheat a chargrill pan over medium–high heat and spray with olive oil. Grill the beef patties for 4–5 minutes each side (*pic 3*) or until lightly charred and just cooked through. (Alternatively, pan-fry the patties for 4 minutes each side.)

4 To serve, place a slice of gruyère, some pickled cucumbers and lettuce on the base of each roll, then top with a beef patty and spoonful of tomato relish and cover with the top of the roll.

VARIATIONS

Gourmet pork and veal burgers: Substitute the beef with 300 g (10½ oz) minced pork and 300 g (10½ oz) minced veal. Replace the HP sauce with sun-dried tomato pesto.

Gourmet lamb burgers: Omit the dijon mustard. Substitute the beef with 600 g (1 lb 5 oz) minced lamb. Replace the HP sauce with barbecue sauce. Replace the tomato relish with tzatziki and the lettuce leaves with rocket (arugula).

1

2

3

TIP Ask your butcher to mince (grind) chuck steak for you. You can also use minced wagyu steak or half chuck and half wagyu.
    HP sauce is a brown sauce available from supermarkets.

Conversion charts

OVEN TEMPERATURE		
C	F	Gas
70	150	¼
100	200	½
110	225	½
120	235	½
130	250	1
140	275	1
150	300	2
160	315	2–3
170	325	3
180	350	4
190	375	5
200	400	6
210	415	6–7
220	425	7
230	450	8
240	475	8
250	500	9

LENGTH	
cm	inches
2 mm	1/16
3 mm	⅛
5 mm	¼
8 mm	⅜
1	½
1.5	⅝
2	¾
2.5	1
3	1¼
4	1½
5	2
6	2½
7	2¾
7.5	3
8	3¼
9	3½
10	4
11	4¼
12	4½
13	5
14	5½
15	6
16	6¼
17	6½
18	7
19	7½
20	8
21	8¼
22	8½
23	9
24	9½
25	10
30	12
35	14
40	16
45	17¾
50	20

WEIGHT	
g	oz
5	⅛
10	¼
15	½
20	¾
30	1
35	1¼
40	1½
50	1¾
55	2
60	2¼
70	2½
80	2¾
85	3
90	3¼
100	3½
115	4
120	4¼
125	4½
140	5
150	5½
175	6
200	7
225	8
250	9
280	10
300	10½
350	12
375	13
400	14
450	1 lb
500	1 lb 2 oz
550	1 lb 4 oz
600	1 lb 5 oz
700	1 lb 9 oz
800	1 lb 12 oz
900	2 lb
1 kg	2 lb 3 oz

LIQUID	
ml	fl oz
30	1
60	2
80	2½
100	3½
125	4
160	5¼
185	6
200	7
250	9
300	10½
350	12
375	13
400	14
500	17
600	21
650	22½
700	24
750	26
800	28
1 L	35
1.25 L	44
1.5 L	52

Index